Best Wish
To Barba

We Chose
Survival

Ruth Lindemann
July 2021

Books by Ruth Lindemann

To Survive Is Not Enough

They Will Not Be Forgotten

We Chose Survival

A Memoir of My Early Life

Ruth Lindemann

Lindemann, Ruth
We Chose Survival

1st edition
Library of Congress Control Number: 2021903850
ISBN 978-1-954604-02-5 (paperback)

Published by

AquaZebra™
Book Publishing
Cathedral City, California
www.aquazebra.com

Editor
Lynn Jones Green

Cover/interior design
Mark E. Anderson

AquaZebra™
Web, Book & Print Design
www.aquazebra.com

Printed in the United States of America

Dedication

This book is dedicated to my mother Mathilde (Hacker) Kohn
in gratitude for her fortitude, which saved our lives.

—Ruth Lindemann

Acknowledgments

My loving appreciation to my daughters, Diana and Tamarra
for their meticulous proofreading of this book.

Preface

This memoir was written to inform my children, grandchildren, and anyone else who might be interested, about my recollections as a Jewish child in fascist Europe. I also want to relate the experiences I had during my first ten years in the United States of America.

The sentences and syntax are, at times, awkward and repetitive. These flaws reflect the fact that I had to translate my memories from the thoughts of a child who had a sparse knowledge of English, and later from the disconnected diary entries of a teenager, traumatized by the dichotomy and mixed messages of her world.

Prologue

Conflagration

The uneven cobblestones make walking difficult as I slowly proceed across the ancient city square, while a cold wind whips around my seven-year-old legs. A bonfire is burning in the center of the square. A group of teenage boys are taking books out of nearby handcarts. With gleeful abandon they rip pages out of the books and throw them into the flames where they quickly turn into ashes. An occasional updraft sends a page or two into the air where they are caught by a gust of wind and flutter away.

The memory of that scene becomes an analogy for the Holocaust. Members of loving families are ripped away like the pages of those books and are thrown into the fire. By mere chance—just like those loose pages—some are wafted away by a friendly breeze and escape the flames.

Part One:

Dark Ripples

The days before March 1938

Chapter 1

At the Montessori kindergarten, we had been rehearsing for weeks, and now all our parents were sitting in rows waiting for the annual Mother's Day performance. Without hesitation I went out onto the little stage, holding my favorite doll, and sang the song about how hard it is to be a mother. I cannot replicate the tune (though I can hear it in my head), nor can I remember any words except the last line: *Ach wie schwehr ist es ya, ya, zu seihn eine mama.*[1]

I gave a deep, heartfelt sigh at the end of the song, hugged and kissed my doll then took a bow. I can still hear the applause and the praise from my parents about my acting and singing. "You were adorable. We are so proud."

That Sunday in May of 1937, I was still a child and my parents were still a young, patriotic, Austrian couple who worked hard and enjoyed the amenities provided in Vienna—a city at the center of Western

Mathilde Hacker and Leo Kohn
January 30, 1931

---

[1] "Oh how hard it is, yes, yes, to be a mama."

culture for hundreds of years. They looked forward to a bright future, raising their daughter in this democratic country. In less than a year, their dreams and plans would be shattered and our very lives in danger.

For the next few months after my little performance, my life went on in its orderly way. Early each weekday morning, Mitzi—our maid, as well as my Nanny, and the most important person in my young life—went to the Ankor Bakery across the street from our apartment house to buy freshly baked, crusty rolls while the chicory coffee brewed on the stove. My parents and I ate a hasty breakfast and got ready to leave.

My mother walked the mile to the wholesale textile company where she had worked for twenty-six years (since the age of fourteen) as a bookkeeper/secretary. My father was a warehouseman at a business that produced liquors. He would leave a few minutes later.

After cleaning up the breakfast dishes, Mitzi got me dressed and we walked to the Montessori school across the Friedensbreuke.[2] In May it was a pleasant walk; but, in the fall and winter, it was always cold and windy on the bridge.

On cold days Mitzi often bought roasted chestnuts from a woman behind a brazier. The newspaper cone holding the treats warmed my hands, while Mitzi peeled and stuffed the warm chestnuts into my mouth. They were delicious.

Sometimes on the way home, Mitzi took me into St. Stephen's Cathedral to warm up. Crossing herself with the holy water from the basin by the door, Mitzi would genuflect before entering the nave. She put coins in a box, lit several candles, and briefly kneeled at the feet of a statue of a beautiful lady.

Back on the street, we hardly felt cold walking over the bridge. In warm weather we walked more slowly, so we

---

[2] A bridge over the Danube Canal that runs through the center of Vienna

didn't have time to visit the church; but we always stopped to admire the windows of the various toy stores along the Wallensteinstrasse.

My parents came home for lunch—the main meal of the day—which usually consisted of noodle soup, and then a main dish which could be schnitzel with roasted potatoes, meatloaf, or chicken with potato salad or a plate of noodles flecked with meat. I remember drinking coffee, which was half milk with two cubes of sugar.

Lunchtime with my parents was always an ordeal. I never ate enough to suit them. I can still hear their strident voices as they argued about the best way to make me eat more food. (We never told them about the chestnuts.)

"The child looks like she has rickets," my father would say. "She needs to eat what is set in front of her, the spoiled brat."

Many references were made to how other children are starving and how hungry my parents had been when they were young. My mother often screamed, "Ruthie, if you don't clean your plate, we will call the policeman on the corner to come and he will take you away!"

"Don't threaten the child with such nonsense," would be my father's retort. "I'll paddle her behind until she begs us to let her eat her dinner."

Their arguments and threats often resulted in my crying and cringing in fear. Then they began to blame each other for making me cry. Mitzi would take me into the other room, the place where she and I had our beds, or through that room, with its oriental carpet and dining room furniture, to my parents' bedroom beyond. Lying on the feather bed, I usually cried myself to sleep.

After my parents returned to work and I was napping, Mitzi would do her countless chores. During the afternoons, I played with my dolls or watched Mitzi work. I had tonsillitis during the winter of 1937, and for several days observed all the things that Mitzi did for our family.

Fifteen years later, I began to appreciate the stamina

and intelligence of this young woman who kept our family fed, clean, and organized. My husband and children were always complaining about something I had not done—or had done, but not to their satisfaction. During those early years of marriage and motherhood—even with several appliances—I felt like a gerbil on a treadmill, getting nowhere and always exhausted. Mitzi had done everything with just her two hands.

While I was in kindergarten, Mitzi went grocery shopping at several small shops, came home, and started preparations for lunch. Then she walked the mile or so to pick me up. After cleaning up the lunch dishes, she would start on her many afternoon chores.

Every other Monday was laundry day. The bed linens and towels were taken to the laundry room in the basement of the apartment house, soaked in a large tub of hot, soapy water, then scrubbed on a washboard; then they were wrung out and dumped into another huge tub of cold water to rinse. It required strong arms and hands to wring out the linen sheets and duvet covers. Mitzi took me along when I was home and I remember the sweat on her face.

Mitzi dumped the wrung-out laundry into a basket and carried the heavy load up four floors to the drying attic. One of those times when I was at home and sick, I helped with the hanging up by handing her the clothespins. I don't think it sped up the process, as I kept dropping the pins which were hard to find in the dark room. Mitzi never scolded me for being clumsy—or anything else for that matter. At that time in my life, I loved no one more.

On Tuesday afternoons, Mitzi and I gathered the clothes from the attic. Since the dry clothes were much lighter, I was allowed to hold one handle of the basket while Mitzi held the other one as we went down the stairs to our apartment. Only once did I drop my end of the basket, and the clothes rolled down the stairs. I felt terrible. Mitzi gathered up the sheets, wiped away my tears and led me into the apartment. Since the laundry was dry the flecks of dust flew off with a good shaking.

Then the grueling process of ironing began. A metal plate was put over the gas burner of the stove. Two irons were placed on the plate to heat, while Mitzi laid several towels on the kitchen table. When the iron on the stove was hot enough (it sizzled when touched with a wet finger) Mitzi began to iron everything in the basket. She often used a small towel to wipe the perspiration from her face so it wouldn't drip onto the clothes being ironed.

Besides the almost-daily dusting, sweeping, floor scrubbing, once a month Mitzi made noodles: A mound of flour was piled onto a board on the kitchen table. Making an indentation in the middle of the mound, Mitzi broke eggs into the flour and began to add a few drops of water to get the right texture to roll it into a ball and knead the dough into a pliable mass. This was then rolled out with a huge rolling pin until it was paper thin. With a sharp knife she cut the dough into long, narrow strips. I got to help drape these strips over the backs of the chairs in the never-used dining room and over the four chairs and small bench in the kitchen. When the noodles were dry, we gathered them up—careful not to break them—and by evening the month's supply of dried noodles were packaged into linen bags and stored in a cupboard.

Our evening meals were cold and sparse. A piece of bread with butter or a cheese that made me gag, or a thin slice of salami or pickled herring. Usually I just had a hard-boiled egg.

I remember Vati (what I called my father) sitting at the kitchen table peeling an apple or a rare orange for dessert. My mother's culinary skills went as far as boiling water for their after-dinner tea. I didn't get anything to drink after five o'clock in the evening, in the vain hope that I wouldn't wet my bed. My nightly bed-wetting was frustrating, especially since my mother had a water closet built into one corner of the kitchen so I didn't have to use the toilet in the hall. This added to the covert animosity the neighbors felt toward us as

the only Jews in this the working-class neighborhood. I overheard my mother being called a "snob."[3]

---

[3] *Die hoch naessige:* "The one with the nose in the air"

Chapter 2

As a special treat, my father took me to a circus. We sat up high in a huge arena, and I could barely make out what was happening below. What I did see didn't make much sense to me. I saw people dressed in strange costumes running around the huge arena. I preferred the graceful tightrope walkers and the acrobats swinging through the air.

When the elephants appeared, I became frightened. My fear only intensified when a huge cage was brought into the arena, and lions began to emerge and gather. I could barely see the lion tamer in his red coat, but I heard the crack of the whip and the loud roar of the lions. I was terrified and began to cry. My crying annoyed the people around us and Vati became angry. While I wept, he clutched me by the arm and dragged me out to the street.

I cried all the way home, and when we arrived at the apartment, Mutti became very agitated when she saw how upset I was. Vati complained loudly to my mother that I was a stupid, ungrateful child and needed a spanking.

Vati often threatened to spank me, but in my memory, he never hit me—or anyone else, for that matter. He was a mild-mannered, peaceful man, but something about me roused his anger. It must have had something to do with his own cruel childhood—which was spent mostly in a Czech orphanage—where he was always hungry and often beaten for violating arbitrary rules. In comparison, he saw me as a coddled, ungrateful, willful, disobedient girl who didn't live up to his expectations. He had experienced a normal childhood with caring parents for only a short time. Living in an orphanage from the age of seven had not prepared him for being a loving father. I only know this history because I overheard my mother tell it to one of her cousins.

On the other hand, my father could be fun. He told me stories about his own childhood before he was sent to the orphanage.[4] He made me laugh with magic tricks, making coins disappear and reappear right in front of me. He entertained me with shadow puppets on the wall who had fights and scary adventures.

Some of those stories were about the hiking club, where he and my mother had met. Since my parents often went to the theater and had season tickets to the Vienna Opera, (in the standing area at the back of the hall), Vati told me stories based on opera plots, but shortened and edited to my level of understanding.

My mother was also a good storyteller. Every night she would tell me a fairy tale. She included the old standards like Cinderella, Snow White, and Sleeping Beauty, but my favorites were the ones my mother made up which were always about poor, orphaned girls who dressed in rags and were always hungry but honest and loving. They met people who needed their help and because they were kind and caring, circumstances developed that they became rich or married rich men. Mutti's original stories always had variations so I never got tired of hearing them.

My favorite story goes like this:

A poor girl had left her home in a village to work on a farm on the other side of a forest. One day a message came that her mother was sick and needed her. The poor girl packed up a basket with bread and cheese and started to walk through the forest to her mother's

---

[4] My grandfather died in a Russian prisoner of war camp in 1917. And my grandmother could not support the three children.

house. Somehow, she got lost. She walked on until it got dark and she had eaten all the food. She sat down on a rock and looked up at the stars. Suddenly she saw the stars begin to fall. She stood up, held out her apron, and soon it was filled with silver coins. The moon came up and lit the way out of the forest and the poor girl got to her mother's house. She used the coins to buy food and a feather bed. Her mother recovered and they lived happily ever after.

In the spring and fall, my parents and I spent Sundays in the Schrebergarten,[5] a small plot of land at the end of the streetcar line in the suburb of Gersthoff. My father took pride in the vegetables he grew there and was especially proud of his apricot tree. A small shack provided shelter, a place to store the implements needed to care for the garden, and a cot where I was supposed to take naps. It was gloomy because it had no windows, so I strongly objected to being left alone there in the dark. My parents wanted to go outside to work in the garden together, but I cried until my mother came back to sit with me. With a familiar expression of exasperation, "Na Yah," she usually let me go back outside.

Permanent residents lived in the neighborhood. One of those was Peter, a boy my age. We played all kinds of games in his family's large, grassy yard. During the spring and autumn Sundays that I spent out in Gersthoff, we were inseparable. I don't remember what we played, but I recall the feeling of freedom and fun we enjoyed when we were together.[6]

As the weather got warmer my mother took me to the Augarten on Saturday afternoons. This huge, walled park—once a private playground for the royal family—was opened

---

5 In 1864 Dr. Daniel Schreber of Leipzig, Germany implemented a program of allotting plots of land to city workers for growing food. In 1904 it was adopted in Austria.

6 Ten years later, after the war, Peter somehow found my address in the U.S.A. and wrote me a friendly letter. We were teenagers by then and became pen pals for several years.

to the public during my grandmother's childhood. Mutti reminded me each time we went there that she had played in that very park when she was a child, as had her mother before her. I could not imagine my mother as a child, or my grandmother, who had died long before I was born. But as I sedately walked the gravel paths or frolicked on the wide lawns, chasing butterflies or watching crickets jump, I felt a sense of belonging.

Sometimes (probably when there was no soccer game), my father volunteered to take me for the Saturday afternoon walk. We usually walked along the main streets looking into display windows then stepped into a Kafehause where I had hot chocolate with lots of whipped cream.

On one of those walks, Vati and I, holding hands tightly, stepped off the curb. A bicycle came around the corner, knocking me down. The front wheel grazed my cheek. It was just a scratch, but it hurt a lot. Vati picked me up, made sure there was no further damage and after yelling at the frightened biker, carried me home.

Mutti washed my cheek with alcohol, changed my panties, which were wet, and put me down in my crib for a nap.

While I dozed, I could hear my mother scolding my father, accusing him of not holding my hand, while he swore that he had been doing just that. Then he yelled that he would never take me for a walk again and he never did.

My parents got along fairly well. I heard them talk and chuckle about incidents at work, or at the athletic club. They seldom argued, but when they did it was always about me. I began to think they would be happier without me.

Chapter 3

In June, Mitzi and I took the train to the small village of Wopfing, where I spent the summers with my paternal grandmother (whom I called "Omama") and her sister, my Tante Franzi. The village, at the foot of the Alps, had no train depot and the tracks meandered through meadows, orchards and across creeks. When a passenger wanted to get off the train, they would tell the conductor where to stop and let them off. To get on, a person stood beside the track and waved a white handkerchief to stop the approaching train.

Wopfing, 1973

From where we descended from the train to my Omama's house was a long walk through a meadow of sweet-smelling grass, sprinkled with daisies and clover. We were always surrounded by the hum of bees and other insects like a welcoming committee.

Tante Franzi, her fuzzy gray hair tied in a bandana and her long skirts billowing around her, always came into the meadow to meet us. After giving me a warm hug, she would take my small suitcase from Mitzi and lead the way to Omama's house. As we passed the latrine, Mitzi would ask if I needed to use it. Then we marched through the courtyard and climbed the high rising steps to the veranda that ran along the back of the house.

Omama had inherited a small grocery store from her parents. The two elderly sisters were born in that very house, grew up in the village and knew everyone who lived there. As a war widow my grandmother was granted a tobacco license, which supplemented their income.

Tante Franzi kept house and Omama ran the grocery store. When Mitzi and I arrived it was usually lunch time. Omama hung the "closed" sign on the grocery door, came into the kitchen and nodded her welcome to me and to Mitzi, then we said a prayer and ate the meal Tante Franzi had prepared. After the meal Mitzi left for Eigen, an even smaller village further up the mountainside, where she helped her family with the summer harvest.

The best part of a meal in Wopfing was the crusty rye bread. All I wanted for lunch was a thick slice, generously spread with Tante Franzi's fried chicken skins. This crunchy treat was called "Kremzl" and my mouth is watering just writing about it.

Saying good-by to Mitzi made me sad. When she gave me that final hug and started out the door, the pain in my stomach and in my throat brought tears to my eyes. She always promised to visit me, but I remember only one visit during the next summer.

For, what seemed endless hours, that summer I sat on a little bench at the far end of the veranda learning how to knit. Omama came in from the store for lunch and inspected my work. If I dropped a stitch or made a mistake, she unraveled my work and I had to start over. Eventually I became skilled in yarn work and actually enjoyed it, but as a four-year old I hated sitting still.

To gain some freedom I told Tante Franzi, who was usually in the kitchen, that I had to go to the latrine. Then I scampered down the steps and ran past the latrine and out the back gate to the meadow.

The Tauber family, Bruno, Chekoslovakia 1937

The path that led to the creek ran along the top of a ridge beside the meadow. The slope from the path to the meadow floor was just the right angle for rolling or somersaulting down to the bottom. I would do this until I heard someone call me. When I got back to the house, my dress covered with grass stains, my hair full of straw, various scratches on my knees, I stood in silence while Omama ranted about what a bad girl I was and that I should get a spanking. Even with the many threats I heard I don't remember ever being spanked.

The tedium of the summer was relieved by a two week visit of my father's sister, (Tante Irma) and her twin daughters. The girls were one year younger and spoke only Czech while I spoke only German, but somehow, we managed to communicate.

Eva was a blonde, chubby, gentle child who liked to play

with dolls and have tea parties with fake tea and real cookies. Vera had dark hair (not quite as black as mine) a wiry body and was an excellent accomplice for the dangerous adventures I devised for us.

One such game was walking along the railing of the veranda. We were oblivious to the thirty-foot drop to the courtyard below. When we arrived at one end we jumped down onto the veranda, making it shake a bit, like a light earthquake. Eva's threats to tell on us irritated Vera and me, so one time we jumped off the railing right into the middle of the corner where Eva had assembled her dolls for a tea party. The little table tipped over, the dishes clattered to the floor and I had jumped on Eva's favorite doll.

Eva yelled for her mother who came running out to the veranda. Not waiting for an explanation, Tante Irma began to spank Vera who wailed loudly, Eva and I wailed too. Then I was scolded, but not spanked.

Back row (L to R), Rosa Kohn, Irma Tauber (Kohn), Mathilde Kohn (Hacker), Franseska Schisha (Kohn). Front row Leo Kohn & Ruth Lindemann (Kohn), 1937.

On one weekend my parents came to Wopfing and brought American Indian war bonnets. They were made from heavy paper, but to us they looked real. Vera and I jumped around the well in the courtyard, whooping and shouting like Indian braves (where did we learn to do this?) while Eva, wearing the paper bonnet sat quietly on the edge of the well watching us.

Ruth Kohn, 1938

Playing ball with mom in the big meadow. Oma's house with veranda in the background, 1938.

Back yard: Leo, Franzi, Thilde, Ruth & Rosa. 1938

(L to R) Vera, Aunt Irma, Eva Tauber, 1939.

Tante Irma came out to the balcony and angrily shouted, "You dark devils stop making that noise! Omama has a headache!" Reluctantly we went back up to our knitting. I still remember the feeling of elation while we could be "wild Indians." I am certain that Vera remembered that afternoon for the rest of her short life.[7]

Ruth, Eva and Vera playing Indians, summer 1938 with Josef Waxhoffer, 1938.

---

[7] Four years later, a week before their eighth birthday, the twins and their mother were murdered in the gas chamber at Auschwitz.

One especially hectic morning filled with accusations and threats of spanking (can't remember what we did, but just running in the house could bring on serious reprimands). I decided to take a walk with Vera. No one missed us in the preparations for the arrival of my parents and uncle Lolo (the twins' father, Lother Tauber). We went out the back gate into the meadow and took the path to the river.

Wopfing Summer (L to R) Maria Waxhoffer, Stefan Waxfofer, Hugo Kohn, Irma Tauber, (Nee Kohn), Lother Tauber, Rosa Kohn, Franceska Schischa (Nee Kohn). Ruth with friends. 1938

I knew the way because twice a month I went this way on washdays with Tante Franzi and the washerwoman who came to help with washing the linens. It was tedious, heavy work for the women, for me it was a fun day.

The laundry room was on the ground floor, under the veranda. First the two women stirred the clothes around in the huge tubs of boiling, soapy water sitting on the wash-room stove. Then they used the long poles to dump the steaming, wet mess into the waiting basket. When the basket was full, they each took one handle and struggled along the narrow path through the meadow, then up the gravel slope to the railroad tracks and down the slippery gravel on the other side, through the tall grass to the riverbank. After each piece of linen was rinsed, Tante Franzi and I spread it out to dry on the grass. While the sheets and the rest dried, I was allowed to splash around in the icy water. It was shallow in the summer and there was little danger of drowning. The baskets were much lighter coming home so I proudly helped to carry them.

The path veered off into an apple orchard where Vera and I climbed the lower branches and filled our apron pockets with green apples. When we got to the river, we took off our shoes and socks and splashed around in the water. In a few minutes, our clothes were soaked and although the sun was warm, we started to shiver. I showed Vera how to lay out our wet clothes on the grass to dry and we sat on one of the dryer aprons eating the green apples.

Four boys I knew, who were about a year or two older, came running up to us and began yelling insults, rubbing their forefingers together in a gesture of "shame on you." The only words I understood were, "You dirty Jewish sows." When they began to throw stones we got really frightened and would have liked to run away, but they were between us and our clothes. The women sitting on their blankets nearby looked up and laughed. Vera began to cry, and the boys ran away before I could ask them why they were so angry with us. Earlier that summer I had played hide-and-go-seek with those boys and they had shown me how to climb the trees and pick green apples.

Vera and I got dressed and ran back to the house where no one had missed us. Tante Irma had gone to meet the train and everyone thought we were with her.

Tante Franzi had prepared a festive meal that night and Omama was wearing her black, silk Shabbat dress. Vera and I had stomach aches and were put to bed early.

A few days later I was alone again with Omama and Tante Franzi. Of course there was Maria Waxhover, who helped Tante Franzi run the household and her husband Stefan, who worked in a brick factory in the nearby town of Pisting.

The Waxhovers lived in a one-bedroom apartment which was located down a dark hallway leading to the delivery door for the grocery store.

Maria did most of the cleaning and helped the washer-woman and Tante Franzi wash the linens on laundry day. She was a strong woman and could haul huge buckets of water from the well, up the steep steps to the kitchen. She was a good cook and I often ate my noon meal with her and her husband. I called him Onkel Stefan and he seemed to be fond of me and I liked him very much.

Omama and Tante Franzi kept a strictly kosher house-hold so everything having to do with food was done by one of them. Keeping kosher in such a remote place as Wopfing was complicated. Omama koshered her own meat. Each piece had to be salted on seven sides, with all blood removed before cooking. Every article in the kitchen was either *fleishig* (beef or mutton) or *milchig* (dairy products). Fish and poultry were neutral. (Pork and meat from animals with fur and shellfish is strictly forbidden). A milchig dish was never to touch a fleishig surface. My mother didn't keep a kosher household, so I was often confused about what to put where. Placing a fleishig dish on a milchig tablecloth could bring harsh repri-mands from Omama.

Maria Waxhover was a laid-back person. She laughed often, and tried to sooth my grandmother when she had a fit of nerves over some incident in the store or in the household. She was the one who defended me when I was scolded for wetting the bed. Omama would shout at me, "You should be ashamed of yourself for doing such a wicked thing!" I tried, but I couldn't feel shame; just sad and confused.

"She didn't do it on purpose," Frau Waxhover would say to Omama and then say soothing things to me while rinsing out the sheet.

Once, after eating the noon meal with the Waxhovers, I told Omama that I liked the rabbit paprikash. Her eyes blazed with anger and she screamed at me, "You wicked child!" I was, as usual, puzzled and frightened by her outburst. It was Tante Franzi who explained to me that rabbit was not kosher.

Chapter 4

In early September, Mitzi walked down to Wopfing to meet me for our return to Vienna. I was surprised when Omama cried as we said our farewells. For the first time during my visit, she told me that she loved me and looked forward to my return next summer. Tante Franzi wiped tears away as she hugged me. I did feel a little sad to be leaving her.

It was always thrilling to watch the scenery fly by on that train ride to Vienna. I remember Omama saying that moving along at such a speed was terribly dangerous and probably a sin. "It is disgusting," she hissed, "how women get on the trains with those short skirts, revealing everything."

After a summer of almost total isolation, the crowded train station in Vienna was an intimidating but exciting place. I enjoyed the streetcar ride along the colorful and noisy city streets. That night, Mutti would tell me wonderful stories, and Vati would do tricks to make me laugh.

Kindergarten in the fall of 1937 was more interesting than the year before. We began to learn the alphabet by singing a song (the same song English-speaking children use, which was helpful in learning to read that language), and we were taught to count. So far, our daily routine was hardly changed since last year.

Wishing to expose me to real theater, my parents took me to the Folkstheater to see *Hansel and Gretel*. The theater was filled with young families for the matinee. The play started out happily enough. The song Gretel sang to teach Hansel how to dance has stayed in my memory, and I often sang and danced it with friends many years later.

I was impressed with how clever Gretel was, strewing white pebbles along the trail so she and Hansel could find their way back to their parents—who clearly didn't want them back.

When the children got lost in the forest, I became uneasy. When they came upon the gingerbread house, I relaxed and I could almost taste the cookies.

As the witch appeared, I remembered the story about the little girl who told lies:

One day, as a little girl was playing outdoors, a witch swooped down and took the girl away. When the girl returned, she was an old, ugly woman, and no one recognized her. (I didn't go outside alone for a long time after Omama told me that story.)

The witch pranced around the stage, doing terrible things to Hansel, and my fear grew. By the time Gretel shoved the witch into the oven, I was trembling and began to cry. The play left me with the suspicion that when parents no longer wanted their children, they took them someplace where they couldn't find their way home. For some time after seeing this play, I was fearful of being alone—even by myself in a room in the apartment.

The cinema was considered low-brow entertainment by my parents; however, I remember going to two films in Vienna. One was with Shirley Temple. She danced and sang, which was entertaining, but I didn't like her because she was such a good girl. The adults in the film were so pleased with her that I couldn't believe she was a real girl.[8]

I also saw a film with Sonja Hennie, the Norwegian figure-skating champion. I loved that movie and Sonja Hennie. For a while, I told people that I wanted to be a figure skater

---

[8] Years later I was disappointed to learn that Shirley Temple didn't speak German.

like Sonja Hennie, but what I really wanted were her blue eyes and blonde hair.

December 6th is called *Krampus* Day[9] in Austria and St. Nicholas day in other parts of Europe. Children put their shoes on the windowsill at night and, if they've been good, they find an orange or other goodies in their shoe. If they've been naughty, the Krampus leaves a lump of coal. I got a tangerine that year—the last one I would see for a long time. Mutti told me that when she was young, she would have been happy to get a lump of coal, which was scarce during WWI.

I remember Christmas that year because Mitzi decorated a little tree in a corner of the kitchen with strands of silky cotton called angel hair and real candles on several limbs. She told me stories of the Christ-child who brought presents to "good" children. I didn't get any presents. I was disappointed, but not at all surprised.

Only once did my parents take me sledding on the Kallenberg, the high peak in the Vienna Woods. After a streetcar ride to the end of the line and a lengthy bus ride up a curvy road, the six of us (Heinzi, me, and both sets of our parents) arrived at the foot of the snow-covered sled run. Then we climbed the steep hill. We would be taking turns on the sled my parents had bought my cousin Heinzi for his birthday. Heinzi's mother, Tante Paula (who was one of several first cousins of my mother) suggested I take the first run as I was the youngest.

I sat at the front of the sled, and Vati sat behind me holding the steering rope. We glided faster and faster down the tree-lined slope. At first it was fun, but as we gained speed, I became afraid. We reached the bottom before I could cry, but I was shaking all over and had wet my pants.

While Heinzi took his turn with his sled, my parents took me into the coffee house. I had just started to drink the hot chocolate, covered with whip cream, when a waiter came to

---

[9] A mythical demon that punishes bad children.

our table. He asked our name, then said there had been a bad accident. Heinzi had hit a tree and broken his jaw. He was taken to the hospital and I was taken home. I don't remember ever going sledding again.

During the month before my fifth birthday (February 15, 1938), I had to take my Saturday naps in my parents' little bedroom. One afternoon I awoke to a "thud thud" sound from the dining room where I usually slept. I got up and slowly opened the door to the larger room and saw Vati standing in front of the mirrored buffet. He was practicing with two marionettes and a ping-pong ball. He saw me in the mirror and stopped, but it was too late; I had seen the whole thing. He put his fingers to his lips and told me I could watch, but I was not to tell Mutti that I had seen his surprise for my birthday party. We giggled like the two youngsters we still were in those days, and I got to watch him practice for the next two weeks.

I also watched Mitzi make the six-layer torte for the party. She baked three layers of chocolate cake, and then, after they were cooled, she put them on a board and cut each one in half with a thin piece of string to make three more thin layers. She filled each layer with raspberry jam and frosted the cake with chocolate icing. Not a crumb would be left after the party.

Finally, the day arrived for my fifth birthday party. It was a festive family gathering and my first childhood birthday party. (It turned out to be my last one.[10])

We drank hot chocolate out of the special china cups that were bought for the occasion; I still have one left. I received a wonderful gift of an almost-full-size pram. I also received a beautiful doll that was much too lovely and fragile for the rough play that my little clown and teddy bear had endured. But she did fit into the buggy, and I could hardly wait to take her for a stroll.

The marionette show was a great success, and the ball

---

[10] Within a year, all the party guests were scattered to different parts of the world.

was only dropped once or twice; the applause was gratifying, and my Vati was so pleased with himself. Laughter filled the house, and guests offered far too many hugs and kisses for me. But it all made me feel deeply loved.

Only a few children attended this party, because most of my mother's cousins—who were also her best friends—were firm believers in the "one child" policy, which they thought would prevent future wars.

Heinzi was at the party and still wearing a brace in his jaw from the sledding accident. A boy named Peter was there; he was very sickly and later died of leukemia. (His mother was not Jewish, and his parents were forced to divorce under the Nazi regime). A girl named Ruth, whom I had seen only once before and whose story I will relate later, was also at the party. Oliver and Helga, six-year-old twins, also came to the party.

Toward evening, when only a few adults were still there, someone turned on the radio. Everyone listened intently to the voice screaming out into the room. I was busy playing with my new toys, introducing the new doll to the old ones. But the voice on the radio was intruding into my thoughts, and finally I just sat there and listened. A man was yelling, almost incoherently, but I understood the word "Jews." Then I heard him say that they were bad people and should all be killed.

Although I remembered only one visit to a synagogue, I knew I was Jewish. Did this mean that I was bad and should be killed? I thought of all the bad things I had done that had annoyed the adults in my life. But I didn't think I should be *killed* for not eating all my dinner or not coming right away when I was called. I knew what "killed" was; I had seen dead birds in the park and heard of death in the stories that Mutti and Mitzi told me. It was an awfully bad thing to happen to people.

The man was still screaming when my mother took me into the next room and put me to bed. The door was always left open a small crack, because I was terribly afraid of the dark.

Although their voices were low, I could hear the adults

talking in the kitchen. I caught a few words of the conversation, which was about leaving to go somewhere else to live. I heard strange words: Argentina, Australia, Uruguay, Montevideo, and—in an especially awed whisper—the word "America." It wasn't so much *what* they were saying, but the tone of their voices that was disturbing. A cold knot of fear began to grow in the pit of my stomach—a pain which has never disappeared.

The next month went by without a change in routine. Mitzi took me to kindergarten, picked me up, and prepared lunch for the four of us. I took my nap before going to my corner to play with my dolls. I often played doctor, pretending to give the dolls shots, or trying to get medicine into their closed mouths.

Sometimes Mausie, the apartment manager's ten-year old daughter, came to play with me. On clear days we took my new pram for a little walk in the front of the building. On rainy days, we played school on the stairs leading to our apartment. Mausie had a little blackboard and chalk, and we practiced the alphabet and numbers and took turns being the teacher. School was my favorite game.

Part Two:

The Undertow

The Anschluss Spring 1938

Chapter 5

One cold morning in the middle of March, I didn't go to kindergarten as usual. Mitzi went about her household chores. When she opened the window to air out the feather beds, I heard the music of a marching band. I leaned out the window and I could hear people singing a familiar song. Lately I had heard it on the radio, usually after many hours of screaming by the man my parents called "that beast." I connected it with the word *Anschluss* (Annexsation).

Mitzi noticed me hanging over the window. "You are not going out today," she said in an agitated tone. She evaded all my questions while she looked through the underwear drawers, pulling out the white knee-high socks and wiping her eyes and nose with them. "You can't wear these anymore,"

she said in a strange voice and left the room.[11]

It was March 15, 1938, the day that Austria became a German state, called "Ostmark." All the anti-Jewish laws that were implemented gradually over five years in Germany went into effect immediately in Ostmark.

That night, Mutti cut her bedtime story short. She could hardly talk, and I asked if she had a sore throat. (She and I often had such problems.) Mutti just nodded, stroked my cheek, and then kissed me softly on both my eyes. I lay awake feeling hurt, because Mutti had not even said, "Goodnight and sweet dreams," as was her custom. Later I heard her crying, and I thought how incredibly bad her throat must hurt for her to cry like that. Loud sobs, and then hushed words were coming from my parent's bedroom. That knot of fear, which had started a month ago, grew colder and larger.

The next day, Mitzi walked me to kindergarten as usual, but Mutti came to pick me up. "Where is Mitzi?" I asked, upset by the change in routine.

My mother looked grim and hurried me along in the cold wind. Between gusts she explained that Mitzi had needed to go home to Eigen to help her family. Her father had become ill. Mutti didn't sound very convincing; and besides, I had overheard a few phrases of the conversation the night before. I knew Mitzi was leaving for good. Fear had always had the same effect on me and soon the cold wind hit my wet underwear and my stockings, making me shiver with cold. I began to cry, and Mutti walked even faster, not hiding her annoyance. I forgot all about looking at store window displays. Was she going to leave me, too?

Before starting out to pick me up that morning, my mother (who had never cooked anything in her life, having been a bookkeeper/secretary since the age of fourteen) had decided to make noodle soup for lunch. She had started the

---

[11] White knee-high socks were to be worn only by Hitler Youth as part of their uniform.

dried noodles in cold water and put them on a low flame to simmer during her absence. She expected the noodles to be ready upon our return. When we entered the apartment my father was standing by the stove looking suspiciously at the lump of dough in the pot.

Mutti looked at the glob and said she had seen Mitzi pour cold water over the noodles and they separated and were ready for the soup. She would do the same. She poured out the remaining hot water, dumped the glob into a sieve and put it over the sink. When she poured the cold water over the glob of dough, it disintegrated.

"I don't understand it!" Mutti wailed. "I watched Mitzi boil noodles once; this didn't happen to her."

Vati gathered up the mess—sieve and all—and threw it into the garbage can near the sink. We ate a piece of dry bread; we must have had the same thing the next day, but I only remember having tea with a dash of rum because I was coughing and had a very sore throat. I did not go back to kindergarten that spring and spent most of that cold March in my kitchen corner playing with my dolls. They were also sick and needed much doctoring.

On one unusually warm afternoon, Mausie took me for a walk to the Wallensteinstrasse, where one of the big toy stores had a beautiful, animated display we both enjoyed. As we neared the wide intersection, we noticed an island of barbed wire with men huddled behind strange-looking machinery. We had no intention of crossing the street, but as we stood watching this strange scene, a friend of Mausie's came up behind us and said, *"Greuse Got,"* ("God greet you") and started crossing the street. There was no traffic, not even a streetcar. As the girl approached the middle of the street, someone yelled, "Halt!" She kept on walking; we stopped to watch her. An explosion of sound ripped through the air. Mausie's friend fell in a brown heap in the middle of the street. We ran back to our street and dashed into our respective apartments. I tried to tell my mother what I had seen, but

I couldn't get a sound past the lump in my throat.

I know now that the machine gun nests at the intersections that morning were there to prevent protests against the Nazi takeover. People who disobeyed an order were summarily shot. It was many years before I crossed an intersection without feeling a tingle of panic down my spine.

From one day to the next, Jews were stripped of all civil rights.[12] They were to divest themselves of their businesses, and they were forbidden to work for or hire an Aryan. They were barred from entering any public place or using public facilities like the streetcars or park benches. Since Jews had no legal right to own anything, an Aryan could walk into a Jewish home and take whatever they wanted. It was a real test of friendship and the decency of our neighbors. Whom could we trust?

My parents were in shock, totally devastated, and the feeling of betrayal never left them. They were cut off from everything they loved doing. Not being able to participate in the athletic club (The Dianabad) was one of their worst deprivations. My mother loved to swim. Years later, I learned that she knew some of the women who had qualified to swim in the 1936 Olympics being held in Berlin. They were forbidden to compete because of the German laws that were in effect regarding Jews.

My father had been leading an exercise class once a week. Both my parents took frequent showers at the club. None of the apartments in our neighborhood had such a facility. The first time I saw my father shed tears was when he realized that he could no longer go to soccer games, and his favorite soccer team *Ha Kor* (the Jewish team) was disbanded.

The strict curfew forbidding Jews to be on the street after dark limited social life, and the proscribed hours that Jews could shop for groceries meant we ate only what was left at

---

12 The Nuremberg Laws, Germany 1935, were based on the racial laws that were in effect in the United States of America to oppress people with dark skin.

the end of the day. The law that forbade no more than five Jews to gather at one place at any given time was a special challenge to religious Jews who needed ten men to properly conduct a service.

Years later, I saw both my parents wipe their eyes as they told me about the moment they found out that many members in the *Wanderfogel* hiking club had secretly been Nazis. These erstwhile buddies, with whom my parents had shared the best parts of their young lives, gleefully kicked them out of the club.

At first, the anti-Jewish laws were implemented sporadically. Austrians were always a bit lax about enforcing politically instigated rules, edicts and ordinances. This attitude dated back centuries to when the Hapsburgs ruled the empire, and the various edicts were sometimes contradictory, arbitrary, and unclear.

Vati was still working at the warehouse because the new laws made exceptions that allowed Jews to be employed in menial jobs. But Mutti was fired after twenty-seven years as a secretary/bookkeeper at Urie & Zwick (a wholesale fabric house). Mitzi had to leave our home because it was forbidden for Aryan females under the age of forty-five to work as domestics for Jews.

Mutti, Vati and Cousin Gieselle began to study English with the help of Cousin Fritzi, who had married an Englishman while working in London. She had come back to Vienna with her twelve-year-old son, Kurt, to help nurse her dying mother; she stayed a bit too long to help her eighty-year-old father to emigrate to his other daughter in Montevideo, Uruguay. Gieselle was planning to emigrate to England with her husband and children.

What I remember of those afternoons of English lessons are the arguments about leaving Austria. My mother was adamant about our needing to leave as soon as possible, while my father kept saying, "Things will get better," "This can't last," or "The Austrians aren't Germans; they will soon come to their senses."

My mother wrote desperate letters to her cousins and an aunt in America, asking them to send affidavits for our admission to that country. The answers were full of complaints about their own lack of funds.

By the middle of April, the weather had turned warm. It had been a habit for my mother and me to take a walk on nice Saturday afternoons. Sometimes we had taken Mausie along, but on this Saturday it was just the two of us as we headed for the Augarten.

Mutti wouldn't walk fast enough so I skipped ahead, running beside the high walls surrounding the park. I started to run through the iron gate, planning to hide and startle Mutti when she came around the corner.

We had gone only a few steps when a teenaged boy, wearing a swastika armband, came running up to us shouting that we were not allowed in the park. Mutti's hand tightened around mine as she turned me around, and we walked quickly past the huge gates out of the park.

I was disappointed because it was only within the walls of the Augarten that I was permitted to run. Living in a big city, children were expected to walk sedately beside an adult at all times, except in the open spaces of a park.

Holding my hand tighter than usual, my mother headed for the esplanade along the Danube Canal, a branch of the Danube River, which runs through the middle of Vienna. Along both banks, trees, flower beds, and strips of grass grew abundantly, flanked by sidewalks and numerous benches. Since we had been walking a long way, I asked to sit down on a nearby bench.

"We can't sit on the benches," Mutti said. "Can't you see the signs that say 'WET PAINT'?"

But I saw other people sitting on some of these benches and, as a precocious five-year-old, I pointed this out to Mutti. She tightened her grip on my hand and, ignoring my whining, dragged me along at a quickened pace until we reached our apartment.

The door from the hall which went into the kitchen was slightly ajar. My father sat at the kitchen table with his head in his hands, staring out the window. Mutti sat down heavily in one of the chairs. I closed the hall door and waited.

"They let me go," he said; my father's voice was flat.

"We are not allowed into the Augarten," said my mother, her voice rising as the hysterical obscenities, learned in her youth in the streets of Vienna, echoed in the high-ceilinged room. She dropped her head and began sobbing uncontrollably. After what seemed a long time, she lifted her head and, in a calm voice, asked, "No mail from America yet?"

Chapter 6

Since Mutti had brought me to Wopfing much earlier than usual, I had come in time for the celebration of Passover. It was all new to me. My parents were not observant Jews, and I had not even heard of Chanukah until I came to the U.S.A.

Omama was extremely orthodox and Passover was a major event in her life. Most families boil their dishes before using them for Passover, but Omama moved all her food preparation and eating into another kitchen, which she kept only for that purpose and called the "summer kitchen." It was located across the hall from the regular kitchen, at the entrance to the dark hallway that went past the Waxhovers' small apartment and ended at the large delivery doors, which opened to the street.

The summer kitchen had a row of tall windows along one wall, which overlooked the graveled courtyard, surrounded by an eight-foot fence. The other three walls were painted white and lined with cupboards containing the Passover dishes. The summer kitchen was a stark contrast to the regular kitchen, which was a dour place with its dark flagstone floor and one tiny, high window. The oil lamps had to be lit most of the day to see well enough to cook.

Passover at Omama's was an impressive experience, and I learned about Judaism and Kosher and Pessachdike food during that week, which served me well the rest of my life.

Onkel Hugo, my father's younger brother, had been fired from his job as a clerk in a shoe store in Vienna and from his position as a "clapper" for the Vienna opera.[13] So he had come to Wopfing to help his mother in the grocery store.

The first night of Passover, we had Seder dinner in the summer kitchen, a white tablecloth covering the table in the center of the room. There were matzoth on the table—which I had never seen before—and a plate with various items that Hugo began to explain. I became sleepy right after Omama lit the candles and Uncle Hugo began chanting. Tante Franzi gave me a little wine to drink and I fell sound asleep.

Breakfast the next morning was a treat. We had the usual coffee with lots of milk and sugar, but instead of the usual piece of bread, Tante Franzi showed me how to break matzoh into small pieces to dip in my coffee. It tasted wonderful. For the next week, I had the same breakfast every morning. I didn't get matzoh again until three years later when the *five* Jewish families in Longview, Washington, got together and ordered Matzoh from Portland; they gave a box to us who were known as "the refugees."

Omama sat down with me that first day and told me all about Passover. She also took the time to explain the separation of dairy and meat products in her kitchen and why she found it more efficient to use a separate kitchen during Passover. Omama was not a patient woman, but she loved her religious traditions; this was the longest conversation we had ever shared. She explained it all so a five-year-old could understand the reasons for all the Passover foods and the rituals. Much later in my life, I began to read about the holiday so I could celebrate it properly with my own family, and her words resounded in my head. I realized that I *knew* all these things already.

Despite her detailed, patient instructions, I managed to irritate Omama daily. I often forgot which dish belonged where and set them down on the wrong surface. I learned to

---

13 A "clapper" for the opera leads the clapping at the proper juncture of the performance and must know every note.

stay out of the kitchen as much as possible.

During the late spring, it was still cold in those mountainous areas, especially during the night. Toward evening Tante Franzi took the bricks she had placed into the oven of the wood stove. She wrapped them in newspaper and put them into each of our beds. It felt so good to get into a warm bed. We had no heat in the house except for the wood stove in the kitchen. I often saw Onkel Hugo sitting in that kitchen with his feet in the oven. He told me funny stories about his adventures in Vienna, and he was usually the person to tuck me into bed—right at sundown to preserve the kerosene in the lamps. I remember telling Onkel Hugo that I wanted to marry him; he said he would wait for me until I grew up. (I believed him.)

The twins didn't come to visit that year, but it was a memorable summer and I can recall almost every detail. I was not allowed to roam outside by myself. I sat for hours learning how to embroider. Threading needles was the worst torture, and I often stuck myself, getting blood spots on the white fabric. When I cried, Tante Fritzi consoled me. She always told me that the blood spots would wash out with cold water, and my finger would heal long before my wedding day.

I missed Mitzi and thought about her daily. I heard that if one made a wish on a four-leaf clover, that wish would certainly come true—but only if you didn't pick the clover. One day, when I had snuck out to the meadow, I found a bed of clover. To my surprise, in the lovely green bed, I saw a four-leaf clover. Thinking of Mitzi, I immediately wished she would come and get me. When I looked up, she was standing over me. I threw myself into her arms, telling her how much I had missed her. She promised to come back when she had more time and even take me to Eigen with her later that summer. Then she was gone. The rest of my life, whenever I see a patch of clover, I take a careful look, but I have never seen another four-leaf clover.

Each Friday, Tante Franzi got up before dawn to prepare

the bread dough for the weekly loaves of bread. She would pound and knead the cartwheel-sized loaves, let them rise on a long board that had a rope strung over it. Later in the day she slung the rope over her shoulder, and we would take the loaves to the village baker to be baked in the huge brick ovens.

I looked forward to Fridays, as going to the baker was a social occasion. Tante Franzi would gossip with the baker for a few minutes; these two had known each other all their lives and called each other by their first names. The baker, dressed in white with the traditional tall, white hat, always impressed me as a warm and friendly man. He had a round, red face with blazing, blue eyes, which twinkled wickedly as he teased my aunt about finding her a husband. She would chuckle, reminding him that he knew that no man was good enough or strong enough for her.

It was fun to watch the baker work. He scooped up the loaves with a long-handled paddle and deftly set them in the oven. While the bread was baking, I went next door to Kampichler's tavern to get a raspberry drink and play with their daughter, Lotti, for a few minutes. Then I went back into the bakery to watch the baker pull the warm, fragrant loaves out of the oven. He set them back on Tante Franzi's board and we would trudge home, the smell of fresh bread wafting around us.

These weekly outings were a break from sitting in one place and having a few minutes of fun with someone near my age. Lottie, a pale, quiet girl, taught me to play Jacks (a game played with a small rubber ball and little top-like pieces), and we enjoyed the drink her father, the proprietor, poured us. Her family also had a dog, and I would have dearly loved a pet, but no one in my family would hear of it.

One Friday, as we walked into the bakery, the baker's face wore a solemn look. His son, a boy of about eleven—dressed in short khaki pants, wearing a swastika armband and the white knee-high socks reserved for the Hitler Youth—stood by his side.

"I'll bake your bread today, Frau Schischa," he said formally to my aunt. "But we cannot serve your kind anymore." He looked at his son who stood there with a frown on his cold face, then he leaned over the counter toward my aunt and whispered, "I'm very sorry, Franzi."

At first, we hadn't been sure he was talking to her. Tante Franzi had grown up in this village and no one had ever called her by her married name. When she realized what he meant, she began to shake, and I could feel her skirts move in my hand. Slowly she put the bread board down on the counter and leaned a little forward.

"Erik"—her voice was low—"your father baked bread for my family and your grandfather before that; you know what kind of people we are. Our families have served each other for over one hundred years, and we have always paid our bill on time; we have helped members of your family when they needed us. You don't really believe all this political garbage?"

The baker looked helpless and shrugged his massive shoulders. Tante Franzi picked up the board. "Come!" she commanded me, and I clutched a larger fold of her skirt. Without a word we walked out of the bakery, past the glaring women waiting to enter. I could feel Tante Franzi shaking as we walked. Was she crying, also? I remember that I was crying with disappointment about not getting my strawberry soda or seeing my friend.

As we came into the kitchen, Omama came in from the grocery store. Before she could speak, Tante Franzi chuckled softly and said, "Can you imagine after all these years, Erik's old oven developed a crack. We'll have to bake our own bread until he can repair it."

With these words she started to put large chunks of wood into the fire box of the iron range. Then she began to cut the bread into smaller shapes to fit into the oven. Omama clucked her tongue in annoyance and went back into the store.

None of Wopfing had electricity, and thus no radio and only a weekly newspaper from Vienna. Yet less than a month after the Anschluss on March 15th, everyone knew that contact with Jews was now forbidden. Most people who had traded at the Kohns' store all their lives now walked to the next town. Omama spent less and less time in the business. Finally, she was forced to sell it for a few Deutschmark to the Waxhovers.

Maria and Stefan Waxhover had no idea how to run a store. They also faced the difficulty of the tobacco license. As I mentioned earlier, Austrians found ways to circumvent laws that were inconvenient. Like all the men in the village, the local Gauleiter smoked incessantly. Making the excuse that Frau Kohn was a war widow—and mostly for his own benefit—he decided to allow their store to keep the tobacco license, while Rosa Kohn volunteered to work in the store. For the time being, the sisters and Uncle Hugo were permitted to stay in the house and work for food.

Chapter 7

The Gypsy

One morning, Tante Franzi woke me early; it was barely daylight. She dressed me in my Vienna dress and a freshly-starched apron. She was wearing her newer housedress, the one with the not-so-faded flowers, and we walked past the latrine and out the back gate. We walked hand in hand through the meadow, following the path that led to the nearby village of Waldeck. It was a cold, clear morning, and my sturdy, high-topped shoes were soon soaked with dew and making a squishing sound at every step. We could have taken the dirt road, but the dust would have choked us before we had walked even half of the five miles.

Tante Franzi taught me some nonsense rhymes along the way. Then I sang some songs from the popular operettas currently playing in the Vienna theaters. I knew many songs from hearing them on the radio and from the people working along the streets. The garbage collectors, the street cleaners, and the construction workers all sang. Everyone knew the melodies from the popular Franz Lehar operettas. Tante Franzi, who had never been to Vienna or heard a radio, was impressed with my knowledge of the theatrical world and my musical talent.

It seemed to me that we had walked forever when the church steeples of Waldeck finally came into view. To the left of the trail we saw a thread of blue smoke drifting toward the even bluer sky. The ringing sound of coins being struck together filled the air. A little further on, we saw the wagons of a gypsy camp. As we came closer, a woman dressed in brilliant colors called to us from one of the wagons.

"Gracious lady!" she shouted. "Come, bring the little one here. I'll tell her fortune." Her voice was deep with a strange accent.

Tante Franzi hesitated, but I pleaded to stop and rest. Slowly we walked to the edge of the camp. I could see a fire and several men sitting around it. They had small hammers and were pounding on an assortment of pots and pans. As each hammer rose and fell, they created a not-unpleasant rhythm. My aunt explained that they were tinkers who came each year and repaired the pots and pans for the households in the valley.

The dark woman jumped down from the wagon and squatted in front of me. "How are you, little Gypsy?" she asked. I noticed that her hair, partly covered by a print scarf, was as black as mine, and when her hand reached out to touch my arm, it was the same color as my own brown skin. She wore gold, hooped earrings that bobbed back and forth as she talked. Her breath was a mixture of stale tobacco and garlic.

"Come, sit here!" she ordered. She took off one of her voluminous skirts and spread it out on the grass. I sat down immediately and gently stroked the shiny, smooth material. Tante Franzi and the woman seemed to know each other. They talked for a few minutes about the weather and more at length about the current hardships and restrictions they'd had to endure under the new regime. Then the Gypsy turned to me.

"Let me see your hand, little one," she demanded. Reluctantly, I held out my hand; I much preferred keeping my hand on the smooth fabric of her skirt. She held both my hands in her gnarled, ring-covered fingers, and studied them for a moment.

"Your hands are cold, little one; that means you have a warm heart." Her smile showed big, yellow teeth, but she had a kind face. I relaxed a little as she let go of my hands and I could go on stroking the skirt. She concentrated on my left palm. Her voice became even deeper, and she spoke in a continuous monotone.

"You will be swept away from your home to a far place. I see much sadness, and you will miss—and be missed—by those you love. You will have children—perhaps grandchildren—before you return. When you do return, everything will be different—and everything will be the same." Her voice stopped abruptly. I could hear the drone of bees between the clanging of the hammers. The Gypsy stood up and held out her hand to Tante Franzi, who dug a coin out of her old leather pouch, and it went into the woman's outstretched palm.

"That was a silly fortune to tell the child," my aunt scolded and led me away.

Thirty-three years later, I stood near the meadow and remembered this scene. The Gypsy had been so right about what she'd told me. I had returned and, although everything in my life was different, I saw that the hills and meadows, the ruined castle on the hill, and the village of Wopfing were the same as the day I left.

We arrived at the home of the cousins. I remember the widowed mother whose husband had been killed in the war (as was my grandfather), and two girls several years older than me. Their names were Charlotte and Miriam, my father's second-cousins.

After we ate cakes and drank lemonade I was put down for a rest on a cot in one corner of the screened-in porch. The ladies settled down for a long afternoon of talk and a game of cards. I wondered, as I drifted off to sleep, if my grandmother would have approved of the cards. I didn't think so, and I decided not to mention anything about that day if asked. Omama disapproved of Gypsies; I could hear it in her voice when she mentioned the tinkers, and she thought fortune-telling was the work of the devil. She had her own superstitions. For example, when she cut her nails, she carefully gathered the clippings in a little piece of paper and put them in a drawer. That drawer held a lot of little bundles, which I discovered as I peeked into it one day. Omama believed that when one dies, all the parts of one's body must stay together. The scattered pieces must be gathered by the soul of the departed before they can rest in peace. Omama knew where to find her nail clippings. She also saved the hair that was shed from brushing and washing.

It was dusk when Tante Franzi and I passed the place where we had seen the Gypsies. They were gone, and only wagon tracks were left. I began to think about what the fortuneteller had told me. I was sure that she had foreseen my fate because that's what happened to little girls who told lies. The witch would spirit me away and I would come back as an old, disfigured hag, and not even my parents would recognize me. For a short while, I was always careful to tell the truth (as I saw it) or else say nothing at all.

The twins didn't come to visit that summer, so I spent many hours alone in the great meadow just sitting in the sweet-smelling grass and looking up at the ruins of a Crusader Castle on the mountain above the village. I made up stories about a princess who was imprisoned in the tower by an evil king. A handsome, blue-eyed, blond-haired prince would come to rescue her. They would ride away on his white horse and live happily ever after.

One of the best memories of that summer was gathering berries and mushrooms with Tante Franzi in the wooded area across the Pisting River. I can still smell the scents that wafted through the air as we walked along the soft cushion of pine needles. Fragrant violets were hidden among the bushes, and tiny, wild strawberries exploded with flavor. I was supposed to fill a small wicker basket with these berries, but few berries ever got that far.

Tante Franzi knew which mushrooms to pick and which ones were highly toxic. She told me that usually the prettier the mushroom, the more poisonous they were. When her basket was full of mushrooms, she tied the corners of her apron around her waist and filled that too. The musty aroma of fresh mushrooms brings back the feel and smell of that forest, and regrettably, the rage and sorrow for the brutal, senseless losses we suffered.

Chapter 8

On a Sunday morning in August (I knew it was Sunday because the church bells were ringing), Mitzi came to take me with her up to Eigen, the small village where her family lived. It was a full day's hike straight up a steep, forest-covered hill.

Tante Franzi packed my things into a small backpack, which I was expected to carry. Mitzi went into the grocery store and filled a large basket with such things as candles, lamp oil, tobacco, cigarette paper, boxes of matches, and a few pieces of candy.

We walked through the town and veered off to the left to climb up to Shmoel's Inn. Annie Shmoel was sitting on the veranda as we walked by and I waved to her. I had played Jacks with her at Kampichler's, but she never had the energy to play tag or climb trees. She didn't wave back, but just stared at me with her wide, blue eyes.

Toward mid-day, Mitzi and I sat down on a log in a small clearing covered with daisies, and she gave me some bread and jam and a peach. I was very tired by then as we had been climbing for several hours. I told Mitzi that I couldn't walk anymore and asked her to carry me.

"I can't carry you," she told me in an apologetic tone. "I need to carry the basket, and besides, you are much too heavy by now to be carried."

I cried and protested but to no avail. Mitzi stood and looked down at me for a few minutes, while I waited for her to change her mind.

"If you don't want to walk up to Eigen with me, you can

either stay here or go back down to Wopfing," she said in a matter-of-fact tone and began walking up the hill. It didn't take long for me to scamper up after her.

The sun was low when we arrived at her parents' house. It was little more than a shack with a low roof and one window facing the road. A water trough was under the window. I could see the outhouse toward the back fence of the dirt yard. Inside the small house, one big room featured a huge stove along one wall, and a narrow side table and a bench filling the opposite wall. A table with benches on either side stood in the middle of the room. Toward the back of the room, behind a ladder, stood some beds. The ladder went up to the loft where Mitzi and I would be sleeping on piles of straw.

Mitzi introduced me to her father. Herr Bauer towered over me, and his tanned face looked like wrinkled leather. Her mother, a small, slim figure standing over the stove, didn't turn around. I don't remember seeing her face and she never spoke to me for the few days I was there. Mitzi told me her mother seldom spoke because she didn't want people to see that she had no teeth.

Mitzi put her basket on the table and helped me up the ladder to the loft. She arranged piles of hay into beds, took my things out of the backpack and arranged them on a low bench against one wall. We went back down the ladder and after a trip to the latrine (it had only one hole, while Omama's had two), we went to the trough to wash up before dinner. The soap smelled awful and I was reluctant to use it, but Mitzi insisted. We washed and wiped our hands on our aprons.

Two men came in and sat at the table, while Frau Bauer filled plates at the stove. The men nodded to Mitzi, ignored me, ate their food, and went back outside to smoke. I must have eaten something that evening, but I was exhausted and fell asleep at the table. The next morning, I woke up on the straw in my wet nightgown, shivering and scared. When I called her, Mitzi came up to get me. She dressed me in dry clothes, helped me down the ladder, gave me a cup of warm milk (straight from the cow), and soon we were on our way to the hayfields.

The men cut the hay, and Mitzi and I grabbed sweet-smelling armfuls and loaded them onto the wagon. The horse slowly pulled the wagon through the freshly-mowed field. At noon, the women of the village brought bread and beer, and we sat under a tree to eat. Afterward, we kept working throughout the hot afternoon. When the sun began to sink behind the hills, we returned to the stone farmhouse. We quenched our thirst with buttermilk, cooled from the creek nearby.

I remember saying that I wanted to stay with Mitzi there in Eigen for always. Mitzi laughed and told me I would soon change my mind. Herr Bauer had come in just then. He grinned at me, and his blue eyes twinkled as he said, "We can't have the like of you up here. You are much too dirty. Why, even your eyes are the color of coal dust."

"I can't help the color of my eyes," I retorted (probably in a sassy voice that I used when addressing unreasonable grownups).

"Yes, you can," he replied. "Wash them out with soap and your eyes will be clean like mine."

It occurred to me that Mitzi had eyes that were almost as dark as mine, but I was quiet.

I was not an ignorant baby, and, instinctively, I knew what soap in my eyes would feel like. But the next morning, while washing my face at the rusty washstand outside the kitchen door, I deliberately rubbed my eyes with strong soap. The pain was excruciating, but I kept rubbing, then rinsed with the water from the basin. Through squinted lids I inspected my flaming eyeballs in the mottled mirror that hung over the washstand. They still looked like two moist coals.

Mitzi came to get me and saw the tears; she assumed I might be homesick. When she saw how swollen my eyes were, she guessed the truth. That evening, while drifting off to sleep on the pile of hay, I heard her talking about me to her father. She was telling him what I had done, and why she thought I might have done such a stupid thing to my eyes. I heard his and her brother's laughter, and one of them said that it served "that dirty Jew brat" right. I wondered why the man thought I was dirty.

The next Sunday, Mitzi and I went back down to Wopfing. Tante Franzi was waiting for us near the large delivery doors at the front of the house. I hugged her, still holding tightly to Mitzi's hand. "I must get back to Eigen," Mitzi told me, and with a quick hug and kiss she was gone. Omama came out and took my hand, exclaiming how dirty I was and needed a bath. Soon, I was sitting in the big washtub, being scrubbed from head to toe.

That Monday was the monthly wash day, and the washerwoman came to help Maria Waxhover and Tante Franzi to boil the linens in the same big washtub in the basement wash-kitchen.

Before hauling the heavy baskets to the Pisting River for the rinsing, the women sat down for a cup of tea and a piece of bread. After the three women left with the hampers, Omama washed out the cups, handing me a *milchig* ("dairy") towel and told me to dry them and put them on the milchig counter. (The *milchig* towels were blue and the *fleishig* towels—the ones for the meat—were red. They were kept in separate drawers in the kitchen.) The cup I was drying slipped from my fingers. My first thought was, *Is the slate floor milchig or fleishig?*

I heard the crash as from a distance. Not waiting for Omama to scream at me, I fled out the door, ran down the steps, and kept running. I reached the meadow near the river where Tante Franzi was laying out the linens to dry in the sun. My eyes were full of tears so I couldn't see where I was going. Someone scooped me up and started pointing at the muddy shoeprints on the drying sheets. I saw what I had done; I knew how much more work I had made for these women. The washerwoman sighed and began gathering up the sheets to re-rinse, while Tante Franzi dragged me back to the house. No one bothered to scold me; they couldn't have been heard over my wailing.

The next day I was still feeling sorry and guilty, so I was unusually quiet and stayed on a chair in the kitchen watching Tante Franzi bustling around. Suddenly the church bells began to ring. They kept on ringing for a long time and, while they were still ringing, Omama came into the kitchen. She was accompanied by a woman from the village who held out a huge bundle of fresh dill toward Tante Franzi. The fragrance filled the kitchen. Omama asked if she knew why the bells were ringing on a weekday—she had to speak loudly to be heard over the clanging bells.

"Little Annie Schmoel died this morning, and the bells are ringing for her Mass," the woman told us. To this day, the smell of fresh dill takes me back to that kitchen and thoughts of death.

The next Sunday, my mother came to take me back to Vienna. I hugged everybody and gave my uncle Hugo a special hug and kiss. I reminded him that he promised to wait until I was old enough and then marry me. (It would be ten years before we met again—and he hadn't waited for me.)

Chapter 9

After Mutti and I got off the train in Vienna, we walked quickly through the cavernous marble hall of the Seudbanhoff. The walls were covered with swastikas and huge portraits of the Feurher. I noticed several groups of surly-looking men, dressed in brown, wearing swastika armbands. My stomach began to churn with fear. Without looking right or left, Mutti lead me through the crowded waiting room and out through the huge doors to the street.

Under a deep blue September sky, we started walking. I remarked that this was not the way to the streetcar. My mother was moving along quickly, and, without slowing down, she told me that we were not taking the streetcar. Of course I asked why not, and she told me that we needed the exercise after the two-hour train ride.

We walked along the tree-lined streets for what seemed an endless time. The shades of red and gold of the foliage, along with the red and black flags that waved from every building and lamp post, looked festive, like the preparation for a big party.

Mutti told me that she had been writing letters to her cousins in America. "It takes a long time for mail to come over the ocean," she sighed.

I had a vision of her letters floating over the waves to America and the hoped-for reply floating back. When I asked about Mausie, Mutti made a vague reply about how busy a person is when they are in the fourth grade.

Finally, we arrived at our apartment. I was so exhausted

that my legs were numb. After a cup of hot milk, Mutti undressed me and Vati carried me into the next room. He tucked me in, carefully pushed my hair back with his big hand, and left the pleasant smell of tobacco in the room as he went out. (Throughout my childhood, I rarely saw my father without a cigarette in his hand.)

In the weeks that followed, my parents spent hours every day studying English. Tante Fritzi (actually, my mother's cousin) came to tutor the inept students. Mutti often remarked how lucky we were to have Tante Fritzi to help us. We were lucky to have her, of course, but she was running out of luck.

Fritzi's son, Kurt, came with her to help with the English lessons. I loved Kurt, not only for his blond hair and blue eyes, but also for teaching me chess with a kindness and patience rare for a twelve-year-old boy. I really enjoyed the game and looked forward to playing it with him whenever we got together.

Kurtie Bader, 1937.

Fritzi, Tilde & Old Uncle, 1939

My mother kept warning Fritzi about delaying her return to England. Fritzi's husband sent entreating letters for her to bring their son home, but she was determined to see her father safely on a ship to Montevideo before she departed. It was a fatal error. The day after *der alter onkel*—"the old uncle," as my mother called Fritzi's father—left for his long journey to the New World, re-entry visas like Fritzi's and Kurt's were canceled. The country known as Austria no longer existed, and all the paperwork had to be started over with the new government, which exacted all new fees. Although she didn't have permission to work, Fritzi managed to earn a little money with her English lessons, since many people were planning to leave Austria for an English-speaking country.

The Montessori school was not considered a public school, so I was able to return to my dear Tante Mary, as all teachers are called in the German Montessori system. At noon, when Mutti picked me up, we meandered along the main streets, admiring the animated displays in the toy store windows. The trains, jumping clowns, dolls that opened and closed their eyes, and even dolls that danced on a platform like ballerinas—these were the only sources of entertainment left for a Jewish child.

During the summer, Mutti had learned a bit about cooking. She had found a cookbook, probably from her mother. Since she could hardly get any of the ingredients needed for these dishes, she improvised. Mitzi had left a large supply of noodles and Mutti had learned how to cook noodles by then, so we usually had soup for our main meal. We also had *Nussnudeln*—the short flat noodles sprinkled with ground walnuts and a little sugar from before the Anschluss, and noodle soup made with bony chicken parts. Only the chicken necks and feet were left at the butcher shops by late afternoon when Jews could shop for groceries. I don't remember eating vegetables and only occasionally enjoying a piece of fruit. A good supply of flour was still in the house, so there was a thickening agent to make the soup seem more nourishing.

Vati was gone almost every day looking for work. Since it was not legal to hire Jews, he must have worked "under the table" for a pittance or just for food. My parents did have Aryan friends, and little by little my mother must have sold furniture and other possessions to the decent people who were not inclined to steal even when it was legal.

Most Jewish homes held little of value by that time. Jews were not allowed to own radios, bicycles, gold or silver jewelry (married women were allowed to keep their wedding rings). All pets were confiscated, which resulted in heartbreaking scenarios of beloved cats and dogs being dragged out of the arms of weeping children.

Against my father's wishes, my mother insisted on taking all their savings out of the bank. She must have hidden the funds well, because even during the Gestapo searches, they never found anything valuable. She also had the foresight to melt her gold necklace into her wedding ring.

One time a black-booted monster tore open my little clown, spilling sawdust all over the kitchen floor. I tried not to cry, but it was hard to wait until they left. My anger at their meanness will never fade.

My parents were used to taking the streetcar to the end of the line and hiking into the Vienna Woods. They must have missed their frequent visits to The Dianabad, where they could exercise, swim and shower. Instead, they spent much of their time in long lines at different embassies applying for visas. My father getting to the United States of America was not possible in the near future, for a quota system was based on how many people from a country were already in the U.S.A. Very few Czechoslovakians were in this country, so the quota was small, and the waiting list was very long. Besides, my father was loath to believe that he was in real danger from the people that used to be his friends. My mother had to make all the plans for departure.

The Nazi who took over the wholesale textile company where my mother had worked needed her to train someone to take over her former position of bookkeeper/private secretary. Thus the laws were circumvented to accommodate the needs of the criminals who now ruled the land.

Whether Mitzi also got a dispensation from the law, I can't say. But one morning, she reappeared. As I mentioned earlier, Austrians were adept at ignoring laws when they found them inconvenient. For me, the nightmare of her absence was over. My mother went back to work in the office. Our routine continued almost as before the Anschluss.

Chapter 10

Every few days, someone in the family came to say good-bye. Uncle Ludvig (my mother's brother, who had fought for Austria in the war) bid us farewell with his wife, Tante Julie, a city girl from Berlin who had never worn a pair of hiking boots. They had plans to walk across the Alps to Italy.

When I visited them in Florence in 1973, my mother's handsome, debonair brother told me the story of how the Nazis came to the village where he and Julie had found refuge along with thirty other Jews. Someone had warned the mayor that these "black-shirted maniacs" were coming to take away the Jews. That night all the refugees were taken by rowboat across the lake to Switzerland where they stayed until the villagers came to bring them back to Italy.

Uncle Ludvig's bright blue eyes were a bit faded now that he was nearly eighty years old, but they sparkled with pleasure as he told this story, which explained his love of Italy and Italians.

Siddie, another of my mother's cousins—who later changed her name to Lydia—had married a successful shoemaker. He had relatives in Brazil who urged him to leave Europe even before the Nazis came to power. Now seemed like an opportune time to head for Rio de Janeiro. Their farewell visit was brief and a bit cool. My mother didn't approve of Siddie, who wore flashy, stylish clothes, and had her hair dyed blonde. The two cousins embraced briefly, and then Siddie patted me on the head and twirled out the door. We heard her high-heeled shoes clicking on the stairs.

Cousin Paula and Uncle Herbert came with Heinzi whose jaw was all healed now, and he could eat anything he wanted (except there was little to eat now). They were on their way to Colombo, Ceylon (Sri Lanka). They talked about the heat there and how one could pick bananas right off a tree. The name was familiar because the tea we drank at night came from this island, and palm trees were pictured on the box. Fortunately, Cousin Paula was an experienced seamstress, a skill she could use wherever she went.

Cousin Minna Gotlieb came one day to tell us she was leaving. Her employer of twenty years—a married, Catholic doctor—had arranged for her to go to Melbourne, Australia.

Years later I found out that Minna and the doctor had been lovers for many years, meeting two weeks each summer in Switzerland, even during WWII. Minna became a talented artist and sent us some of her paintings, which hang on my walls to this day.

Mutti's favorite cousin, Joshi, was leaving for Shanghai, China. He advised my parents to get tickets for that city. "No visa needed, just a steamship ticket." (My mother bought tickets for Shanghai; we never used them, so she must have sold them to get badly-needed cash.) Joshi pinched my cheeks and told me how cute I had become, then hugged my mother. "I can never thank you enough," he said in a husky voice, while she bit her lips, tears streaming down her ruddy cheeks.

During October of 1938, my parents spent most of their time at home studying English and standing in long lines at different government offices and at food stores. We had received some answers from Mutti's relatives in America. Most of the letters were offers of help—if and when we got to the U.S.A. People in our circumstances needed an affidavit (a signed document—costing $300—that guaranteed that the sponsor had means to support the immigrant for at least five years) to get a visa to enter the country. I heard my parents talk about this daily while they nervously waited for the mail. The month went by with little change in our situation, or any knowledge of what was happening around us. Our radio had been taken away and the newspapers printed only propaganda.

Fritz Schischa, Tante Franzi's only son and my father's cousin and best friend, came to visit us late one evening. I know it was late because I had been asleep when the raised voices in the kitchen woke me up. The door was open a crack because Mitzi had not come back yet from her nightly church service.

Fritz, who made his living as a pastry chef, was a founding member of the Wanderfogel hiking club, a trail guide and a mountain climber. He had come to persuade my father to join him and some friends who were planning to flee the country.

My mother's voice was shrill as she asked Fritz, "What about Ida and the baby?"[14]

"They are already in England," was his calm reply. "The whole family left together. Ida's mother, stepfather and her two brothers."

I heard a loud gasp from my mother, followed by a long silence. Ida had not even stopped by here to say good-bye. Then my mother started to scold, scream, curse everything and everyone, from God to the fiends who now ruled us. This was followed by the heart-rending sobs that had become familiar to me.

"Things will only get worse for us," Fritz said. "There are plans for a pogrom, an *Aktzion*. Every Jew in Germany will be arrested."

My father's voice was calm, almost jovial, as he replied, "The Austrians are not going to go along with those German thugs. Things are getting better here already. Thilde has her job back and Mitzi is still with us. I get work here and there. I am a decent, innocent person. Why would anyone arrest me?"

My mother had calmed down and I could hear her talking

---

[14] Ida Schischa was my mother's best friend since school days, and she had persuaded my mother to join the hiking club where she met my father. The "baby" was two-year-old Erwin.

but couldn't make out what she was saying. When Fritz started to talk again, I realized she had been asking him questions. He answered in the drawling dialect of the Wopfing region. It would be many years before I heard it again.

"I have friends, well, actually business acquaintances at the pastry shop who have contacts in Belgium. For a price, they will get us papers, put us in touch with 'safe houses' and get us over the border near Aachen. Once we are in Belgium we just need to get to Antwerp. Ships leave for England every day."

I was getting sleepy, and as I dozed off, I heard Fritz yell at my father, "You are an idiot, a stupid coward. Come with me right now. It is your last chance to escape. The people that warned me are in on a dreadful, vile plot to destroy every Jew in Germany."

As I had often heard before, my father made light of such talk. He told Fritz he could not leave his wife and child behind, and besides, he was sure the whole story was greatly exaggerated.

"Leo, haven't you heard what that maniac plans to do?" Fritz was raising his normally soft, lilting voice. Before my father could answer I heard Fritz yell, "Leo, you are an idiot!" Then there was a loud bang as the hall door was slammed.

Once again, I heard my mother crying as she walked by my bed to get to her bedroom. She had not told me a story that night. A few minutes later, Vati stroked my hair as he also passed by on his way to bed.

Chapter 11

The next morning while Mitzi helped me dress, gave me my usual crusty roll and milky coffee, I noticed her hands were shaking. It took her an inordinately long time to tie my shoes and button my coat. Finally, we hurried downstairs.

A sharp wind cut across my legs as Mitzi and I walked to kindergarten that morning. When we arrived at the Montessori school, instead of the expected quick hug, Mitzi held me a few moments and I felt tears on her cheeks. I thought nothing of it since my cheeks were damp also; my eyes had been watering from the cold wind.

There was the usual morning ritual of hanging up our coats, gathering around the tables in our classroom. When Tante Mary came in, the seven of us five-year-olds stood up and said *"Guten Morgen"* in unison.

We were just having our ten o'clock snack when I saw Mutti in the doorway. She motioned me to come with her and seemed agitated as she helped me on with my coat. She was in a hurry, and we walked quickly through the back streets. I began to object, as Mitzi and I usually walked along the main streets on our way home, enjoying the window displays, especially now that they were decorated for the coming Christmas holiday. Mutti didn't acknowledge my complaints, just pulled me along. She had not given me time to use the toilet before we left, and she was not about to stop and let me go to the public one, which she considered dangerously dirty.

When we were near our apartment building one of my mother's cousins came running up to us. "They have taken away all the men!" she shouted in a high-pitched scream. Mutti ran past her to the apartment house entrance where the manager was sitting on her low bench. We ran past the manager and up the stairs to an empty apartment. "Leo! Leo!" my mother called out, but no one was there. Ignoring my demand to use the toilet, she dragged me down the stairs and accosted the manager.

"Have you seen my husband?" she asked the grim-faced woman. Mausie's mother answered in her nasal twang, "I told him that there was an order from the Gestapo for all Jewish men to report to the police station. He didn't believe me at first, so my son arrested him."

My mother screamed obscenities that I had never heard from her. I only understood the word *luder*[15] which was seldom used in my presence. Sadly, this term applied to many of the people my family had trusted and loved.

Clutching my hand, Mutti marched us to the police station, up the long flight of steps, into the great hall, and up to the officer behind the desk.

"Franzle, where is my husband?" she asked in a demanding tone.

For a moment he squinted at us from his perch at the raised desk and then he recognized my mother. "Thilde," he said in a quiet tone. "The men were all taken to the train depot, they are under arrest for crimes against the state, and they're being transported to Dachau. (The informality of first names meant that these two had known each other from childhood) The policeman continued: "We know that your Leo is a decent man, no one is going to hurt him. It is just a political action."

My mother turned abruptly, and we started down the steep marble steps. When we got to the street, she tightened her grip on my hand and hurried me along at an even quicker pace. Suddenly I realized that we were on the main street and

---

[15] A despicable, abominable and corrupt female. (In American English: "Bitch")

that we were walking ankle deep in glass. I shuffled along as best I could. When we passed an intersection, I looked down the narrow street and saw the red glow of a fire. The flames and sparks were shooting high into the air and I was fascinated. I wanted to see what was happening and dragged my feet to slow us down. But Mutti would not slow down and urged me to go faster. (The synagogue was burning and the bonfire in front of it was being fed all the books and Torahs that the frenzied mob had dragged outside.)

By the time we reached the Nordbanhoff, the station where the trains left for Munich, it was getting dark. We walked into the almost empty depot. A few people were standing around, some of them in the brown uniforms of the SA. I wanted to run away, as I knew that these were the most dangerous men in Vienna. I had heard this from my father as he described them as the worst criminals in the country. Mutti walked up to one of these scowling thugs and asked what had happened to the men being transported that day.

Kristallnacht (Aftermath) November 10, 1938.

"We sent the Jewish swine to Dachau about an hour ago," he said and smiled down at my mother. We scurried out of the building and started walking back to the apartment. It began to snow, adding more moisture to my stockings and shoes, which were already soaked with urine. I was shivering and my teeth were chattering. It was almost dark when we finally arrived home. Mutti changed me into my night shirt, gave me some hot tea, and put me to bed.

I didn't have a story that night, and I lay awake for a while trying to make sense of the day. Vati was gone. Mutti was angry, and I heard her pacing the kitchen until I finally fell asleep.

I don't remember much of the next few weeks as I was sick with tonsillitis, a cough, and eventually an earache. We weren't allowed to go to an Aryan doctor, and all the Jewish doctors in Vienna (actually, in all of Germany, all the men who didn't have the sense to hide) had been sent to Dachau that day. Nothing could be done but just wait for the infections to subside. (This was long before the time of antibiotics.)

The world we knew was gone. For the rest of her life, when my mother spoke of the tenth of November 1938, her voice changed, and I would get chills just to hear her say "Der Zenta." It was like a deep chasm separating our lives. Everything that happened or that we remembered was always referred to as being either before or after "The Tenth of November 1938."

The pogrom *(Kristallnacht)*—ostensibly a spontaneous riot in response to the shooting of an official in the German Embassy in Paris—had been meticulously organized for months. In the aftermath of the nationwide destruction of Jewish businesses and the looting and burning of synagogues, the German government cancelled all insurance policies. They confiscated all bank accounts held by Jews and ordered the Jewish Cultural Association *(the Israelische Kultus Gemeinde)* to pay for all the damages. Until these damages were paid (a purely arbitrary figure), the Jewish men—about thirty thousand of them—who were now in concentration camps would not be released.

It had been an easy task for the Nazi thugs to find *every* Jewish man left in Germany as they had the address and religion of every resident in the country. For hundreds of years, every child was registered at the local police station at birth, indicating their name, religion, address, and name and occupation of parents and grandparents. This information was updated to include their school, current residence if they had moved, marital status, club membership (sometimes including their political affiliation), arrest record and, by the 1920s, an updated photo. A copy of this information had to be carried by every citizen at all times. Failure to show one's "identity papers" when required was a serious offense.

Chapter 12

After that night of horror, Mitzi did not come back, nor did I return to Montessori Kindergarten. A month went by before I recovered sufficiently to get out of bed.

A notice had been sent out to all the Jewish women, notifying them that the men being held in the concentration camps would be released with payment of a fee. If specified papers were filled out, verified, stamped, and submitted with a certain amount of cash, a release form would be issued.

Ascertaining which forms were required, filling them out with the correct information, and then getting them stamped by an official meant standing in line at various government offices. Each time we climbed those steep marble steps to the second floor of the Gestapo headquarters, the knot of fear in my stomach took over my whole body. Almost immediately after being ordered to sit down on a black, leather-covered bench to wait for my mother, I had the urge to urinate.

My mother disappeared behind huge wooden doors, while I waited in the hallway for what seemed an eternity, wondering if I would see her again. When she reappeared, I shook with relief, leaving a trail of urine as we descended the stairway to the street.

I asked Mutti to take me to a toilet. Her answer was brusque: "There are no toilets in this place." I knew that was a lie, since I had seen a good-looking young woman standing guard in a doorway that had the word "TOILETTE" on a sign above the door.

I lost respect for the authority of uniforms, titles, and

adults—including my parents—who had grown up in an authoritarian society. My attitude caused constant friction.

Many years later, I understood that my mother was trying to protect me from the horrors that were developing around us. Even before the public had any knowledge of the atrocities of which these people were capable, Mutti was ashamed of her fellow countrymen. It wasn't only the German/Austrian people who, totally against their own self-interests, persecuted decent, productive people who had lived peacefully among them for many generations. Almost all of Europe was involved in this crime.

As time went by, I encountered Anti-Semitism at each of the fourteen schools I attended and in each European country I visited. I began to believe that prejudice against Jews is a contagious mental disease, endemic to Christians. It is totally irrational to persecute Jews; they have proven to be an asset to any nation where they are permitted to live in peace.[16]

One afternoon we heard a knock on the door—always a cause for alarm. In those days anyone could walk into a Jewish home and take whatever they wanted. We had no legal rights to possess anything, and we heard stories of neighbors just coming in and helping themselves to whatever they wanted. We waited quietly, hoping whoever it was would go away. Then a familiar voice said, "It's me." Mutti opened the door and saw a woman wrapped in a large shawl with a peasant scarf over her head, carrying a small suitcase. It was Omama.

Omama came in quickly and set down her small bag. She was shivering and frightfully pale. Mutti was so surprised to see her that she was speechless. Omama burst into loud sobs, and Mutti led her to the bench by the stove. She began to tell us her story.

She and Tante Franzi had been arrested, loaded onto a truck, and taken to the prison in Wiener Neustadt, which was the nearest large town in the area. Prisoners could take a

---

[16] I found no trace of Anti-Semitism in any Asian countries I visited.

small bag of personal things and their purses. The police took all the money in the purse except for a few coins. Omama and Franzi were searched for valuables and then put into prison cells overnight. They slept on the straw-covered floor.

In the morning, an officer told them that the "Jewish sow," Francesca Schischa, could go back to Wopfing for the time being. The "Jewish sow," Rosa Kohn, being the widow of a soldier who had fought for the fatherland, was urged to go to Vienna and make arrangements to pay the fee for the release of her sons.

"How did you get here?" Mutti asked, completely astonished tone.

"I walked to the outskirts of Vienna. I used the coins they left me to take a streetcar into the city. I had your address, but I had to ask for directions many times."

"Do you know that Jews are not allowed to ride street cars?" Mutti asked.

"Yes, I know," Omama gave a mirthless chuckle. "No one stopped me. I look like a peasant coming to the city to sell produce."

Uncle Hugo had also been arrested on the night of November 9th by his best friend and fellow violin player. The grocery store—no longer owned by Jews but managed by Omama and Onkel Hugo—was vandalized and looted that night.

Hugo talked about his arrest many years later. He had been taken to a cellar in the nearby town of Pisting by a man whom he thought to be his best friend. They had played together as children and, as adults, often performed duets on the violin. The local SS guards were busy beating the men in their custody when Hugo was shoved down the steps by his erstwhile friend who was now the local *Gauleiter* (the district commander). He gave orders that Hugo was not to be beaten up like the others. Several men were lying around in bruised and bloody heaps, but the thugs only slapped Hugo few times, knocked off his glasses, and then allowed him to pick them up.

Mutti prepared some hot tea and soup for Omama and filled a hot water bottle to put into Mitzi's bed where Omama would sleep. Mutti told Omama that she knew where to go to start the release process and that we would leave early in the morning. Then we went to bed.

During the night there was a commotion. Omama called out to my mother, "Thilde, come here at once!" My mother came running out of the back bedroom and I sat up to see Omama standing beside the drenched bed, empty hot water bottle in hand. With abject apologies my mother took Omama into the back bedroom to sleep and came back to hang the wet sheets over the dining room chairs. I was disappointed to learn that it was a leaking hot water bottle that had wet the bed, but I couldn't help the little giggle that escaped from me before I went back to sleep.

The next morning, after a roll and some coffee (mine with the blue milk that was allotted Jewish children), we started on the long walk to the Gestapo headquarters. Passing the burned out Seitenstettengasse Temple (the synagogue where my parents and grandparents had been married), Mutti and Omama paused for a few moments; then, wiping their eyes, they each took one of my hands and we went on our way.

Winter is extremely cold in Vienna, and while my mother and I had warm coats, hats and mittens, Omama had only her shawl and a peasant scarf to put over her head. As we carefully stepped over the wet and slippery cobblestones, I could hear her dentures clattering.

At the first office the women were given papers to sign and told to take them to another office in the building. Eventually the three of us were standing in front of a caged window where my grandmother was told that both her sons were in Dachau. The woman behind the bars seemed sympathetic.

"As a war widow you shouldn't be treated this way," she whispered. "Even if you are a Jewess." Then she gave Omama another set of papers and directed her to another building in the area.

We went from one place to another, not stopping for food since we were not allowed into restaurants. At each office we were told that we needed to go to another office to pay for yet another stamp.

At last the three of us arrived at the apartment and Mutti began to prepare a meal of noodles sprinkled with garlic and onions. We drank hot tea without lemon or sugar; only a few drops of rum were added for a little flavor and some warmth. We went to bed right after eating. It was Friday night and, for the first time in her life, Omama didn't light the candles.

The next day was Shabbat and my very observant grandmother said she would take me for a walk while my mother should get some rest. So Omama and I set out for the Wallensteinstrasse. We caught a glimpse of sun and the streets were dry. We walked along seeing mostly boarded-up windows. There was a Konditorei open for business that had a chewing gum machine sitting outside their door. For a *pfennig* (penny) you could get a gum ball. I asked Omama for a pfennig to get one and she looked at me with a shocked expression. "It is the Sabbath, and we do not handle money on the Sabbath!" she hissed at me. But I kept on begging and wouldn't move, so finally she told me to reach into her open purse and find a coin that would fit—all the time muttering about how only common, uncultured people chewed gum. She also remarked that I lacked a religious education and what else could one expect from a woman like my mother.

This was not the first time I had felt that there was hostility between the two women, but this was the first time I had heard a complaint. The gum was both sweet and bitter and soon got hard in my mouth, but I didn't dare spit it out where Omama might see me, so I swallowed it—along with the words about my mother.

The next morning Omama said she was leaving to go back to Wopfing. Mutti urged her to stay and try some more offices on Monday, but Omama replied that she couldn't sleep well except in her own bed, and she couldn't eat anything in this house.

"You never did care much about your children," my mother reproached her.

I had always sensed friction between the two women. Not so much what was said but the tone they used. That day Omama's disapproval and Mutti's resentment became obvious. The truce was over.

Chapter 13

One day my mother met Lottie, a longtime friend, on the street and invited her to come upstairs for a cup of tea. The conversation, as always these days, turned to emigration and staying alive until departure. Lottie told my mother that she had found a way to solve the problem: "Conversion."

Lottie told us she could not become Catholic, because her gentile husband had divorced her in compliance with the new laws, but there was a sect of Christians (new to Austria at that time) called "Evangelical" and they would convert anyone who wanted to join them in their adoration of Jesus. The whole idea horrified my mother and she said as much to Lottie. (As it turned out, conversion was not considered valid, and no remedy existed for being a Jew. It was considered a capital offense and soon there was a law that made the murder of all Jews legal.)

The discussion turned to how difficult it was for my mother to take me along to her daily rounds of standing in line and waiting in offices. Lottie suggested she enroll me in a kindergarten class. Mutti sighed deeply and said that the Montessori school would no longer take Jewish children nor would any other public school, and the Jewish schools had been disbanded because all the teachers were in Dachau or in hiding.

Lottie suggested the Catholic kindergarten in the convent just around the corner. A long silence hovered in the room as the women looked at each other and began to smile. They remembered that one of their best friends in school was now a nun in that very convent. Lottie offered to go there and talk to their friend.

A few days later Mutti and I were entering the Convent of the Sisters of the Holy Cross.

Many years later my mother told me how she had always crossed the street when she saw nuns approaching. She had been told they kidnapped Jewish girls and forced them to become nuns.

There were heavy doors on either side of the long, cold hall and we could hear murmuring of voices coming from behind them. Finally, the nun who had let us in pointed to a door at the end of the hallway. Mutti's hand was clammy as she held mine and knocked softly with the other. A woman's voice called, "Come in!"

Sister Maria Augusta had been expecting us. She was a corpulent woman with bulging blue eyes that dominated her ruddy face. From behind her huge desk she motioned us into the spacious study and offered me a cup of hot cocoa from a tray on her desk, and then poured tea for my mother.

She started to make light conversation. She explained that the hand-painted Japanese tea set had been a gift from a former pupil and was a bit gaudy for a convent, but it was a gift of love and must be accepted. I thought it was lovely; mother and I spent some time admiring it, remarking on the artwork and the varied and deep colors.

All the while, Mutti sat nervously on the edge of the straight-backed chair, while I sat on a low footstool beside her and looked around the room.

A tall bookcase stood against one wall, and a fireplace glowing with hot coals took up another wall. The gilt-framed painting hanging over the mantle—depicting a man nailed to a wooden cross, blood dripping from wounds—simultaneously fascinated and repelled me. (Variations of this ghastly scene were to be seen in every classroom of the convent and seemed out of place in such gentle, serene surroundings.)

Sister Maria Augusta had a soft, soothing voice. I could

sense that Mutti was beginning to relax, as she asked if she could enroll me in the convent preschool.

Sister Maria Augusta was reassuring. "Yes, it would be entirely appropriate for a five-year-old to attend the kindergarten. No, the sisters make no distinction between Catholic and non-Catholic students. Aren't we all God's children?" Then she added, "The new regime be hanged, but for safety's sake, we won't *officially* enroll the child."

My attendance at the Kindergarten of the Sisters of the Holy Cross was a new experience for me, as well as for the two new postulants who taught the nine little girls in our group. They spent a few extra minutes each morning teaching me the correct way to cross myself, when to genuflect, and how many "Hail Marys" to say after which prayer. I was an able pupil and learned to execute these rituals quickly and accurately. Almost as if my life depended on it. (Which, of course, it did.)

This was, to my mind, a much superior preschool. Instead of silly games with blocks and pegs, we spent the mornings singing melodic hymns and coloring pictures of landscapes and angels. Best of all, no disruptive, noisy boys were there to tease and annoy us.

One day, Sister Maria Augusta came into our classroom and announced that we would all be in a Christmas Pageant, and she would assign the parts the next day. When my mother came to pick me up later that day, the sister asked her permission for me to play the part of Mary in the tableau, which would be our group's contribution to the pageant. Mutti gave Sister a tight smile and said she regretted that we would most likely be out of town that day. But she would let her know.

Sister Maria Augusta then told us that I was the only girl in the class who looked the part. The irony of that statement must have struck my mother because she laughed aloud. I remember it so well because I had never heard her really laugh. Of course Sister was right, I thought. The other girls were blonde and blue-eyed and were suited for the part of angels. In the manger scene, Mary would have her head covered. The other girls, depicting angels, would hover around her, their beautiful blonde hair flowing free of the tight braids most of them wore to school.

On the way home Mutti asked, "You don't really want to be in the Christmas Pageant, do you?" Her tone made it clear that this was not a question.

"But I *do* want to be in it," I whined.

Mutti began to sniffle like she had a bad cold, and I realized she was crying. I thought she would be proud of me for getting the lead part, and I was very confused by her reaction. The sisters were delighted when she gave permission for me to participate in the Christmas pageant.

I continued to enjoy my mornings at the convent. The gnawing fear that the sisters would find out who I was began to recede. Like the other little girls in the school, I viewed the sisters with awe and admiration. Encased from head to foot in shapeless habits and confining wimples, they nevertheless exuded an aura of gentle femininity and managed to fill our mornings with a sense of fun that alleviated their often-monotonous lives.

Imitating Sister Maria Augusta was a favorite sport for the young nuns. They would walk with an exaggerated swing of the hips from side to side or wave their arms up and down as she often did when trying to quiet us as we knelt for prayers. We each had our own pillow with little fringes around the edges that we used for kneeling during the Hail Mary prayer, and we used them for our heads at rest time and to muffle our laughter. The sound of any disturbance always brought Sister Maria Augusta out of her study and waddling into our classroom. Each time she came in the suspense was almost unbearable. Who would she scold—the novices, the students, or both? Most of the time she ignored the mischievous grins, just asking us to behave more ladylike.

It was Friday, December 23, 1938, two days before Christmas. The aroma of baking gingerbread greeted us as we arrived for school. We noticed that the sisters had hung evergreen boughs along the drab hallways. A festive mood prevailed as we made decorations for the tree in our classroom. The Pageant was to be held after class, followed by a social hour. We were all incredibly excited at the prospect of having cookies and hot cocoa with our mothers for the ten o'clock snack time *(Zehner Jause)*.

It was strange to see the grownups sitting in our little chairs, sipping from the child-sized mugs. The pageant went well, as did my short speech about my blessed motherhood. When I joined her for the refreshments, Mutti smiled, but her eyes were blank.

A tall, blonde woman stopped near us and greeted Mutti by her first name, using "Mathilde" instead of the "Thilde" that her friends and family used. The woman gave me a friendly smile then pointedly turned her back to us. Mutti and I drank our cocoa and said goodbye to Sister Maria Augusta, and then, as unobtrusively as possible, slipped out the door.

The next day I went to the convent as usual. During the opening prayers (led by Sister Maria August who sat in a chair in front of the room), three men in black uniforms strode into the room. Two of the men, holding rifles, stood at attention in the doorway; the third, wearing a pistol strapped to his side, approached Sister Maria Augusta. He raised his arm to touch the visor on his hat, but he quickly changed its course, throwing out his arm and clicking his heels as he shouted, *"Heil Hitler!"*

Sister Maria Augusta got up slowly. *"Greuss Gott,* Karl," she said as she made a brief curtsy.

"Excuse the intrusion," he apologized. "We have a report that you may be harboring an enemy of the Reich." His hand rested on the pistol while he stared intently at each of the little girls and the novices.

We remained frozen on our knees, our palms still pressed together in supplication. The blood pounding in my ears was deafening. Suddenly he clicked his heels again, startling us with the shot-like sound. Then he turned sharply and led the other men from the room. The sound of their boots rang through the hallway. Sister Maria Augusta sat back down and calmly led us in a prayer about guarding us from our enemies.

As Mutti and I were leaving the convent that day, Sister Maria Augusta stopped us at the Gothic doorway. No words were exchanged, just sad glances between the two women and a gentle pat on the head for me. My Catholic kindergarten days were over.

On the way home I remembered that Sister Maria Augusta had called my mother "Mathilde," just as the blonde lady had done. It was then that I realized that they had known each other as children and had even been good friends who played together.

Mutti and I walked home through a thick curtain of gently falling snow. I knew by the looks my mother and sister Maria Augusta exchanged at the door that I would not be returning to the Catholic kindergarten. With every step, the knot of fear grew colder and bigger in the pit of my stomach. I tried to think of what I might have done wrong to be expelled.

Chapter 14

We entered the front hallway of Webergasse 13, and Mutti reached inside the mailbox. Her trembling hand came out with a letter stamped with the official German seal. In a moment we were in the kitchen, and Mutti sat down at the table and picked at the censor's wax seal. With shaking fingers she slipped the flimsy piece of paper out of the envelope.

"It's from Vati," she said, in a voice choked with tears. I waited impatiently while she read the letter in a half-sobbing whisper.

I made out some of her words, others were muffled in the sobs. Strangely, the letter had hardly been censored. My father, a painfully honest and humane person, was completely bewildered why he had been arrested and sent into hell.

After several weeks of starvation, torture and other degradations, the men could write to their families. The idea was that the more dire the circumstances that the men described, the sooner their families (actually, their women folk) would pay for their release.

Toward the end of the letter Mutti began to read aloud, "When we arrived, we were ordered to undress and shower. While standing there unfastening my clothes, I saw a man with one foot on the bench near me, unlacing his shoes. His bald head reminded me of Hugo. It is difficult to believe that these things happen in real life, but it really *was* Hugo. There was also a round up in Wopfing. His friend, Rudy the violin player, had tried to warn him, but like me, he couldn't believe he would be arrested. We have managed to stay together. This reminds us of the years we spent in the orphanage, which was good training for the concentration camp."

Mutti took a deep breath, and I noticed her hands were no longer trembling. She was gripping the paper tightly and continued reading in a steadier voice. "We have been promised release upon payment of the amount requested by the government for each man in custody and proof that we will be leaving the country immediately. Since our mother is a war widow, we may be able to pay a little less. There are forms to fill out for this process.

"There is little food here. Some fortunate few have money to buy food from the guards, some get food packages from family. None of these men are inclined to share. Please send money for food. Do whatever you can to help us get out. I can't survive much longer.

"As ever, your Leo."

Mutti looked at me. "Where will I get the money?" she wailed.

"You have money; I saw it in your purse." I was trying to console her.

The clank of her enhanced wedding ring on my front teeth was such a shock that, for several seconds, I didn't feel the pain on my lips. The chip from my front tooth slid into my hand, with a thick drop of blood from my fast-swelling lip.

Even with all the threats of a thorough thrashing, no one had ever hit me before. Mutti looked horribly angry, and I groped around in my mind for a reason. She ignored my pleading question about what I had done that was so wrong. Without warning I began to scream; loud, rhythmic, animal like shrieks. All the fear, anger, bewilderment, confusion, frustration and sadness of the last few months exploded from somewhere deep inside of me.

Mutti grabbed my arm, yelling at me to stop. I was helpless to do so. My eyes were closed, but it seemed I was watching myself from a distance, powerless to stop screaming.

When the screams finally subsided into throaty sobs,

they were muffled by the clothes hanging in the wardrobe closet. I could hear Mutti, as from a great distance: "When you can be quiet, you can come out."

I didn't answer. In that moment I was ready to stay in the closet and suffocate. The necessity to breath finally won out and I pushed the door open, crawled out, and went to the kitchen.

Mutti was standing over the stove, and when she turned around her face looked serene. She put two plates of noodles on the table and motioned for me to sit down and eat. I sat down, but I couldn't eat. Fear and resentment closed my throat. Mutti ate while I kept sitting in the straight-backed chair staring at the cold noodles.

The twilight had faded into near darkness when we were startled by a soft knock on the door. Mutti put a finger to her lips and laid the other hand on my wrist. The knock was repeated, a little louder. There was a short pause, and then a familiar voice whispered, "It's Mitzi. Let me in."

I ran to the door and shot back the lower bolt but had to wait for Mutti to undo the upper one and the chain lock. Mitzi almost dropped the packages and large basket she was carrying as I threw myself at her. As she came into the kitchen and embraced my softly-weeping mother, I saw Mausie standing in the hall holding a small but well-shaped spruce tree.

"Come in, Mausie," Mitzi ordered softly, and then quickly shut the door behind her. "I have come to celebrate the holiday with my little one," she said and led the way into the parlor, where Mitzi had slept near me for the last four years. On the low table near my crib, she set up the little tree. She fastened candles to the tree limbs and lighted them. A soft glow filled the room and we stood back, arm in arm, to admire the lovely sight.

Mausie helped me open the presents. There was a wide, red, satin ribbon for my hair; a pair of full-length, black woolen stockings; a decorated, metal box filled with an assortment of home-baked cookies (which we began to eat immediately); and best of all, a hand-sewn, red velvet dress.

We gave Mausie some of the cookies to take with her as she left. Then the three of us were alone. I hugged Mitzi tightly, dreading the moment when she would leave. I was overjoyed when she told me she was staying overnight. She helped me get ready for bed and tucked me in with her large, rough hands (which I had missed so much). She blew out the candles on the tree and placed a chair next to my crib.

In a soft and soothing voice, she retold me the story of how the Christ child sent an angel around the world on this one night of the year to bring presents to all the good children. I knew this story did not include me, but I enjoyed hearing the fairy tale again. Mitzi assured me she was spending the whole night, but she needed to leave the next afternoon to return to Eigen. She kissed me goodnight and called me her little treasure. Hearing her say this made me feel warmer and safer than I had felt since my birthday, a lifetime ago.

I awoke to the scent of the spruce tree and the sight of Mutti standing over the crib. As she lowered the macramé side, she carefully studied my face.

Gingerly I touched my swollen upper lip, but neither of us spoke of it. She helped me out of the crib, and I noticed—with relief—that my bed was dry. We went out to the kitchen. Mitzi was setting the table. She turned to me, gave me a hug then bowed in an exaggerated curtsy.

"Breakfast is ready, your highness," she said with a little smile.

On the table were fresh poppy seed rolls, spread with homemade butter, and a small jar of my favorite strawberry jam. Mitzi poured us each a steaming cup of coffee, sweetened with real sugar. Next to my plate, waiting to be peeled and filling the room with its tangy scent, was an orange.

After we had eaten, Mutti peeled and sectioned the orange. Mitzi started to unpack the huge basket and oddly-shaped bundles she had brought. I watched in wonder. There were eggs, a wheel of cheese, a plucked goose, several potatoes, a bag of flour, and a bottle of homemade wine. She laid all these things out on the table, then tied a cotton, print kerchief over her hair. As I watched Mitzi fasten the ends at the nape of her neck, I remembered how we wore such kerchiefs when we were in Eigen for the haying. I could almost smell the fresh cut hay and taste the cool buttermilk.

Mitzi showed Mutti how to cook the goose. The aroma of the baking foul began to fill the kitchen and set my mouth to watering, Mutti asked many questions about the procedure and Mitzi answered with resigned patience, all the while preparing the rest of the meal.

In the midst of this activity, Mutti took off her apron, put on her coat, took her purse off the paper laden desk and left the apartment.

I helped Mitzi clean up the kitchen, set the table for the noon meal. To pass the time, we sang some of the songs we had heard while we still had a radio, and we were waltzing to a familiar tune when we heard Mutti's key in the door. Mutti came dejectedly into the kitchen.

"No luck?" It wasn't really a question. "After the New Year things will be better." Mitzi tried to comfort my mother who continued pacing up and down the room, twisting her red, gnarled fingers.

"My poor, naïve Leo. He can't last much longer. He isn't emotionally strong." Mutti's voice rose as if she were in terrible pain. "I don't have the money," she wailed. Finally, she sat down, mechanically eating the soup.

After we finished eating, Mitzi offered to show Mutti how to iron clothes using the two heavy irons. Mutti mastered the fundamentals of ironing that afternoon, and the burn hole in the sleeve of her first attempt would be covered by a jacket.

With a sinking heart I watched Mitzi leave. "Don't look so sour, little one," she coaxed. "I'll be back for your birthday." That reminded me of my party, and I was enveloped in my sense of loss.

Chapter 15

Two days later (the day after Christmas), while Mutti and I were eating the last of the poppy seed rolls for breakfast, we heard a loud banging on the door. At first, we sat very still in the hope they would think we weren't home. The banging was persistent; obviously they knew we were there. "That bitch, the manager, must have told them we were here," Mutti muttered and went to the door.

Four men in shiny black boots came into the kitchen. Three of them were dressed in the hated brown shirts, with guns at the ready. First, they asked who else was in the apartment. Not waiting for an answer, they began a search. We just stood beside the door, hearts pounding. While the three brown shirts proceeded into the next rooms, the man without a gun, who was dressed in the black Gestapo uniform, told Mutti that the apartment was being confiscated by the Gauleiter.[17]

"You have one week to move to the new place," he said in a cordial tone. I was thinking that I had seen this man before; the voice was familiar,

"I want to see the Gauleiter's apartment," I heard my mother say in a normal voice. "I need to see the place in order to decide what we can take along." It was a reasonable request, and to my surprise, the man agreed.

While the three men with the guns filed out, I heard my mother ask, "Karl, why are the Nazis persecuting the Jews?"

---

[17] The Gestapo leader of the district.

"The Romans persecuted the Christians, even fed them to the lions. Now it is the turn of the Jews to suffer," was his senseless reply.

Mutti uttered one of her many versions of "Na Ya!"[18] (This one meant, "What a stupid answer!") and gave a mirthless chuckle as she closed the door.

That very afternoon we went to see the apartment in Heinzelmanngasse #5, which was not far from the Webergasse #13, but nearer to the Augarten (which we were forbidden to enter). The cubby hole was divided into two sections, with windows looking out to an air shaft. The kitchen and sitting room contained a narrow shelf with a gas burner. The sleeping area was through a low archway. From that window we had a partial view of a small courtyard. There was no electricity or running water. We would need to use a kerosene lamp (like in Oma's house), and water had to be carried in buckets up two floors from a tap in the courtyard. Four other apartments shared the water closet in the hallway. The walls were crawling with huge bedbugs. They had eaten away at the ancient wallpaper, which hung in tatters.

Mutti was outraged. We marched to the Gauleiter's office, and I waited in the hallway as I heard Mutti demand that he get rid of the bedbugs before we moved in. I was standing just outside the door as he ushered my mother out of his office. They seemed to know each other, and I heard him apologize for the deplorable state of his apartment.

It would be another two weeks before we moved to the hovel in Heinzelmanngasse. My mother went to inspect the place several times and would not set a date for our vacating our apartment until the vermin were entirely gone.

During that time, Mutti was able to sell most of the furniture, the oriental rug (the pride of her possessions, inherited from her parents), and most of her beautifully-tailored suits.

---

[18] *Na Ya* is like the English expression "That's just great." Depending on the intonation, it can mean, "Very good," or, "That's bad."

(She kept the navy blue, pin striped suit, with the felt beret to match.) With this money she bought steamship tickets for Shanghai, China. At my father's release, we would be ready to depart.

A letter came from Mutti's aunt, (her mother's sister) who lived in Washington, D.C. The gist of the letter was that this aunt did not have the funds to help us. She suggested that we write to Mutti's cousin, Rudy Menkes. The aunt wrote, "He has a dental practice in New York, married an American woman from an observant family. They have a house in Long Island and send the children to a Jewish school, thank God!"

By European standards, he was a wealthy man. We could only hope that he could and would send an affidavit. (The application cost $300 and the sponsors had to prove that they had sufficient income to support the refugee for at least five years. The $300 fee was not refundable in case the application was denied.)

Mutti sat down at the kitchen table and began to write a letter to her cousin in New York. He was the oldest son of a favorite uncle who had emigrated to America before WWI. He and my mother had played together as children. "He was a likable boy," Mutti said. "I loved him."

It was New Year's Eve, the last day of 1938. The letter from America lay on the kitchen table like a small emblem of hope. We sat at the table watching the light fade from the window, as the short winter afternoon turned to night. I walked to the wall by the door to turn on the overhead light and just as I turned the switch there was a soft knock on the hall door. Mutti opened the door a crack. It was Lottie; but when we saw the man, dressed in black, standing behind her, Mutti started to close the door.

"It's all right," Lottie whispered. "It's Karl Mikel."

S.S. Captain Karl Mikel strode into the kitchen, stifled the salute he was about to make, lowered his hand and bowed over my mother's limp one.

Mutti's voice was icy as she mumbled, "Good evening."

With a shock I recognized this man as the one who had come to the Catholic kindergarten to look for "enemies of the Reich." I was further astonished to learn that evening that Mutti and Lottie had known Karl for many years. They had attended school with his sister who was the tall blonde lady who had spoken to us at the Convent Christmas party.

Mutti served tea (sweetened by the sugar cubes that Karl had brought) and Lottie's homemade apple strudel. The three old friends talked openly about their political views. Karl had been in Germany for the last two years, working with members of the banned Austrian Nazi Party planning for the Anschluss. On March 15, 1938, Karl had come back to the German state of Ostmark, and Austrians were issued German passports. "Even the Jews," Karl reminded us.[19]

"The Nazis have the answer to solve all of Europe's problems and, eventually, the world's as well. Eliminating the Jews is necessary," he said and quoted a slogan that appeared everywhere: *"Di Juden sind unser umgleuck."* ("The Jews are our misfortune.") "I was unemployed for years," Karl continued. "Now I have an important position with good pay.

I was sitting in my play area of the kitchen, and the adults were ignoring my presence; but I found myself listening to their conversation. Also, I could hardly take my eyes off Karl. He had taken off his hat and his thick blond hair glistened in the overhead light. I enjoyed seeing his deep blue eyes when he glanced my way. His voice was soft, and he sounded so reasonable.

Lottie talked sympathetically about the "unbaptized," as she called the Jews. She said that they should become Christians and that would solve the problem. "My husband and I had to get a divorce because of the new laws. The priest in his church won't baptize me." I heard tears in her voice as she said those words. Then her voice rose as if she wanted to

---

[19] Jewish passports were stamped with a huge, red J. Jews were stripped of their identity. Females were Sara, men were Israel.

make sure I heard her too: "The Evangelical Church will baptize willing converts with no regard for their past situations. Thilde, take Ruthie to my preacher. He will help you convert."

My ears perked up at that comment. *If being a Christian is an option, let's do it,* I thought. But Mutti only shook her head, twirled her index finger near her temple to indicate insanity.

Lottie believed everything she read in print. When Mutti pointed out that Jews were not the traitors who caused Germany to lose WWI, or that stories about Jews committing heinous crimes were blatantly untrue, Lottie would say, "But I read it in the newspaper!"

Karl was more skeptical of the newspaper stories which he called "exaggerated" or just "propaganda." He nodded his head for emphasis as he remarked that he knew many "decent" non-Aryans. "They just don't have the same goals as we have in the Nazi party." To this last comment, my mother agreed most heartily.

One New Year's custom that was new to me was telling fortunes with a melted piece of lead. Karl had brought a stick of lead for this purpose. He broke off small pieces and we each dropped it into a cup of boiling water. It melted into peculiar shapes. Karl and Lottie found that their pieces foretold a productive year ahead, while Mutti and I both saw a sea voyage in the cup.

Having Karl in our apartment, smiling and talking with my mother as if she were a real human being, was confusing for me. It seemed that not all the men in black boots and uniforms were barbaric robots. Even after Mutti put me to bed and I heard the three adults in the kitchen chuckling and talking, I felt that cold knot of fear growing in the pit of my stomach.

Chapter 16

In the first weeks of 1939, Mutti spent hours every night writing letters to America. During the day, we waited in long lines at many different offices. The only time I got out of the cold wind was when I waited in some hallway while Mutti went into an office, clutching a fistful of papers.

Piece by piece, the furnishings disappeared out of the apartment. Some decent people paid for items they could have just taken away. Finally, only my crib, the narrow bed that Mitzi had used, one chair, and my grandmother's sewing machine were left in the kitchen. The brass headboards were sold, but Mutti kept the featherbeds.

A few days before we were scheduled to move, a telegram arrived from America. Telegrams were always disturbing, since they seldom contained good news. But this one was from Rudy Menkes: "Sending affidavit. Yours, Rudy."

Mutti clutched the telegram to her chest with one hand and wiped her eyes with the other. She read it to me over and over. Then she folded it carefully and put it among the pile of papers on the sewing machine.

I don't remember how and when exactly we moved into the tiny apartment on Heinzelmanngasse, nor how my mother squeezed my crib, a narrow cot, and her mother's treadle sewing machine into the sleeping cubicle. In the front area there was barely enough space for a small table and bench under the window. A lone chair stood against the wall near the shelf where the two-burner gas hotplate stood. Two shelves above it held the dishes, pans and utensils for cooking. Mutti arranged with one of the men who helped us move to place a cupboard above my crib for folded clothes and to pound some nails along the walls to hang her good suit and a nail next to the stove for her apron.

Although Mutti had brought along a large pot, it was not nearly big enough for taking a bath. Besides, heating enough water for even a pot of soup was nearly impossible. Yet Mutti managed to keep me clean. Every day she washed out our undergarments and hung them from a line stretched across the room.

We spent most days waiting in line at different vendors for each essential of existence. There were endless lines at the stores to get bits of food for a meal. At the baker we were allotted a quarter-loaf of stale bread; at greengrocer we waited an hour for a head of garlic, a small onion, and a pint of blue milk. Kerosene was strictly rationed, so it took a whole day to get that.

In the evenings, I learned how to embroider on small squares of linen cut from worn out pillowcases. First, I drew flowers on the linen with a pencil, embroidered them with my mother's careful instructions, then hemmed them with the colorful yarn that had been in the family for nearly a century. I also embroidered upper case initials in one corner to personalize each one.

At bedtime Mutti told me stories about beautiful, blonde girls who became princesses as a reward for being kind and obedient. She described the elegant gowns they wore to the grand balls, then hummed the music that was playing while the dancers twirled in the elaborate ballrooms. I fell asleep wishing for Mitzi to return and that Vati would come home soon.

One morning, just as I was sitting down on the bench to eat the piece of bread and drink the warm, blue milk—my usual breakfast—I heard a soft knock on the door. Although we knew it was not the SS officers—they always banged loudly when they came to take people away—we were hesitant to open the door. When the knock came again, even softer, Mutti opened the door. And there stood Mitzi.

"I had to come wish my little treasure a happy birthday." Mitzi was smiling broadly as she saw my happy, surprised face. It was my sixth birthday, and she was keeping her promise. Handing me a sprig of lilies-of-the-valley, my favorite flowers, (their fragrance filled the room), she put a cloth covered basket on the table. Inside was a paper bag of cookies and fresh, crunchy rolls.

My mother gasped with delight when Mitzi pulled out a can of Gerstel coffee (a mixture of real coffee and grain). We hugged, I cried, and Mitzi promised to return soon. (It would be a year-and-a-half before we saw her again.)

That afternoon we visited Cousin Fritzi and her twelve-year-old son, Kurt. He had very patiently taught me to play chess, and when I heard they were leaving for England shortly, I was very sad. Besides being a patient teacher, Kurt was very handsome. He had soft, straight golden hair that hung down his forehead, over his pale eyebrows and into his deep blue eyes. Looking into those eyes was like looking at a patch of blue sky on a winter day. Fritzi and Kurt had planned to return to England as soon they could get permission to bring her father, "The Old Uncle" (as my mother called Fritzi's father who was her mother's brother) back to England with them.

That afternoon we learned that because of his advanced age (Mutti's uncle was eighty-two), the British government denied him entry into England. So Fritzi and Kurt were staying in Vienna a bit longer, while Fritzi arranged for her father to travel to Montevideo, Uruguay, where Fritzi's sister had fled. The revised travel plans would take several months to complete. I was relieved.

While we waited for the Jewish Cultural Society to start a school, my mother enrolled me in the evangelical school recommended by Lottie. The class met in a large, basement room with long tables around the walls. There were about fifteen boys and girls of different ages. The younger ones, like me, sat most of the day just coloring pictures of people I had never heard of. The two gray-haired ladies in charge led us in vigorous prayers before the noon meal, which was the highlight of the day for me. Each of us got a plate with a boiled potato and a boiled red beet. I mashed these items together and loved every bite. I could hardly wait to get to school each day.

The celebration during the week before the Lent season is a festive time, especially for Catholics. In many countries it is called "Carnival," but in Austria it is called *Fasching*. Many organizations sponsor masked balls. Everyone dresses up in a variety of costumes pretending to be someone from a fairy tale or history. The idea is that one can do or say things that one would never do or say as themselves.

Lottie convinced my mother to bring me to such an event. Lottie dressed me as a fairy in a thin, gossamer skirt and white tights, and we walked to the dance hall in her neighborhood. It was a clear, but extremely cold afternoon and by the time we arrived at the dance I was shivering. Lottie led the way up the flight of stairs to the ballroom. Many people were there in strange costumes. I didn't see any children. It was noisy with talking, laughing, singing, and the rattle of dishes.

Obviously Mutti had been persuaded to come because of the promise of something to eat. We followed Lottie to a food-laden buffet table. Mutti filled her coat pockets with rolls and an apple. Then she took my ice-cold hand, turned me around and we headed for the stairs as Lottie called out a reluctant farewell. It was my first and last glimpse of a Viennese Fasching celebration.

One morning as Mutti and I descended the stairs to the schoolroom, a table blocked part of the doorway. A strange woman in a gray uniform with a red cross on a white armband handed Mutti some papers and in a foreign accent asked her to sign the documents. I don't know if my mother signed the papers because I proceeded into the classroom and went to my assigned seat.

Later that morning, all of us children in the class were led into another room. A man and woman dressed in white coats were sitting behind a table. Benches lined the wall opposite a window. The woman in the white coat told us to take off all our clothes, except for the shoes and socks. Obediently we did so, laying our clothes on a bench. Then we were told to line up in a single file.

I was cringing with cold and shame and could not raise my eyes as one by one we were told to go out and walk past the doctor. He told me to stand still in front of him and then to turn around. I kept my eyes firmly on the floor. At last I heard him say, "Next." I ran to the bench and hurriedly put on my clothes. Most of us returned to the classroom, but some of the children did not come back.[20]

Eventually, we were taught how to write and do some simple addition. The teachers were old women who made us sit still most of the day. I know there were other classrooms in the building because we could hear the commotion out in the hall as the older children left the building to go home for their midday meal; we were given our plate of potato and beet in the classroom. After the meal, blue mats were laid out on the floor and we were to lie down and sleep, which I never did. Mutti usually came to pick me up right after the end of nap time. When she was even a few minutes late I became nervous.

One day, I was the last child left in the room before my mother came in the door. By then I was shaking all over and fighting down the hysterical screams that were gathering in my throat. As it was, we barely made it home before the curfew would go into effect. I was acutely aware of the danger of being out after dark. I had overheard adults talking about those who had been shot. Every night, just as it got totally dark, we heard shots. I lived in constant terror of losing Mutti.

---

[20] These children were sent to France and then to England on the *Kindertransport*. My mother declined to sign the required papers.

Chapter 17

The summer of 1939 was very warm in Vienna and the air in our little apartment was stifling. Late one night while Mutti and I were trying to fall asleep, we heard a soft knock on the door. A voice whispered, "Thilde, it's me."

Mutti opened the door a crack and I looked over her shoulder to see who was there. I saw an old, stooped man wearing a wide brimmed hat and very baggy clothes. He tried to smile at us with a toothless mouth. Mutti opened the door a bit wider and the man came into the room, but I didn't recognize him.

It wasn't until Mutti began to moan, "Leo, Leo," and gathered the small form into her arms that I realized it was Vati. The three of us just hugged and cried for a long time. Then Mutti told me I must go to bed right now. Her tone was such that I knew better than to argue. I crawled up into my crib and pretended to go to sleep.

A short time later my parents came into the sleeping area. I continued to lie curled up in my usual sleeping position with my eyes closed. However, my ears were wide open. They sat on the narrow cot and between stifled sobs my father told what had happened to him during the last nine months.

On November 10th of 1938, my father, Leo Kohn, was summarily taken to the police station and shoved into a room with hundreds of other Jewish men. They were taken, by army trucks, to the Nordbanhoff (the North train station). As the men were herded through the entrance of the train station, they were lined up in single file.

Each man was asked what he did for a living. Next, each man was sent through a gauntlet of brown-clad SA men, who punched the hapless prisoners with their fists or hit them with cudgels. If the Jewish man said he was a laborer—like my father who had a menial job in a warehouse—the brown shirts just punched him in the face and body a few times, and then let him get on the waiting train. If a Jew admitted to being in a profession or the owner of a business, he was punched and beaten all the way down the line until he was bloody and his half-conscious body would be thrown onto the train.

The men found themselves in passenger train cars where they were told to sit very still in their seats and look directly into the overhead lights. If anyone looked away from the light they would be shot.

"Some were shot," I heard Vati sob. "They were left to bleed all over their seat mates. They threw them off the train like sacks of flour when we arrived in Dachau."

Upon their arrival the men were driven with whips along a fenced area and into a large room lined with benches. There, they were ordered to undress for the showers. As my father sat on one of the benches to untie his shoes, he saw a man bending over next him who looked like his brother (my Uncle Hugo). To their total astonishment, the two brothers found themselves sitting side by side. Somehow, they managed to stay together and wound up in the same barracks.

For the rest of the night I lay motionless in my crib, listening to my father talk about the things he had experienced and witnessed. Those images remain with me and made me aware of the infinite depravity of humans. I heard more stifled sobbing and then Vati continued his story.

There were terrible beatings for breaking arbitrary rules. Men were beaten to death with shovels or shot for disobeying conflicting orders. The prisoners were ordered to clean the barrack floors with toothbrushes, and then they were beaten because it took too long to do a good job. This was an excuse to not give the men their once-per-day piece of bread and watery soup. Every day, men threw themselves against the fence and were electrocuted. The prisoners were kept busy digging graves from early morning to late at night.

The civilian guards were criminals from all over Germany and Austria, chosen for their history of brutality and sadism, and given full authority to do whatever they wanted to their hapless charges. These criminals often stole the food packages that relatives were urged to send the prisoners. When a prisoner was allowed to keep a package, he was attacked by the others who grabbed it away. Many formerly-decent men had become like animals.

"Thilde," I heard his whisper, "I could not have survived much longer."

He told about how the guards never talked in normal voices. They constantly bellowed orders and shouted demeaning names to humiliate the prisoners. Men who had been in important positions were especially sought out for beatings. These prisoners included many doctors, teachers, and former soldiers—people who had been respected until these thugs came to power. The screams of prisoners were mixed with the shouts of the guards from daybreak until the prisoners were finally allowed a few hours of sleep.

According to my father's narrative (and many stories I heard later from survivors), sleeping was impossible except for a few snatched minutes at a time. Hundreds of men (as many as ten on each set of hard planks) were laid out in three tiers with just enough space for a man to lie on one side. Turning over was a team effort. During the night, the guards stopped bellowing, but there was the constant noise of men weeping, groaning in pain, and coughing (many were coughing up blood during their last night). The few who slept tended to snore loudly. With the beatings, starvation and lack of sleep, many men died each day. The prisoners worked long hours digging graves and hauling bodies to the various sites. An oven was erected for burning the bodies, but it was seldom used.

I heard my mother talk about professional smugglers who could help my father get over the Belgian border. Their voices became seriously low, and soon all I heard was soft sobbing. I soon fell asleep.

When I awoke in the morning my father was not there.

A few weeks later, on a hot day of August 1939, my mother, in an agitated state, came to the school to walk me home. I could see she had been crying for a long time, her face and eyes were red and swollen. The familiar knot of fear expanded in my stomach as she hurried me along.

"We are going to Cologne tomorrow," she said between sobs. "Your father is in prison and I need to get him out."

The next morning Mutti put on her navy pin-striped suit and the jaunty, navy blue beret. She dressed me in my best dress, which her cousin Paula had made for me before she left for Ceylon. The dress still fit, but the winter coat she had made was more like a jacket. Mutti made me wear it anyway, and although it was a warm day, she pulled a wool knit hat tightly over my jet-black hair to hide as much of it as possible. When I objected to being dressed so warmly on this hot day, she mumbled something about, "Going north and it might be cold."

We walked to the Nordbahnhoff and found the train for Cologne. Since Austria was now a German state, we were not crossing a border, thus no one asked for identity papers. We arrived in Cologne without incident and took a taxi (my first ride in a car) to a place where we were to spend the night. Since Jews were not allowed to stay in commercial facilities, the Jewish Committee (which had notified my mother of my father's imprisonment) had arranged lodging for us. Mutti paid the taxi driver, and he said, "Thank you, gracious lady," in a normal tone. Obviously, he didn't know we were Jews. (If he had suspected we were Jews, he would not have transported us in the first place.)

We climbed up several floors to a small apartment, which seemed very luxurious to me since it had a toilet and electricity. Pictures with ornate frames covered one wall, and a cross like the one in the convent hung over the door. When one of the two elderly ladies who lived there offered us coffee, I asked for milk and sugar (like in the old days). My mother gave me a sharp, embarrassed look and the ladies just smiled; my mother apologized for my bad manners.

One of the ladies showed me where we would sleep and after taking off my dress, Mutti tucked me into the huge feather bed. I was very hungry, but I didn't dare to ask about food. I did sneak out to the toilet and I overheard Mutti tell the ladies why we had come to Cologne.

For a fee, a smuggler had led my father to the German side of the Belgian border and to a supposedly "safe house" where he was to wait, with several other men, for another smuggler to take them over the border. For a small reward, the smugglers, who were Jews, told the Gestapo where to find the Jewish fugitives. The other men managed to get away, but my father was caught and sent to prison in Cologne. The authorities notified the Jewish Council in Vienna that if sufficient funds were paid, he might be released, and if not, he would be sent back to Dachau.

Even though I was only six years old, I understood exactly why we were in Cologne and hoped that Mutti had brought enough money. With the cold knot of fear expanding in my stomach, I began to wonder if the authorities would arrest her also. I finally fell asleep.

The next morning, after a few bites of stale bread, we walked a long way to a building surrounded by high walls. Inside was the prison where my father was being held. We walked past the gates and many men with guns, into a long corridor with high windows that shed a gray light on the straw-covered floor.

We came to a gate with thick iron bars. An overweight guard was standing behind the gate. He opened the gate and told my mother she could go down the dark hallway to the prison where she would be allowed to see her husband. But children were not allowed to go into the prison, and I would need to wait for her in the cell-like area just inside the gate.

The guard pointed to a little bench against one wall and indicated I was to sit there. The walls were so high I could not see the ceiling; a small, barred window was several feet over my head. I was surrounded by gray stone walls.

A different man approached from the gloom, called my mother's name and ordered her to follow him. Mutti did not look at me, just turned her back and followed the man to the area behind the bars. As she disappeared from my sight, I could feel the panic rise into my throat. The overweight guard must have seen my distress. In a low and soothing voice, he told me not to worry, my mother would be back soon. He led me to the bench, and I had no choice but to sit. It took all my strength to swallow the screams but the whole bench shook with my quiet sobs.

Somehow, I managed to sit still and keep quiet until my mother came back. I don't know how long I sat in that gloomy corner, getting up only once to add my own body fluids to the human waste in the straw. The stench in that place was overwhelming; I will never forget it.

When Mutti reappeared I was so overjoyed to see her that I wet my pants. I couldn't tell from her face how things had developed. She clutched my hand, and we walked the long way to the train station. We just made the noon train to Vienna and, fortunately, arrived in the middle of the next day so we could get to our apartment before dark.

A few days later a letter arrived, stamped with the official insignia of the government, informing us that (Leo) Israel Kohn had been returned to Dachau until further notice.

I don't know any of the details, but somehow my mother got my father and his brother, (my dear Uncle Hugo) accepted to a Zionist program *(Hech Ha Lutz)* for sending Jewish men, under the age of thirty (by now my father was thirty-two), to learn how to run a dairy farm in Sweden, then immigrate to Palestine and join a Kibbutz.

That second time in Dachau was, if possible, much worse than the first time. My father never spoke about it, but for the rest of his life, he had nightmares about those times. He sat up in bed, screaming at the top of his lungs, his nightshirt and the sheets drenched with sweat.

Chapter 18

In Vienna, our lives were getting more and more restricted. It was not safe for Jewish children to be outdoors, even in the daylight, as ruffian boys would cruise the neighborhood looking for easy marks to brutalize. The Nazis accosted young girls and women with impunity.

During those warm, humid summer days Mutti and I would sit by the open window hoping for a whiff of a breeze. I practiced embroidering while Mutti told me winter stories in the hope that we would feel cooler. My favorites were about how there was a terrible snowstorm the night she was born, and the storm lasted for many days. By the time her father, Zev Hecker, got to the city registrar, he was not certain of her date of birth and put down the twentieth of December.

When Zev brought the birth certificate home, there was a row. Zev tried to convince my grandmother, Jetti that she had forgotten exactly when this baby was born, and Jetti berated Zev for not remembering that Mathilde was born on December 18th. Every year, on December 18th, the same argument arose as to Mathilde's birthday. Jetti wished my mother a happy birthday on the eighteenth, Zev on the twentieth, and my mother never knew which was the real date of her birth.

Another winter story involved Mutti's much older sister, Amalia. Jetti and Amalia were accomplished dressmakers who designed and sewed fashionable garments for socially prominent women. In the early part of the twentieth century, skirts swept along the ground. On wet, winter, days, traversing a slush-covered street would leave the skirt hem a soggy mess.

Jetti and Amalia invented a garter belt, made of the same fabric as the dress, to be worn over the dress. The matching strips with garters attached to the skirt hem on four sides. It raised the skirt just enough to keep it out of the mud, or manure, on the street (still covering the ankles), freeing the hands to carry an umbrella, a muff, or parcels. Hundreds of these garter belts were sold and worn until the fashion changed and women no longer had to hide their ankles. But for several years, this accessory provided extra income for the Hacker family.

During that fall of 1939, my father arrived in Sweden, where he was reunited with his brother, my dear uncle Hugo, who had preceded him to that peaceful, neutral country by a few months.

Soon we started getting letters from Sweden. It seems that Vati wrote at least once a week, but there was a limit to how many letters Jews could receive at a time. Sometimes we got two or three at once. My father wrote poems in capital letters so that I could read them. These letters often made us laugh. What a blessing that was. He also sent beautiful poems that made Mutti cry.

He wrote detailed descriptions of the Swedes and Sweden and told what life was like for my father and my uncle. Both were impressed by how kind and polite everyone was. It took him a few days to get used to hearing people talk in a normal tone instead of the shouted commands of the concentration camp guards. The farmers were considerate of their farmhands and gave them delicious, plentiful food (although some of the fish dishes were strange to the Austrians, who seldom ate fish). Desserts were often made up of bite-sized chunks of seasonal fruit mixed with milk. This was certainly different from the rich, cream-filled pastries of Austria.

Vati told about the custom of keeping a pot of real coffee (not the chicory variety) on the back burner of the wood stove. People came in and out of the kitchen and drank coffee all day. One chilly morning, he tried some of the coffee and found that it contained a good deal of brandy.

Uncle Hugo was on another farm a few kilometers away, so every Sunday the brothers took turns visiting each other. Soon they acquired bicycles, which allowed them to spend more time together.

Hugo also wrote many letters to us, but while Vati's letters were usually humorous, entertaining and educational, Hugo's letters contained words of wisdom, encouragement and advice to keep looking toward a better future and not to dwell on the past. These letters were in answer to the ones my mother wrote to them about how helpless and unhappy she felt. Years later, my father showed me some of her letters. They were heavily censored, but enough of the words were left to make out how terrified, lonely and depressed she felt.

Eventually the leaves began to fall, and the days were shorter and cooler. One day Mutti announced that she had word from the Jewish Cultural Society that they had organized a real school for the Jewish children left in our district.

Getting ready for school kept us busy. I needed new shoes and my winter coat would need to be altered. Cousin Fritzi let out the seams and lowered the hem of my coat. She also gave me Kurt's outgrown backpack and a pair of high-topped shoes. Both items were like new and fit me perfectly, as did my one good dress.

One afternoon in Fritzi's courtyard, Kurt took pictures of me in my "ready for school" outfit. I took pictures of Mutti, Fritzi, and Kurt standing around the "Old Uncle," who was leaving for Montevideo the next day, Friday, August 31, 1939. Fritzi and Kurt planned to leave for England on the coming Monday.

After a year of separation, in which her husband wrote countless letters begging her to come home, Fritzi and Kurt were finally packed and ready to go home.

On Saturday, September 1, 1939, Germany invaded Poland. On Monday, September 3, 1939, England and France declared war on Germany. All travel to England was cut off. Fritzi and Kurt were now enemy aliens placed under strict house arrest. No one was permitted to visit them, and they were not allowed out of their apartment. Being Jewish made their situation dire since they were not allowed to hire someone to bring them food. They were, effectively, trapped.

About once a week, my mother took a chance, and we visited Fritzi and Kurt. We usually did this on a Sunday when the patrols were less frequent. We brought a little food and helped bring water from the hall faucet into the apartment. Only a few pieces of furniture were left for us to sit on. Kurt and I played chess on the floor in the light of the kerosene lamp, while Fritzi and Mutti drank tea made from dried leaves from a tree in the courtyard. The apartment had no electricity, and the curtains in the front room were drawn as Fritzi and Kurt were afraid of the neighbors who often yelled insults at them through the door.

One day, while furtively walking home from a visit with the totally depressed Fritzi and a very frightened Kurt, I heard my mother bemoan the irony of Fritzi sacrificing herself and her son to save a man who had already lived most of his life. Wiping away tears of frustration and sorrow she told me some stories about the "Old Uncle."

He had been the personal financial advisor to Kaiser Franz Josef, an important position at court. It was due to his contacts that he arranged for his niece, my mother's older sister Amalia, to be invited to one of the royal balls.

Jetti designed and sewed Amalia's ball gown which was admired by some of the ladies of the court. Amalia swore one of the more friendly women to secrecy, before she revealed the name of her dressmaker. This event enhanced the reputation of Jetti Menkes and assured her success.

The Old Uncle had kept up his Jewish observances, but not openly. Jews were not usually allowed to be government officials. However, Kaiser Franz Josef had Jewish doctors and financial advisors, and members of his court had Jewish mistresses. When the Nazis came into power, almost all the former officials of the Kaiser's court (which had been disbanded in 1918) were arrested and/or executed or sent into exile if they could find a place to go. The fact that the Old Uncle survived to emigrate was proof of his cunning and intelligence.

Chapter 19

In the fall of 1939, The Jewish Cultural Society rented a two-room building for a school. I was excited the morning that Mutti and I walked the ten minutes to the school. Numerous cement steps led up to the huge front door of the brick building. Inside, there was a wide, dark hallway. Toward the end of the hallway, a few steps went up to the larger room with a window to the street. Rows of desks faced a blackboard. Across the hall, two steps down, was another classroom with bench-type desks, and a window open to a wall. While the upper room was light, this room had an air of gloom.

At the end of the hall, behind a flowered curtain, was an old-fashioned English-style water closet. (A water tank was mounted high up on the wall, a pipe ran down to the back of the toilet, and a cord was pulled to release the water into the toilet bowl.) The water tank was seldom filled with water—thus the stench that filled the hall.

When Mutti and I arrived, several children had already gathered in the hallway. We looked at each other with interest, while the mothers exchanged greetings. The teacher came into the hall and told the girls to go into the upper room and the boys to go into the room across the hall. We girls climbed the three steps to the room indicated, and we started looking for our desks. The mothers stood in the hall, and we could hear them talking. Then the teacher, a stone-faced, gray-haired lady, rapped her long stick on a desk. She waited until we were quiet, and then announced that there were twenty girls and ten boys and only fifteen desks in each room, so five girls needed to go to the boys' room. (In those days, boys and girls did not go to the same schools. The fact that we were going to school in the same building, albeit in different rooms, was already a social stigma—a sign of the sub-humanity of Jews.)

I was one of the five girls ordered to take my things and go to the boys' room across the hall. We were immediately teased by our classmates and even by the mothers that were still lingering in the hallway. My own mother was still there, and when she saw I was one of the outcast girls, instead of consoling me, she pointed out that I had a pimple like a raspberry on my nose that morning; that must be why I was chosen to be exiled. She thought it was funny, but I began to cry. She called me a sissy, reminded me to come straight home, and left the building.

It was a horrible morning for the five of us outcasts. The girls who were left in the girls' room called us boy-girls, made jokes about what would happen to us as we became more like the dirty, stupid boys. Even after school these girls would not talk to us; they just pointed their fingers at us and laughed at us as if we were being punished.

The teachers, an old man who hated children and made no secret of it and the ugly, mean-faced woman who taught the girls, ignored the bullying or joined in on the jeers, depending on their mood. Admittedly, the five of us ousted girls were a bit different from the other six-year-olds in the girls' room.

Hedy was short; she barely came up to my shoulder. She huddled down in her desk to make herself as unobtrusive as possible. The teacher would yell at her to "Sit up!" often striking her across the shoulders to emphasize his command. This made her cringe down even lower.

Sonja was half-Gypsy with long, uncombed curls trailing down her back. The rumor was that her father was Jewish. She had dazzling white teeth and a fierce fire in her black eyes. The teacher stayed away from her.

Marta had a mop of orange hair and pale white skin with a sprinkling of freckles across her huge nose. Her upper teeth protruded over her lower lip and she lisped for the lack of lower teeth. She was the tallest student in the class and my mother always referred to her as "The Ugly One" *(Die Miesse)*.

Ursula had no unusual features. She had smooth, brown braids that always looked freshly plaited. She wore a white, starched apron every day and smiled readily whenever someone talked to her. Most days she brought her own food for the ten o'clock break *(Zenerjause)* and shared some of the little sandwiches with us four other girls. One day, she brought a tangerine; we had never seen such a fruit. Ursula gave each of us a section. I still remember the explosion of flavor in my mouth. She told us her non-Jewish father, as was mandated by law, had divorced her mother, which explained her presence among us.

My best friend was Susie. She had a halo of curly black hair, dark laughing eyes, a pretty, pixie face, and a club hand. Her right hand had five little toe-like bumps protruding from a lump of flesh at the end of her wrist. She had perfect dexterity with her left hand and wrote more legibly than I did. This vexed the teacher. Sometimes he stood over her and hit her left hand with his stick until she was unable to hold a pencil, then ordered her to use her right hand, which was impossible.

It was obvious why I was chosen to be among the boys. I had dark skin, black eyes and jet-black hair. I resembled the Gypsy girl, except my hair was smooth and so straight that a ribbon would slip off no matter how tightly it was tied. From the very first day I hated the teacher, and the feeling was probably mutual since I had the tendency to question authority.

One morning, Ursula, who was usually so punctual, came a few minutes late. She was sobbing loudly as the teacher stopped her at the door. "You are late!" he barked at her. "Put out your hands."

She put out her hands, palms up as was the custom, and he smacked his stick sharply across her palms, one smack for each minute she was late. No one asked her why she was crying. At the ten o'clock break, she told us that her mother was not there when she arrived home from school and had not come back by morning, so she decided to come to school.

We just stared at her. There was nothing to say. Her mother was gone just like all our fathers and we all had the same thought: *Hopefully, my mother will be there when I get home.*

That day I ran home from school as fast as I could (which I did most days after that), my heart pounding with fear. The relief I felt when I saw my mother filled my whole body and I could breathe again.

Ursula didn't come back to school. We heard she was sent to an orphanage. For us, she was as good as dead—which she soon would be. (All the children from that orphanage in Vienna were sent to Terezine [*Teresienstadt*] and subsequently to the gas chambers in Auschwitz.)

The desks were connected two-by-two, and the students had to share a desk—except the boy the teacher named "Strumpel Peter"[21] (we never knew his real name). He had to sit on a little stool near the door. Every day the teacher, who had a scraggly beard, foul breath and body odor, remarked on Peter's dirty clothes, his smelly little body, his dirty face, his messy hair, his long, dirty fingernails and his stupidity. I don't remember ever seeing him look up.

Some of the boys laughed, hearing the slights and insults, but Susie and I boiled with hatred for the teacher and cringed for Peter. One day I overheard two mothers discuss how unfortunate it was that this little boy, not yet six, had to take care of his blind grandmother. He wasn't old enough to go to school, but just followed the other children to school hoping to get something to eat.

Susie and I shared a desk, and I admit we giggled often and disturbed the class. The teacher tried to separate us at

---

[21] "Strumpel Peter" is a boy in a children's book who never bathed, combed his hair, cut his nails, or ate his soup. His tombstone with a picture of the disheveled boy is the last page in the book.

times, but we always managed to get back together. One day, when the teacher was being extra mean to Susie, hitting her hand till she cried, I asked him to please stop hitting her. "It's not her fault she can't write with her right hand," I had said. "Please, please, leave her alone," I pleaded. The teacher came around to my side of our desk, dragged me up by the collar of my dress and shoved me into the aisle. "Go stand behind the blackboard." He barked. I noticed that everyone laughed except Susie and tiny Hedy.

I stayed behind the blackboard until school was dismissed. The teacher told me not to move. He went to the other classroom and ordered the female teacher to come and guard me until my mother came to get me. By the time my mother came to the school, the light was fading, and she was in hysterics. I heard her yell at the teacher who was guarding me, and then she saw my legs behind the black board.

I heard Mutti question the woman about why I was behind the blackboard and the answer was that I had committed a terrible crime. "Such behavior would have resulted in a serious beating if she were a boy," I heard her say.

Mutti gathered up my coat and backpack, all the while berating me for being such a disrespectful, disobedient child. "Aren't you ashamed of yourself?" she asked me in an exasperated tone.

When I told her that I was not ashamed because I had not done anything to be ashamed for, she finally gave me a minute to tell her what I had done.

"That just goes to show how willful and stubborn you are." She continued scolding me while we walked quickly to get home before dark.

Even at the age of six, I realized that some of Mutti's anger was the result of the terror she must have felt when I didn't come home from school on time. She had waited two hours, trying not to panic. Finally, she hurried to the school, fearing that I might not be there.

When we were safely inside our apartment, she turned to

me. "Must you always take up with the misfits of this world?" she asked me. "Why can't you be friends with the normal girls?"

At that moment I knew there were discussions I could never have with my mother. From that day on, our relationship followed a predictable pattern. I only told her what I thought would make her proud of me. I never discussed my real feelings or complained or criticized the establishment—and especially not the teachers.

Over the years, on rare occasions I forgot myself and mentioned a complaint about my husband, a friend, or my children. This revelation usually brought on a tirade of how it was my fault that I had this problem.

Ruthie & Mother, 1939.

Mitzi Bauer & Ruthie, Winter of 1939.

Chapter 20

In early November 1939, snow began to cover Vienna. Piles of snow lay beside the sidewalks and around the base of trees. One afternoon, as several of us students were leaving the school, someone threw a snowball. Soon we were throwing snowballs at each other like the children we should have been. Boys across the street began to get into the game, and we started throwing snowballs at them too.

Suddenly one of the boys in our group let out a scream; we saw blood running down his face. The boys across the street had put rocks into their snowballs. The rock-filled snowballs came at us, accompanied by threats of how they were going to kill all us "dirty Jewish pigs." They were reminding us of who we were. The boys across the street were older and bigger, so fighting was out of the question. We scattered and ran home as fast as we could go. It was our last snowball fight.

As the winter days dragged on, we sat with our four fingers flat on the desk, with our thumbs underneath, while reciting the answers to problems in addition, subtraction, multiplication and division. A wrong answer meant a smack across the knuckles with the stick. Clutching tightly to our stubby pencils we learned to write cursive letters without the basics of printing them first. Each night we had two or more hours of homework, which included dates and places of historic events.

Mutti and I subsisted on a piece or two of garlic toast, sometimes a boiled potato and for me the cup of blue (all cream skimmed off) milk. In the morning, we had a piece of bread with strange-tasting, yellow fat spread on it, and the brown water we called coffee. I took a thin slice of bread, wrapped in a piece of paper (that I had to remember to bring back), for snack time. We never saw fruit or vegetables. Sometimes there was a hardboiled egg for lunch when I got home from school. Usually there was just garlic toast and hot water, which we called tea.

Each day there were fewer children coming to school and one morning the teacher for the girls' class did not come in. Since there were only eighteen children left, the classes were combined and the students had to sit three on each bench. Susie and I shared a desk with Sonia. There was no heat or electricity in the building, so we were grateful for the warmth we gave each other.

Since Sonia didn't come to school regularly, she seldom knew the answers to the questions the teacher asked her. When he raised his stick in preparation to hit her hands, she glared at him with those fiery eyes; he stopped the stick in midair and quickly moved away. Susie and I admired Sonia's fearlessness, but we were also a little afraid of her.

It was a sad day for me when Susie did not come to school. I kept hoping she might be sick and come back when she recovered. A week went by, and then I overheard a conversation between the teacher and another student who lived near Susie. Susie and her aunt, with whom she lived after her parents were taken away, had disappeared.

I kept going to school, did my homework, learned to embroider, and listened to Mutti's stories; but I missed Susie terribly, and just thinking of her made me cry. When Mutti asked me why I was crying, I didn't answer. I remembered her criticizing me for being friends with misfits and cripples. Of course I loved my mother, but I became aware, at an early age, that even the nicest people can have callous and cruel streaks and blind spots.

Sonia and I were the only two girls left from the original five who had been moved into the boys' room. We became friends with some of the more civilized boys—the ones who treated us like equals instead of pulling our hair or untying our apron strings as we walked by. The other girls from the original girls' room just ignored us.

After the day of the snowball fight, most of us were picked up by our mothers after school. One day, Sonia's mother approached my mother and asked her if she had anything she could spare. "Anything at all," I heard her plead. "A piece of lace, a bit of yarn or cloth that I could make something to sell."

Mutti told her to follow us home and she would see what she had. When we got to the apartment Mutti told Sonia and her mother to wait in the kitchen area. She searched the cupboard over my crib for something to give the Gypsy woman. She found a yard of lace and gave it to Sonia and her mother. They both thanked her profusely and left.

At that moment Mutti discovered that the bread was gone from the counter. Quickly she checked her purse on the table and saw that the ration cards were also missing. A tirade rained on me for having such bad people as friends. Eventually she said that doing a favor is usually rewarded with punishment, and she took some of the blame on herself.

It was not a pleasant night without even a bite of bread, and an even more miserable week, until Mutti was able to replace the ration cards. I had strict orders not to consort with Sonia again. She wasn't hard to avoid because Sonia didn't come back to school after that day.

A few days later I began to scratch my head. Several of the girls at school also had head lice. The word went around that they had surely come from Sonia. The modern cure for head lice was to shave the heads of people who had them. However, my mother remembered having lice when she was my age. Her mother had combed kerosene from the lamps through her waist long hair. According to Mutti it had taken weeks to get rid of the vermin. My hair was short and not nearly such a challenge.

For several days in a row, my hair was saturated with the kerosene from our lamp and I went to school with a cloth torn from an old pillowcase wound around my head. At home, my hair was yanked and pulled through a special louse comb. The dead lice piled up on the white cloth around my shoulders. After a week I was finally lice-free.

It snowed almost every day that winter of 1939–1940. Our room was icy cold, and we went to bed immediately after eating our evening garlic bread.

One night, loud knocks came on our door, and we were paralyzed with fear. Had they come to take us away? We had heard those knocks on other doors in the middle of the night; we knew what they meant. People were disappearing every day. Mutti took a long time to open the door, and by the time she had her hand on the handle, the hinges were beginning to splinter the wood. The men were angry and tried to grab us to come along, but my mother began to argue with them, saying things like, "I cannot take a six-year-old out of bed to shovel snow all night. She has to go to school in the morning."

The men paid no attention to her, but they allowed her to get our coats, hats and mittens. They walked us to a street near where we used to live. It must have been a ten-minute walk, but we were freezing by the time we started shoveling. Hundreds of Jewish women and children were lined up in rows, shoveling snow off the street until near dawn.

Several more snowstorms came through March 1940, and more nights on the street shoveling snow. Each time we heard the knock after midnight we froze with fear that, this time, we would be taken away.

One time, when the men came to get us for snow shoveling, I had trouble waking up. The men were rushing us because of how slow I was to get up, and they began to shout insults at my mother for being a "lazy, Jewish sow" and threatened to throw her down the stairs if she didn't move faster. I peed into my nightgown in terror while Mutti struggled to get me into my coat. When we got to the shoveling site, I realized I had forgotten my mittens. My hands were so cold, they froze to the shovel. A man came toward me and asked me to come warm my hands at the fire that was burning in a nearby barrel.

I looked around at the guards, with guns, whips and dogs, and I shook my head. I was not about to leave my mother's side with a strange man. Now I know that this man risked his life since it was forbidden to offer any type of kindness to a Jew. People were sent to concentration camps for such transgressions.

A few days later, we were walking home from another futile visit to the American Embassy when we heard shouting and laughter coming from a

Going to school after a night of shoveling snow, 1940.

huge ice-skating rink surrounded by a heavy chain-link fence. I pulled Mutti to a stop and she reluctantly allowed me to watch a few minutes as the children and some adults glided around to a waltz. It looked like such fun. Before I had a chance to ask about going skating, Mutti said in a sad tone, "Too bad you can never ice skate, since you have such weak ankles."

I wanted to argue, but I remembered that Mitzi had once told me I needed to wear the ugly, high topped shoes because they supported my ankles. When we passed the iron rod gate to the rink, I saw the large sign: "JUDEN VERBOTTEN."

I could read by then and knew I didn't really have weak ankles. I had seen the sign on nearly every door to a public venue in Vienna. Jews were forbidden to enter all places of entertainment, medical and cultural institutions, as well as sports clubs, parks and skating rinks. The irony was tragic beyond all reason. The very doctors, artists and philanthropists who had helped to make Vienna world-famous for its culture and medical advances were now barred from entering those buildings that housed their work.

Chapter 21

One afternoon the girl named Ruthie, who had been a guest at my fifth birthday party, and her tall, blonde mother, Anna, came to visit. Anna wanted to thank my mother for arranging for Ruthie to go to France on a transport for Jewish children. My mother assured Ruthie's mother that she needn't thank her. It was the least she could do under the circumstances.[22]

She went into the bedroom and came back with her little, black-banded wristwatch. It was one of the last valuable possessions we had. Seeing my mother put the watch on Ruthie's wrist, then giving her a warm hug, I felt a twinge of jealousy. With tears in all our eyes we said farewell. My tears were for the watch I had thought would be mine someday.

Toward the end of March, an envelope arrived from America. It contained the long-awaited affidavit. Rudy Menkes had sent an affidavit to the old address at Webergasse 13, and the apartment manager (the *luder*—the "bitch"), who knew exactly where we now lived, had returned it to him marked "Address Unknown." By the time he had received the returned affidavit, it had expired.

When Rudy received my mother's pleading letters with the new address, he re-applied with another $300 fee which, in those days, was a small fortune.

Now we had the precious document which meant we could

---

[22] Anna, a devout Catholic, became pregnant during an affair with mother's cousin, Joshi Menkes. They came to my mother to ask for funds to get an abortion. My mother refused; instead, she offered to help with support if Anna agreed to raise the child Jewish. (My mother's best friend, Ida Schischa, told me the story sixty years later.)

apply for papers to immigrate into America. Again, we did much standing in line at various offices. Permits had to be obtained for riding the streetcar, documents to allow border crossings, and other endless papers to be signed and/or stamped.

Steamship tickets were bought after Mutti sold the Shanghai tickets. She arranged for a large, wooden, packing crate to be brought to our little apartment. It filled the room and we had to squeeze around it to get into the sleeping area. I could fit into it if I stooped a little.

Deciding what to take to America filled my mind, I continued going to school but, by the time I came home, I had thought of a few more things for the crate. Soon it contained dishes, pots, lids, and linens. The last things packed were the feather beds and my eider down pillow.

We had a short debate about my best doll, Irma Puppe. She had real hair and eyes that opened, an extravagant gift from the mother of the twins, and I named her in honor of this generous aunt. I was told I could take only one toy. When I insisted on taking my Teddy Bear (who was my best friend), Mutti decided to take the doll too.

Then it was time to say goodbye to the cousins who were still in Vienna. Heinzi and his parents had left for Ceylon. Mina had left for Australia. Sidi (known to her Rio friends as Lydia) had gone to Brazil with her shoemaker husband.

One day we went to visit Gisele & Herman and their children, Helga and Oliver. I vaguely remembered them from my birthday party two years ago. Oliver was chubby with a big, round face; Helga was taller than I was, very pale and shy.

The family lived in a house outside the city, and it was a full day's walk to get there. On the way, Mutti told me many things about her cousin as we made our way through the city, watching the streetcars glide by. She told me in a lowered voice that they were *Nichtglauber* (Atheists). I didn't know what that meant, but from Mutti's tone, I knew it was not a good thing to be. She went on to tell me that they were Jewish, like us, but denied the existence of God and felt that the world would be better off if there were no religion. They were also vegetarians, which meant that they didn't eat any meat or animal products. "They raise their own food," she said in a tone that sounded respectful. "We will need to stay overnight because we can't get back before dark." I could hear the apprehension in her voice as she told me to eat what they gave me and not to complain about the food. I was thinking it couldn't be any worse than the garlic bread and blue milk I got most days.

The house sat in a patch of tall grass with a narrow, muddy path going to the door. It had two rooms, no electricity, and no running water; the latrine was a few steps from the back door. We sat on rough benches around a plank that served as a table and ate the bowl of cooked vegetables that came from their garden. To me, the children sounded rude and aggressive as they addressed their parents by their first names. They never said a word to me or my mother. The family spoke only English with each other because they expected to go to England and then on to Palestine, where they had friends who lived on a Kibbutz.

Only the low flames of the old wood stove heated the house, and it smelled musty. The kerosene lamp was the only light. We children were put to bed not long after we had eaten our midday meal. From what I overheard while presumably asleep on the moldy, smelly couch in one corner, their hopes to emigrate were slim, and, if necessary, they would stay in their dank, dark little house until the British chased out the Nazis.

When she heard their plan, my mother gave an ominous chuckle. Then I heard her say, "You talk like ignorant or very naïve children. No one with any Jewish ancestors is safe from those fiends. If you don't leave as soon as possible they will eventually kill you." Her voice had risen, and I knew she was crying.

"Don't be so upset, Thilde," I heard Gisele say. "Our friends are all Free Thinkers (Atheists), like us. They will hide us if that becomes necessary."

I must have gone to sleep after that conversation. When

my mother came to lie down beside me, I awoke briefly. Before I fell asleep, I heard her quietly weeping into the coat she was using as a pillow.

The next day we tried to say cheerful goodbyes to the cousins, who, like so many others in our family, would disappear without a trace, from our lives and the earth.

The sky was gray, like our mood, when we went to say goodbye to Fritzi and Kurt. The Old Uncle had left for Uruguay, and by then, Fritzi and Kurt had lost all hope of getting back to England. Kurt and I played chess while our mothers talked and cried and lost all track of time. The final farewells were very emotional, and by the time we were at the door, it was dark. Mutti decided we would take a chance and go home. It was not far, and she knew the way even in the pitch dark. (It was like walking blindfolded that rainy April night.) We heard the boots, but luck was with us, and we made it into our building before they turned the corner. My heart was pounding when we entered our apartment, but Mutti was still softly sobbing, oblivious of the danger we had narrowly averted.

Part Three:

The Tidal Wave

Those who were swept away,
others tossed out to distant shores

Chapter 22

Early in the morning of the last Sunday in April, exactly two weeks from the date set for our departure, we heard a knock on the door. And then Mitzi's voice was calling out to Mutti. She came into our cramped little room and, carefully stepping across the packing box lid, she gave me a long hug. After putting a few bundles of vegetables on the table she said brightly, "I'm taking my little treasure to the Prater."[23]

At first Mutti said that this was not possible. She would not let Mitzi put herself into such danger. But Mitzi persisted. "I can't let my little treasure leave Vienna without once visiting the world-famous Prater." Mitzi's voice was firm.

Mutti relented after Mitzi told her she was taking me to the *Stefans Turm* (St. Stephens Cathedral) first. She would ask for protection from the holy Maria. Mitzi tucked my hair into the scratchy wool hat that I hated. Not a strand of my coal black hair could be seen. "Just in case," Mitzi said, as I objected to the hat. It was a warm day, but the hat stayed on my head. I knew exactly what "just in case" meant. Coal black hair was suspiciously "Jewish" and if we were caught breaking the law it meant a concentration camp for Mitzi, and I would "disappear" as had so many children already.

After lighting a candle at one of the huge altars at the famous church we took a streetcar back across the river toward the Prater. It had been a long time since I had been

---

[23] The huge amusement park near the center of Vienna, famous for its giant Ferris wheel with gondolas the size of streetcars.

on a streetcar. As much as I wanted to look around, I kept my very dark eyes lowered. My hand was sweaty as I gripped the pole in the middle of the car; the other hand was firmly in Mitzi's grasp,

I tried to avoid looking at the huge sign in the middle of the gates that forbade me to enter the Prater. My stomach was churning as we walked into the midway area. By the time we had taken our first ride in the *Liliputen* ("dwarf") area, I had forgotten that I was forbidden to enter this park and just enjoyed the day. While watching the Punch and Judy Show, I was surrounded by other children, and we all laughed at the antics of the puppets. We enjoyed many other rides, and we ate the famous *Wiener Wuerstel,* drank raspberry soda, and just before we went on the *Riesenrahd* (the giant Ferris wheel), Mitzi bought me my first ice cream cone. I was a sticky mess by the time we reached the top of the ride. I had never been that high before. It was wonderful.

On the long walk back to the apartment, Mitzi needlessly admonished me. "You must never tell anyone about being in the Prater today." After a last (and it was the very last) hug, Mitzi left. I remembered that day as my happiest in Vienna and in all my seven years.

One morning Mutti woke me up early. "We are going to Wopfing," she told me as she got me dressed and urged me to hurry and drink the warm milk that she had fixed for me.

We rushed to the train depot, and two hours later arrived in Wopfing. Walking through the fields I asked why we didn't go by the road, which was an easier walk. Mutti just kept walking until we arrived at the back gate of Oma's house. We used the latrine before we climbed the stairs to the main floor. I thought I heard the voices of my cousins. Entering the kitchen, I saw Vera, Eva, their mother (my aunt Irma), Tante Franzi and Oma. The three women were sitting at the table and the girls were having a tea party in a corner on a towel. After hugs all around, I joined the girls and their dolls.

While Eva and Vera were chatting to each other in Czech,

I listened to the women talking in German. I heard and understood everything. We had come to say goodbye before departing for America, and everyone was very sad. Oma was crying, and between sobs, I heard her wail.

"Why do they have to scatter us like this? It is such torture. I can't stand it! They want to kill all of us, so why don't they let us all stay together and drop a bomb on us?"

One of the women told her to hush and think of the children.

Aunt Irma told my mother that they had no intention of leaving their home. "The Czech people are not Austrians," she declared emphatically. "They suffered under the rule of the Austrian-Hungarian Empire for hundreds of years. The Czech people distrust, even hate, Austrians, and will never emulate their brutal behavior."

The conversation turned to a present that my grandmother wanted to give me. She held out a black velvet box. Inside were deep blue sapphire earrings, a wedding present from her groom. I heard Oma say, "Ruthie should have them because she is the oldest girl."

That sounded good to me. The two little stones nestled in a black velvet box, twinkled at me as if to assure me they would be mine. Then I heard Tante Franzi say she could easily pierce my ears and I could wear them. I knew what the word "pierce" meant, and I quickly lost my desire for the earrings. "No!" I screamed out and they all looked at me, puzzled. "I don't want my ears pierced. I won't let you do it."

It was Mutti who came to her senses. "She can't wear those stones in public; the fiends will rip them from her ear lobes."

The other women began to argue with her. "Who would deprive a child of an heirloom?" Oma said. "But we will hide them, and when you are safely in America we will send them to you."

Aunt Irma said, "She doesn't want to get her ears pierced so give them to Vera; she is the next oldest."

It was during this discussion that a neighbor came into

the kitchen through the door that led into the grocery store (now owned by an Aryan). Her face was contorted as she hissed in a loud whisper, "They are coming to get you!"

Everyone became quiet and we could hear the boots on the gravel road. As they came closer, we also heard dogs barking. In the next moment, we heard a loud banging on the huge delivery doors, which were at the end of a dark hallway that led to the street. Oma rose slowly and headed into the hallway. My mother got up and with a firm grip on my arm pulled me along behind Oma. The banging on the huge doors got louder as Oma went towards them.

My mother stepped to the left into the little apartment where the Waxhovers lived. Strangely, Maria was not home that morning. As we entered the apartment Mutti closed the door behind us and pushed me under the window seat across the room. She squeezed in behind me then pulled me up between her legs. We heard the loud creak of the street doors swinging open, heard boots clomping, people screaming, men barking commands.

Mutti held me tightly with her arms across my chest so I could hardly breathe. The fur trim on her coat sleeve tickled my nose, but she wouldn't let me move a muscle. We sat under that window seat for a long time. It must have been many hours, as it was getting dusk when she finally let me loose and we crawled out from our hiding place. We went out into the hallway, along the veranda to the kitchen, which was empty. The whole house was empty. Not even the Waxhovers had come home.

Quietly we made our way down the stairs, out the back gate, then hurried through the meadow toward the train tracks. Wopfing had no train depot. When people wanted to take the train, they stood by the tracks and waved a white handkerchief. The train would stop for a few moments to let them on and they would pay the conductor according to how far they planned to travel.

Grandmother's grocery store and tobacco shop where we hid under the Window in May, 1940.

It must have been late in the evening by then because when we walked through the meadow, the grass was very wet and my socks and shoes—as well as the hem of my dress—were soaking. We waited for what seemed a long time and when the train came Mutti waved her hanky and we got on the train.

When we arrived in Vienna it was pitch dark. No street-lights were allowed as it was war time and heavy blackout curtains covered apartment windows. Fortunately, Mutti knew her way. When we arrived in our neighborhood, we heard the clomping of boots from the Gestapo Patrol. We had no way of knowing which way they were coming because of the echo in the narrow streets. With hearts pounding, we froze in our tracks, expecting to be shot. Suddenly we saw a man coming toward us from across the street. As he came closer, we saw it was a regular city policeman. Without a word he pushed us into the nearest doorway and spread out his gray cape. He stood there in front of us as the patrol marched by. He greeted them with a "Good evening." When they had passed, he stood aside, and we hurried to our apart-ment which was only a few steps farther. The policeman didn't exchange a word with us, and I don't know if he knew my mother (which is likely), but he took a chance with his life and he saved ours.

Chapter 23

The day after our trip to Wopfing and our narrow escape in the street, I went to school as usual. I didn't find out that it was my last day until I came home. Although my satchel was full of homework, Mutti didn't make me sit down to work on it immediately. Instead, she took the satchel off my back, replaced some of the papers with my favorite books and put it carefully into the nearly full crate. It was the last item to go into the crate before Mutti stuffed the featherbeds and pillows around and between the items in the crate.

Then she pulled me down beside her on the bench under the window and began to tell me about how we would travel to America.

"I have all the papers." Mutti was breathless with excitement. "We have permission to ride the streetcar to the *Seudbahn Hoff* ("South Station") where we will take a train to Genoa, a beautiful port city in Italy." Then she described the ship as being as big as the village of Wopfing. "Five other people will be sleeping in our cabin, so you must be very careful not to wet the bed." She gave me a stern look and continued to admonish me about being quiet during the voyage.

The next day would be the last day in our tiny room when a representative from the Jewish Cultural Society was to bring us the final papers we needed and instructions on where to stay and how to get to the ship. While we waited for this person to arrive, Mutti told me about Italy. She told me that I would see palm, lemon and orange trees. She planned to take me for a walk to see this most beautiful city where we would see the ocean. She had never seen it; she managed to describe the vast emptiness, but to me it was unimaginable.

Later that morning the man from the Cultural Society brought us the fat envelope with instructions and information about Genoa and getting to the ship. A special hotel for Jewish transients was there because, as in all other countries ruled by the Nazis, Jews were not allowed in places open to the public. He told us that a man from the Jewish Agency in Genoa would contact us at the hotel and give us further instruction.

He was getting ready to leave when my mother asked him if he had any news of the *Kinder Transport* on which the girl Ruthie had been traveling. He looked at her for a moment then asked, "Didn't you know?" I could see Mutti's eyes getting wider behind her eyeglasses as she shook her head, indicating ignorance. The man continued speaking in a low, even tone. "The train was intercepted by the Germans at the French border. The children on that train have disappeared."[24]

The scream that burst forth from my mother's tightly clenched teeth was high pitched like a whistle, but loud enough to echo around the little room. The she clutched her stomach as if someone had punched her and sat down abruptly on the only chair. She rocked back and forth as if in great pain. Her head was touching her lap as she began to wail. "What have I done? Oh God, what have I done?"

The man and I just stood and watched for a few minutes. Then he turned to me and said, "Bon voyage," while backing out of the door and closing it behind him. As I watched Mutti rock back and forth in the chair, her arms still clutching her stomach and sobbing openly, the cold knot of fear that usually stayed in my stomach spread throughout my whole body. I had never seen my mother in such pain. That scene has stayed in my memory as clear as the day it occurred. I

---

[24] Two boys escaped and told what happened. The German SS took the two hundred children off the train, led them, at gunpoint, to an open field, ordered them to undress, relinquish all valuables and money. As some of the men set up the machine guns, others raped several of the girls. Then they mowed down the children like stalks of ripe wheat.

don't remember how long she sat in that chair, but eventually she got up and prepared some food for me.

The next day, two men came to the apartment. They worked hard to stuff the feather beds below the rim, and then nailed the lid on the wooden crate. It took a long time to maneuver it down the narrow stairs and load it into a waiting truck. In the meantime, we managed to put a few more things into two small suitcases.

Although we had permits to ride the streetcar to the train station, the permits forbade us to carry any luggage. Lottie, our Evangelical/Jewish friend, was dating an Aryan doctor who had a car, so when we got downstairs a big black automobile was waiting at the curb. A strange man was at the wheel, but I recognized Lottie beside him. Lottie got out of the car and helped us put the suitcases into the back seat, and we squeezed in beside them. I had never been in an automobile before and the ride to the train station was almost as exciting as those rides at the Prater.

Lottie and my mother hugged briefly; Lottie pinched my cheek with her gloved hand, and I could see tears running down her face. Mutti was also crying softly. I was too excited to cry. As we hurried into the station, heading directly for the train, it seemed to me that everyone was crying in that place.

The train was different from the ones we took to Wopfing. Instead of rows of wooden seats there were closed off compartments in each car. With a great effort Mutti, who was only five feet tall, got the heavy suitcases into the overhead shelf. Clutching her big purse, she sat down and carefully arranged her hat into place. Then she pulled my cap down to my ears, my dress below my knees and sternly admonished me to sit perfectly still and be totally quiet.

The whistle blew and we were on our way out of Vienna. The woods and fields went by the window, and soon there were mountains and eventually lakes. I fell asleep, and when I awoke, we were at the Italian border. The conductor came by, calling out "Passports!" which were inspected by two men in black boots and SS uniforms. I was too frightened to look up at the other passengers in the compartment, but I saw them holding out passports with trembling hands. My heart began to pound as I looked up at Mutti and saw her lips were pressed into a thin line, but her hands were steady.

One of the women in our compartment had to get off, accompanied by the men in the SS uniforms. She asked if she should bring her suitcase, but they told her not to bother. Then the train began to move and as I looked out the window, I saw the woman between the SS men, being dragged into the station. No one in the compartment said a word; we all looked at her suitcase up on the rack, but we did not look at each other.

In the morning we rolled into Genoa. Somehow, we found our way out of the station and to the street. A man with a sign from the Jewish Agency came up to us. He knew our names, helped us into a taxi, and gave the driver directions to a small hotel in a narrow, alley-like street. After we checked into the hotel, the same man came up to the room with us, sat on the bed, and asked my mother if she had any lira. Of course she had only a few German Marks. He said he would be happy to help her exchange the money, as she would need lira on the Italian ship. So Mutti gave him most of her money (she kept five dollars' worth of Marks, just in case) and he said he would be back by five o'clock with the lira.

After a rest in the little room, Mutti decided we would explore this city, touted as the "most beautiful in the world." Being careful to note landmarks, we began to walk through the narrow streets. We walked a long time and saw only old, shabby, apartment houses with clotheslines strung across the streets. After about an hour of seeing nothing but clothes flapping in the wind, we returned to the hotel. Mutti produced an apple out of her purse. Since she didn't have any money, I suppose she took it off a fruit stand when I wasn't looking. This was our lunch.

At long last we heard the church bells chime five o'clock.

Mutti began to pace up and down the narrow room, muttering, "Where is he? Where is he?" over and over. By six o'clock, it was obvious the man was not coming back with the money. Mutti was frantic. She began to talk louder and berate herself as a trusting idiot and many other words that I had never heard. Although I was very hungry, I knew better than to mention it to Mutti that night.

In the morning Mutti asked the woman at the hotel desk (who spoke a little German) how to get to the ship. She said her son would take us in his donkey cart as part of the hotel service. If the young man expected a tip, he was sorely disappointed.

On ship to America. Newlyweds on diving board. Other shipmates, cabin mates Ruth and girlfriend.

Chapter 24

We arrived at the dock just in time to board the majestic SS Conte di Savoia, pride of the Italian shipping line. The ship was, as my mother had described, like a floating city. A porter took our suitcases and we followed him to our cabin, deep in the hold of the ship. Three bunks lined each side of a space the size of a closet, with a sink and toilet behind a door at the far end of the room. We were to store our suitcases under the beds and, since we could not get them out to open them until we docked, we took out a few things we might need for the next five days of the voyage. We had no shelves or cabinets, so we squished everything to the foot of our narrow bunks.

We went up on deck to watch the departure. As we drifted out of the harbor, I saw Mutti crying. I was surprised at her tears; much later I realized that she had good memories of her native land, while I remembered only fear.

Several long tables, covered with red-and-white-checked tablecloths, filled the spacious third-class dining room. Wide windows let in the afternoon sunlight which reflected on the bouncing waves around the ship. We sat on rough wooden benches while waiters brought in platters of strange looking food. Noodles covered with tomato sauce, cooked and uncooked vegetables, platters of what looked like green grapes. (I was so disappointed at their taste that it was many years before I learned to like olives.)

Although I was very hungry (the last thing I had eaten was an apple the day before), the only thing I ate that first day was the fruit served after the main meal. I could hardly believe the abundance of oranges, tangerines, apples, green grapes, apricots and slices of red and yellow melons.[25]

After the meal we went next door to the equally spacious lounge. Desks were spaced around the room, complete with writing paper, fountain pens and inkwells. The bookshelves contained books and magazines in German and Italian. Cushioned chairs and couches provided an ambiance of comfort.

The people scattered around the room were reading, playing chess, writing letters or just chatting in several languages. It all looked very dull to me. I saw no other children my age, and I began to complain to Mutti that I was bored. "You can walk around the ship," she said, "Just remember where our cabin is located. In fact, let's go there right now."

When we got to our cabin (I had taken careful note of where it was), Mutti dashed into the toilet. When she came out her face was white. She lay down on the lower bunk, and I crawled into the middle one. One of our roommates was already asleep in the top bunk and snoring loudly.

"Go brush your teeth," Mutti muttered feebly from her bunk.

I found my toothbrush and the little bag of salt we had taken from the dining room, and I went into the cubicle where the toilet and wash basin stood. (We found out, just before we arrived in New York, that there were showers at the end of the hallway. Somehow, we had kept clean with just the sink and the small square of soap provided by the shipping line).

Lying down on the narrow bunk I thought, narrow as it was, it was certainly more comfortable than my little crib. The linens were clean and smooth, and I luxuriated in the fresh smell of real soap. My stomach started to growl, and I thought of waking Mutti to see about an evening meal but fell

---

[25] For breakfast, each day, I had a soft-boiled egg, delicious white bread with real butter, and hot chocolate to drink. Baskets of fruit sat on each table. I filled up on tangerines. The meals on the ship were wonderful after two years of garlic toast and thin onion soup.

into a deep sleep.

When I woke up, the occupants of the other bunks were still sleeping. I did not need to get dressed because I had fallen asleep with my clothes and shoes on. Slowly I made my way to the floor being careful not to disturb Mutti or any of the other women. After a quick trip to the toilet, I left the cabin to look for food.

I followed the fragrance of freshly brewed coffee to the dining room and found I was just in time for breakfast. The rolls and butter were like the ones we used to have before the Nazis took over our country. I ate a couple of rolls and stuffed several into the pockets of my dress, while gulping down the milky coffee.

When I got back to the cabin, Mutti was just getting up. I gave her the rolls and she tucked them away in our bundle of clothes at the foot of her bunk. Then we went upstairs to the third-class lounge. Mutti immediately began to write letters on the stationary. In fact, she spent almost all her time, when she was not seasick, sitting at a desk writing letters to Vati.

During the noon meal, the captain announced the next morning we would be sailing through the Straits of Gibraltar. Passengers were not allowed to leave the ship, but a tender would take mail ashore to the post office.

Mutti spent most of that day writing letters to Sweden, to Austria and to New York. Then she used the last of the few Deutschmarks she had left to pay for postage. Luckily, all food aboard the ship was included in the passage because now we really did not have a cent to our name.

The next morning the ship eased its way through the narrow waters of Gibraltar. Hundreds of small boats, laden with colorful fabrics and a variety of handmade objects, approached it from all sides. The dark-skinned vendors, wearing multicolored, flowing garments that flapped in the light breeze, shouted, in several languages, to the passengers hanging over the rails.

I was fascinated, not just by the variety of beautiful objects that were being held up for our inspection, but by the system of paying for and delivering the purchased object. There was much bargaining, but when prices were agreed upon, little baskets with the desired purchases were transferred by long poles to the buyer on the ship who put the money required into the basket. An honor system on both sides.

I knew we had no money but sometimes I blurted out, "How pretty" or "That would be nice to have." Mutti would snap at me, "We have no money" or "Don't be so stupid, you know I haven't any money." She was always so angry.

The sun was sinking into the ocean in front of us as the ship passed through the towering cliffs and out into the brilliant sunset. I was dazzled by the colors and wide expanse in front of us. On our way to the dining room for our evening snack, I saw a girl near my age walking in front of us. We sat together at the table and started to talk. Her name was Else, she was traveling with an aunt. We met again the next morning and started to explore the ship together.

We climbed the outside stairways to the first-class deck where we saw a huge swimming pool, surrounded by cushioned lounge chairs and tables spread with white linen. In the dining room the small tables were also covered with white tablecloths with many sets of flatware beside porcelain plates. Crystal goblets gleamed in the light from cut glass chandeliers. It looked like one of the banquet rooms my mother had described in the fairy tales about royal princesses. We didn't dare enter such a splendid setting. However, we did bend down and run our hands over the thick, velvety carpet. It reminded me of the time I had been allowed to stroke a rabbit.

The second-class dining room was one deck down and not quite as luxurious as the one we had just left. The tables, set for two, four, or six people had colorful center pieces of real flowers. Lunch (the main meal of the day) was served buffet style and Else and I got in line and helped ourselves to the various dishes and took our plates out to the open deck.

The ship rocked in the choppy water and we stumbled to the nearest deck chairs and ate every bit of the delicious food. While returning the empty plates to the dining room, without any warning, I threw up everything I had eaten. My delicious lunch splattered all over Else, down to her shiny black shoes. We were standing in a doorway so she couldn't back up as the doorframe was against her back. She stepped sideways, turned and ran away, screaming for her absent mother. I made my way down to our cabin.

The next day Else and I met up at breakfast, but she went back to her cabin right after the meal and I didn't see her again until late afternoon. My mother and her aunt had not left their cabins for two days and this was our third day at sea. That afternoon my mother recovered sufficiently to go to the lounge and write more letters.

I made friends with a young, newlywed couple. They were very friendly and walked the deck with me, telling stories about how they had met. When my mother saw them in the dining room, she remarked that they were so ugly that they were meant for each other. I told Mutti that it was an insulting thing to say. With a fierce glare, she told me that she was sick and tired of my rudeness and walked away.

Later that day we all happened to meet on deck while the ship's photographer was taking pictures. He gathered Mutti, Else, her aunt and the young couple to the railing of the ship where a lifesaving ring showed the name of the ship. We didn't notice the Italian boy who squeezed in with Else and me, until we looked at the photo several days later. People often asked if he was my brother.

One morning I met the young couple on the deck and the man offered to hold me up while I walked along the rail. It was a great feeling watching the ocean glide by below me and I hoped he would let me walk the whole length of the ship. Just then my mother, who seldom had left her bunk, came stumbling out to the deck. When she saw me on the rail, she screamed my name and began to berate the young man. He lifted me down and just laughed. This made Mutti even angrier. While dragging me away she forbade me to see these horrible, ugly people again. Since we were landing the next day, I promised to obey her.

Chapter 25

America: May 1940

This was to be that fateful day when we would enter New York Harbor and see that symbol of freedom, The Statue of Liberty. Mutti was finally able to pull the suitcase out from under the bunk bed and stuff in the things we had used on the voyage. The porters came to pick up the luggage, which we would claim when we got on shore. We started up the stairs to the open deck with every expectation of seeing the famous landmark and the New York skyline with the tallest buildings in the world.

When we reached the hallway that led to the stairway to the deck, we saw a heavy chain across the stairs. A sailor standing on the top step told us to go back down to the lower deck foyer where we were to wait until it was time to leave the ship. A ship's officer came to the top of the stairs and yelled out in German and Italian that third class passengers were not allowed on deck until the ship was docked. Immigration officials would inspect each person and their papers before any of them could leave the ship.

We were not allowed back into our cabins or into the locked dining room. I had been too excited to go to breakfast that morning and my stomach began to growl. We were being held prisoner in the area below deck. Two sailors stood at the bottom of the steps blocking anyone from going up even a step or two. Looking past the men I got a glimpse of gray clouds. Then someone pushed me back in among the adults. I heard some German speaking women discuss the situation.

"How can they be so mean? Not letting us see the Statue of Liberty?" A man near me mumbled that he didn't think the Italians could be so cruel. Even at the ripe old age of seven I knew exactly how mean and cruel adults could be and always wondered why.

Clutching Kasper (my sawdust leaking clown) in one hand I managed to keep a tight grip on my mother's skirt. I looked up to see her clutching her purse with our precious identity papers against her chest with both hands. I tried to see her face, but the crowd was getting closer and soon I was squeezed tightly between many people. I felt the panic rise in my throat and for a moment I felt I would suffocate. I couldn't breathe. Suddenly I heard myself screaming. Mutti yelled at me at the top of her lungs. "Stop! Stop yelling, be quiet." Did she really mean it when she threatened to throw me overboard if I didn't stop screaming? I wanted to stop but couldn't.

I kept screaming until the ship docked and the debarkation process began, and the crowd thinned out a bit. We finally got to go up the stairs then started down the ramp which had a canvas covering, turning it into a tunnel, which led into a large room, where we found our battered suitcases. Mutti carried both suitcases into an adjoining room. We waited in a long line for getting our passports inspected and went into another room, where, eventually, we met up with cousin, Rudy Menkes.

Rudy a tall, mustached man in a brown suit with a felt hat to match, uttered a terse greeting and guided us to a long table against one wall. A man behind the table looked at us sharply, inspected every piece of paper Mutti handed him, stamped each piece, then waved us on. We stepped into the daylight, our feet still feeling the rolling of the ship. The clouds had parted, and a bright sun blinded us as Cousin Rudy took one of the suitcases from Mutti so she could hold my hand as we crossed a street and found Rudy's car. He put our suitcases into the trunk, pushed me into the back seat (I was still holding Kasper, but he was little more than a limp rag by then.) and indicated Mutti was to sit next to him.

We drove off in his spacious car, the skyscrapers swishing by, making me dizzy trying to see the tops of the buildings. I was excited about riding in a car, but also exhausted from the stress of the debarkation and the long screaming session on the ship, so I promptly fell asleep on the two-hour ride to Long Island. When I awoke, we were in front of, what looked to me, a stone mansion, set in the middle of a flower garden. I thought I was dreaming.

We stayed with Cousin Rudy and his American wife (who spoke no German) for about three days. I don't remember much about them. They were friendly and served us dinner every night, but we needed to find food for ourselves during the day as they both worked in Rudy's dental office. The two-bedroom house seemed large to us and the fact that they had two bathrooms proved to us that they must be very rich. They also had a telephone, which really impressed me.

One morning Rudy and his wife drove us to a bus depot, and we got on a bus headed for Washington, D.C. Upon our arrival in Washington, D.C., we spent a few days at the Basseches house owned by" The Old Aunt" as my mother referred to her mother's younger sister. Aunt's youngest daughter was an unmarried lady, probably in her forties, who was the designated care giver for her mother. I was to call her "Aunt Gussie." (Her full name was Augusta.) She had a soft voice and was very kind to us, in contrast to Old Aunt.

Old Aunt held court in her parlor, sitting upright in a high-backed chair, her feet on a low stool, her hands resting on the ornate handle of her huge cane. That very first day she began a sequence of lectures while my mother sat, like an errant schoolgirl, nodding when it seemed required. Old Aunt talked to my mother in a gruff Viennese accent that had accusatory overtones. She made it clear that she was blaming my mother for being a refugee and a pauper. My mother was already convinced that our dire situation was her fault, so she never tried to defend herself; but she wound up crying after every encounter.

The parlor was a large room with low and high tables scattered around and in each corner. Every surface was covered with figurines, framed pictures and small plants. There was a low chair near the door where I usually sat while Mutti and Old Aunt talked. Being terribly afraid I would break something in the crowded room, I made sure my hands were folded tightly in my lap. But my ears were wide open. I learned about family history. Old Aunt didn't stop at berating my mother, she ranted about the stupidity and stubbornness of her older sister, who insisted on marrying that Polish umbrella maker and staying in Austria instead of coming to America with her and her husband. "I warned Jetti thirty years ago that the Jews in Austria will wind up back in a Ghetto." She declared. "My sons are lawyers, dentists, and my daughter, Fanny is married to a government official." Her voice would soften when she talked about her sister, but the words remained harsh. "Thilde, you take after your mother" She would sigh. "My sister was a good woman, a good seamstress, and mother, although she lost two babies, but stupid and stubborn."

From the very first day she made it plain that the plan was for us to stay in her house only for the time it took for our shipping crate to arrive, then we were to go live at a chicken ranch in Maryland with Old Aunt's older daughter, Fanny.

While we waited for the crate to arrive, Aunt Gussie arranged for me to attend a Neighborhood House children's facility to get me out of the house and away from Old Aunt. "Children make her nervous." Aunt Gussie explained.

The ladies at the Neighborhood House treated me as if I were retarded, or just ignored me. One of the women understood a few words of German and tried to communicate with me as if I were a real person. It was when this kind lady began to talk with me that the other children found out I was German. When we were in the playground, they began to call me a dirty Nazi and hit me, pull my hair and even knock me down. I didn't have the words to explain to them who I was and that I hated Nazis more than they did. The other ladies ignored us except when I tried to defend myself. I didn't know what they were saying, but they clearly thought, just like the Nazis, that I should not be there.

The Neighborhood House playground had swings; I had never seen one before. They had wooden seats and iron chains held them to a bar, high above me. I watched the children fly back and forth like magic. Then It was my turn to sit in the wooden seat, my hands gripping the smooth, cold chains I waited for something to happen. The boy in the next swing began to yell "push" and one of the ladies stood behind him, pushing his back and he was flying past me and squealing with pleasure. So I began to yell "push" as he had done, and someone set me in motion. The sensation of flying was wonderful but being able to use a word in the new language was even more exhilarating. I had learned a new English word. The knot of fear in my belly shrank a bit.

Until that day my English vocabulary consisted of "yes, no, please, and thank you" and, although Mutti knew a few more words, she had learned about life in England and British English from Aunt Fritzi, which was almost like a foreign language to Americans.[26] We had no orientation or explanation of American customs and mores. We felt disoriented, disconnected, confused.

A week later the crate arrived. I knew that meant we were going to leave the spacious rooms of Old Aunt's house and travel to a chicken ranch in a place called Maryland.

Before we were picked up by a cousin with a car, for our journey to Maryland, we spent a long time in the basement of Old Aunt's house, deciding what things we would take along that we had brought from Vienna. Gussie told us that the house we would be using was fully furnished and

---

[26] American English words compared to British English: truck=lorry, umbrella, bumbershoot, eyeglasses=spectacles, cookies=biscuits. Even the Yiddish words were different, as I found out at Hebrew School.

we wouldn't need anything but our clothes. "It is a temporary arrangement until you find a permanent place." Cousin Gussie told us. I decided to take my teddy bear and Mutti bundled up our down pillows.

Chapter 26

I slept through most of the trip out of Washington, D.C. but woke up just in time to see green hills spreading endlessly on both side of the car. Mutti was in the front seat of the two-door car, trying to talk with the young man who was driving. The car windows were open, and their voices were lost in the wind. I hugged Teddy with one arm and told him about the scenery we were passing. After what seemed a terribly long time, we turned off the main road, stopped at a round box, sitting on a post, where Uncle David, which is what I was instructed to call this young man, opened a door in the box and took out some letters.

We drove along this gravel road for what seemed another half hour. Then turned into a narrow lane, with bushes on both sides, that opened up to a wide graveled area. On a low rise behind the gravel patch stood a big white house surrounded by a grassy meadow. As we climbed out of the car, Mutti's cousin, Fanny Schaeffer came out of the front door and across the screened in veranda. She stood at the top step watching us walk up the gravel path. When we reached the steps she came down and put her arms around my mother then bent down to hug me.

Tante Fanny, as I was told to call her, was a little taller than my mother but had similar features. Her dark hair was rolled around her head in the same fashion and the similarity was remarkable. They could have been sisters. Tante Fanny directed Uncle David to drive us to the guest house a few yards along a dusty trail and behind a huge building that I learned was the barn.

The guest house really was completely furnished. It even had some strange looking jars in the cupboard which we later learned were such unheard-of things like peanut butter and a sticky, white substance called marshmallow spread. The house was small, but the windows all around made it light and friendly. A narrow kitchen area with a table and two chairs took up one end of the large room. The refrigerator was noisy, but to us a real luxury and there was a double burner electric hotplate. A single light bulb, dangling from a cord over the table, was the sole electric light in the house. An upholstered couch, on which I was to sleep, and a rocking chair were the only furniture on the other side of the room. My mother had a bedroom with a double bed and there was the luxury of a real bathroom with hot and cold water coming out of faucets. Using the shower was an adventure.

That first afternoon we were invited to the big house for dinner. Walking by the barn I heard horses whinnying. I was terrified of horses and couldn't walk fast enough to get by the barn. We went in the back door and through the kitchen. The adjoining dining room had a long table set for four at one end. Tante Fanny and the man who had driven us to the farm were standing by the table.

The adults communicated in Yiddish. A language that was never used in our home, and I didn't understand it. My mother must have spoken it with her parents, but this was the American version, and she wasn't always certain about what was being said. I don't remember what was served for dinner, but I do remember eating only a piece of bread, then waking up in the kitchen on a chair. I saw Mutti standing by the sink with her back to me. When I called her, she turned around, wiping her hands on a towel.

"Be good," she whispered and handed me a wobbly, red blob on a plate with a spoon. "It's dessert," she said and ate a spoon of it to show me it was good to eat. It was my first taste of American Jell-O. I still don't like it.

I watched Mutti finish washing the dishes and after she had dried them, she put them away, cleaned off the counter, swept the floor, rinsed out the milk bottles and put them in a basket by the back door. Finally we walked back to our little house.

On the way Mutti explained our situation to me and I could hear the resentment in her voice. Mutti and I were to stay with Fanny and her husband (I only saw him once) for the summer until their housekeeper returned from her summer vacation. Mutti was to help the cook prepare meals and clean up afterwards, leaving the kitchen spotless. The laundry was sent out once a week, but we were to do our own laundry in a washtub outfitted with a washboard and hang it up on a clothesline behind the little house. "Be sure to take it down the minute it is dry," Tante Fanny had told my mother. "Clothes flapping on a clothesline is so low class."

That first night in Maryland, I tried to sleep on the couch in the living room. It was so narrow that Teddy had to lie on the floor. I tried to cover him with part of my blanket so he would know I was there. Suddenly there was a loud bellowing. It was like nothing I had ever heard before. It thundered through the house, rattling the windows. I called out to Mutti, but she was already running out of the bedroom. We sat on the couch shivering in wonder and fear. "What is it?" I asked.

"It must be a sick animal, maybe a cow, in terrible pain." Mutti tried to reassure me.

There were several more bellows, not as loud as the first one, and gradually the noise faded away. It was days later that we found out it was the whistle from an American train. (In Europe trains use a high-pitched tweet). Fortunately, the train didn't come by every night. But when it did, the sound always set my teeth on edge and I wanted to scream. Eighty years later the sound of a train bellowing still has that same effect on me.

In the morning we went to the main house, hoping to get some breakfast. The cook gave me a glass of milk and a piece of bread while Mutti got to drink coffee with her piece of bread. The cook was busy frying something in a pan on the gas stove. When it was done, she put it on plates. Motioning Mutti to take the plates to the dining room. When Mutti came back, the cook sent her to pour coffee while I sat on a chair by the door waiting to see if I would get anything more to eat.

After helping to serve the meals in the big house, Mutti could take food back to our little house where we would eat our meals. The cook, a large woman with very dark skin, never spoke to me and only seldom to Mutti. We noticed that the fruits and vegetables she packed up for us to bring back from the main house were usually over ripe and there were only the ends of tomatoes and cucumbers and other parts of vegetables that were obviously not used by the cook. The brown bag we took back every night contained only ends of bread.

The resentment Mutti was feeling for this treatment was festering in my mind also. Even when Tante Fanny was kind to me, I was suspicious of her motives. One afternoon she came into the kitchen where I was sitting on the chair assigned to me, listening to Mutti tell me a story while she washed the endless dishes. Tante Fanny motioned me to follow her through the darkened living room, out to the screened in porch. A card table was set up in the middle of the porch with chairs around it. On the table were folders with colorful pictures of girls on the covers. Inside were pages with pictures of clothing printed on them. Tante Fanny showed me how to cut out the clothes and the dolls and how to put the clothes on them. I was absolutely delighted. When Mutti came to get me I brought the paper dolls, with their many outfits, along to our little house. Those dolls gave me much enjoyment and I kept them with me through numerous re-locations.

One morning as we got to the kitchen, Tante Fanny presented me with a colorful metal tower that turned out to be a savings bank. There were four open spaces below the slots on the top of the tower. One for each type of American coin: Quarter, dime, nickel, and penny. When the coins were dropped into the bank, one could see them accumulate in the four separate rows. Tante Fanny, in broken German and some English, told me that when each section was full there would be five dollars inside. She showed me the key and said that when it was full, she would unlock it for me, and I could have the money. "This will teach you how to count money" She said and added, "You also need to learn how to earn money." Then she went on to tell me that I could earn money by picking bugs off the potato plants that grew in long rows beside the barn.

We went out to the potato patch where she showed me the black insects on the green leaves. She picked a few and put them into the little tin can I was holding. Then it was my turn to pick one. The bug was soft and left black marks on my fingers. I felt like I might throw up, but Tante Fanny didn't seem to notice. She urged me to try it again, and I did as I was told. It wasn't that hard to do and soon the bottom of the can was covered. "I'll give you a penny for each bug." Tante Fanny told me. She counted the bugs, and we went up to the house, where she put a dime in the bank.

Tante Fanny said I was a good girl, handed me the savings bank and sent me to the little house where I hoped my mother would have something for me to eat for lunch. "You can start picking potato bugs again in the morning." She called after me. "There will be a new can at the end of each row. Your bank will be full in no time."

The next morning Mutti and I started walking to the main house, as we approached the barn Mutti told me to go to the potato field until lunch. To get to the field I had to walk by the barn and that morning the horse was grazing just outside the barn door. I desperately looked for a way to get to the potato field without walking anywhere near the horse. I thought about calling for help, but there was no one around. Eventually, with a pounding heart I made a wide path around the horse, who didn't even look up as I passed by. Fortunately, I never saw the horse again.

Picking potato bugs was very boring, the bugs smelled awful and left sticky black marks on my hands. I stuck with it until Mutti called me for lunch. When I brought the cans to Tante Fanny, she gave me a few pennies to put in my bank. I told Mutti, who was standing nearby, that I was not going to pick potato bugs anymore. She didn't say anything, but Tante Fanny, given the look she gave me, understood enough German to know what I said. I didn't understand what she was saying to me, but by the tone of her voice I knew she was not pleased.

The next day Tante Fanny came into the kitchen, where I sat on my usual chair watching Mutti scrub the floor and took my hand and we walked to the rows and rows of chicken coops located on the far side of the main house. I had been in this area with Mutti to collect eggs while the laying hens were feeding out in the yard. I had not come close to the chickens and although they didn't terrify me like the dogs and the horses, I didn't like being near them. Now I was expected to feed them. Tante Fanny showed me how to throw hands full of grain out of a bucket at the cackling forms that milled around in the fenced in area. That was my morning chore for several days, until one morning while on my way to the chicken coop Mutti, standing near the big house, called me back.

We walked by the barn where a man stood in front of the open barn door holding a huge axe in one hand while grabbing a chicken by the neck with the other. I saw him throw the chicken onto a wood block and chop of the head with one blow. The headless chicken ran around for a few seconds before another man grabbed it and threw it into a vat of steaming hot water. I watched this procedure for two more chickens before my mother turned me around and drew me away. As we approached the area between the big house and the barn, I saw a long wooden table covered with headless chickens. Women were sitting on the benches on either side of the table plucking the feathers while another woman went around the table stuffing the loose feathers into a burlap bag.

Mutti motioned me to sit down on a bench next to her, then handing me a steaming chicken, demonstrated how to pull out the feathers on one side, turn the chicken over and pluck out the feathers on the other side. The plucked chickens were handed to a man collecting them into nearby crates. I just kept my head down and concentrated on pulling feathers, one after the other until one side was bare, turning the lifeless body over and plucking the other side. The odor drifting around the table was making me a bit nauseated, but not enough to vomit, I swallowed and kept plucking.

When I had plucked one side of the third chicken and while turning it over a loud groan came from the limp body in my hands. I dropped the chicken, jumped up from the bench and screaming, ran towards our little house, horrified by my own screaming, but unable to stop. Mutti caught up with me, grabbing me by the arm and shaking me until I stopped screaming. Then she began to scold me for being a useless, lazy, ungrateful brat who should be ashamed of myself. "Go into the house." She ordered, "Stay there until I come back."

While I sat on my cot in the stifling heat of midday I tried to think of what I had done and why I should feel ashamed. I was puzzled by the word "ashamed". My grandmother and my mother often told me that I should feel ashamed (rarely by Mitzi, and then always with a smile.) I only felt confused by the anger that I seemed to provoke in the adults around me. At some point I did realize that shame was something people should feel when they purposely hurt another person. Since I had no control over the acts of which I was told to be ashamed. (i.e. bedwetting, screaming when I was terrified) I could not bring up that feeling. It was that day that I understood an eternal truth: *People can control their actions, but not their feelings.* You can't order people to feel ashamed any more than you can order them to feel love.

It was late afternoon before Mutti came back to the house.

In the meantime I looked for food. I found some crackers and tried the marshmallow spread. In the heat it had softened enough to spoon on to the crackers. I was making a crumbly, sticky mess which attracted flies and other insects, When Mutti saw the mess she silently swept up the crumbs, stuck me under the shower, then into a clean nightshirt. We ate ends of tomatoes, with a plate of beans and a piece of watermelon for dessert. Then, like most evenings, we went up to the main house to clean up after their dinner.

While Mutti washed, dried and put away the dishes, swept the floor, scrubbed the counters and the stove, she told me stories about beautifully dressed princesses who went to lavish balls in ornate royal palaces. She described in detail what everyone wore, how they danced and whirled to lovely music. Those stories kept me entertained and calm during some very stressful times. Although our lives were no longer in imminent danger, I needed to hear those stories.

Chapter 27

Early the next morning Tante Fanny came to our house just as we were having breakfast. She was pleased to see I was having cornflakes with milk, (I would have preferred a crunchy hard roll from a Viennese bakery) but made a grim face when she saw Mutti pour coffee into a cup for me. "Children don't drink coffee in America." She said in her strange Austrian accent. I couldn't understand that attitude. American coffee was very good, and I drank it with half milk and lots of sugar. After two years without sugar we could hardly believe how plentiful it was in America.

After I finished eating, Tante Fanny said she had a job for me that would help me fill up the savings bank she had bought me. She led me down to the, chicken coops. We stepped inside and it felt eerie to see the rows of empty roosts. Tante Fanny gave me a knife-like tool with a wooden grip and showed me how to scrape the chicken shit from the rods that ran the length of the narrow building. It wasn't difficult, but it was boring.

Tante Fanny said she would give me a nickel for each clean coop. The job looked endless, but I worked on the horizontal poles all that morning until Mutti came to fetch me for lunch. After lunch she came back to the coops with me and swept the scrapings out the door. We were soon choking in dust, so Mutti got a bucket of water and dumped it on the floor, which caused a gunky mess that was impossible to sweep. After that we endured the dust and by the end of the day one of the coops was cleaned, but there were many more. After four days I developed a bad cough. Two more days went by and my throat was beginning to hurt. Later that same afternoon I had a high fever. Mutti went to the main house and asked Tante Fanny to send for a doctor, which she did immediately. He told me to stay in bed, gave me cough medicine and suggested I stay out of the chicken coops. "That is no place for a vulnerable child." He advised my mother.

Maryland tends to have very hot summers. In 1940 few people had air conditioning but kept cool by spending time on their screened in porches, in the basements, or running electric fans, if they had electricity. Since there were no screens on the windows of our little guest house, we had to keep the windows closed. I felt like I was going to suffocate in that hot and airless room. My cough abated somewhat, but I was nauseous all the time and couldn't eat the peanut butter sandwiches Mutti made me for lunch every day. (It took many years before I could abide being in the same room with peanut butter.)

One night I told Mutti I didn't want to live there anymore. She began to cry and told me we had no choice since we didn't have any money or any prospect of earning some. I offered her the coins in my savings bank, but she only cried harder and then began to pace the floor. It was a good sign. I knew she would find a way to get us out of there.

By the middle of July I was better and back in the kitchen with Mutti. (There were electric fans throughout the main house, and we dreaded going back to our little house each night). One evening we were invited to have dinner with the Schaeffers. Their son was home for the weekend and they wanted us to meet him. He was tall, with sandy colored hair and a toothy smile. What struck me most about him was that his mother had to cut his meat, which was something I had done with dexterity since I was four years old.

I can't remember much of what he said, but during dinner he mentioned he would teach me how to ride a horse that summer. I was terrified of the prospect of getting near a horse, but he obviously thought I would be delighted. Tante Fanny told me what a good horse man he was and how lucky for me to have such a kind offer. I fervently hoped that Mutti would find a way for us to leave before he came back to spend the rest of the summer.

On Monday morning after the son's visit, Mutti was cleaning the kitchen. One of her chores was to clean out the half dozen glass milk bottles then take them to the wire carrier by the back door for the milkman to pick up the next day. I had two bottles in each hand with fingers in the neck to get a good hold. We started down the cement steps when I tripped and fell into the broken glass. My hands were scratched, and my right thumb was nearly cut off.

For a moment I was too stunned to scream, then the pain took my breath away. I saw the blood gushing down my arm, heard Mutti scream while she dragged me back up the stairs into the kitchen. She wrapped a dishtowel around my thumb, but the blood kept running out, drenching one towel after another. Eventually the bleeding slowed down. I was lying in the middle of the kitchen floor, trying not to cry. I didn't need to scream, Mutti was screaming loud enough for both of us. She kept wrapping clean towels around my thumb until the bleeding stopped. Then she put a towel under my head and began to clean up the broken glass. I watched Mutti as she swept up the glass and sponged at the blood. She kept nodding her head and mumbling to herself between sniffles. She had come to a decision.

When Fanny came home for lunch and saw me lying on the floor with my hand wrapped in a kitchen towel she asked. "What's the matter now?" in an exasperated tone I knew well by now.

Mutti started speaking in an even tone as she told Tante Fanny what had happened, but as she continued talking her voice rose until she was close to screaming. The gist of what she said was that she couldn't live like this anymore. We needed to get to a place where she could work for money. "We are educated people." She told Tante Fanny. "We must live near cultural and medical facilities. We want to leave right now!"

To Tante Fanny's credit she understood my mother's frustration. In the next few days she arranged for us to live in Washington, D.C. in a room above a grocery store. She had found a housekeeping job for my mother with a friend who lived in Arlington, Virginia, (A suburb of Washington, D.C.). The grocery store belonged to a young couple who were distant relatives. Judy, the wife, would keep an eye on me while my mother was at work.

We packed up our few belongings and Fanny drove us to the train in the nearby town. We arrived in Union Station towards dusk on a warm July evening. Judy and her husband, David (the man who had driven us to Maryland) were there to meet us and drove us to their grocery store on 4th Ave. North. On the ride we saw the Capital building. The huge dome was framed in lights. It was a dazzling sight. Where we were going to live was within walking distance of the capital and soon I was walking there almost every night. I would lie on my back on the low wall surrounding the grounds, just staring at those wonderful lights. After years in a war time blackout, this was the highlight of my time in Washington, D.C.

The room above the grocery store had a two burner cook top in one corner next to a sink. It was not too different from the room we had in Vienna. However here was a full bathroom down the hall and the window looked out to an alley and part of the street. A view of the sky and a tree nearby was a welcome sight. A wide bed took up most of the space. A chair, table, and bridge lamp were against one wall, and a small dresser with a mirror was next to the door. We had no closet, so we kept our clothes in the suitcase under the bed. Mutti and I were to share the bed, but I don't remember Mutti ever sleeping in the bed with me. She got up long before I woke up and went to bed long after I was asleep. I remember watching her sit in the chair reading and re-reading Vati's letters or the newspaper she brought home from her job. Summer is hot and humid in Washington, D.C. and our room, even with the windows open was very stuffy. When Mutti wasn't reading it, she sometimes used the newspaper to fan herself and me, until I fell asleep.

Most of our belongings were still in the wooden crate at Old Aunt's house, but little by little we started bringing things to our room above the grocery store. I was especially pleased to have the books that we had brought from Vienna. *Firlefanz Der Puppen Doktor* (the Doll Doctor) was my favorite, but I had missed them all.

David and Judy opened the grocery store at 7 A.M. six days a week and closed it officially at 6 P.M. But they often stayed later to accommodate last minute customers. When they were finally able to leave, they drove their little Chevrolet coup to the "White" suburbs where they lived.

After Mutti left for work in the morning, I went down to the grocery store where Judy usually gave me a roll and glass of milk. Most of the time I went back to our room and played with the paper dolls until I got hungry and went back down to the store. Judy was very kind to me. She taught me English words while she prepared lunch for me. Usually I had a cold sandwich, sometimes a warm bowl of soup. Then I went back up to the room and sat around waiting for Mutti to come home.

One morning I heard children laughing and talking. I tried to see where the sound was coming from, but I could not see them from the window. I went downstairs and stood in the grocery store doorway. I saw some girls my age involved in an activity I had never seen before. There was a long rope with a girl at each end turning it while the other girls stood in line and took turns jumping the rope. When a girl missed and stopped the rope, she had to let the next one in to jump. It looked like fun. I hardly noticed that these children had black skin.

I stood at the doorway and stared. Then one of the girls called me over. She indicated that I could join them by taking a turn holding one end of the rope first. When it was my turn to jump, I was clumsy at first, but the girls were patient. Of course they laughed but I didn't feel embarrassed. We were all laughing together, and we became friends. By the end of the summer I was able to jump "Double Dutch" which is done with two ropes going at once and requires much skill and dexterity.

The girls all lived in the neighborhood and were out on the street every day. They accepted me without any hesitation and even shared their treats with me. Snow cones were the favorite treat. The cones, bought from a man with a hand cart, were a nickel and one or the other of the girls always seemed to have one. One day I asked my mother if she could give me a nickel for a snow cone. She said an emphatic "No" accompanied by a lecture of how there was only frozen water and a few drops of artificial flavor in those cones and we didn't have the money to waste on things that had no food value.

One morning while she was in the bathroom, I stole a nickel out of her purse. After she left for work, I went outside to play and later that afternoon I bought a snow cone from the vendor. I shared some with the other girls but enjoyed most of it for myself. I did keep looking over my shoulder and was afraid that Judy would see me and tell my mother. As it happened my mother missed the nickel, (she needed it for bus fare). That evening when she came home, she didn't even ask me about the nickel because she saw the blue spot on my blouse where the cone had dripped blueberry flavoring.

Her anger was fierce. She shouted at me, calling me a worthless, dishonest and ungrateful child. When I began to cry, she threatened to leave me if I didn't be quiet. I only cried louder and Mutti, her nerves frazzled to the edge after a day with two spoiled little boys, ran down the stairs and out to the street.

"I am leaving right now" she shouted at me as I chased after her, screaming at the top of my lungs by now. She ran to the corner bus stop. I can still feel the terror that engulfed me as I caught up to her just as the bus pulled up. I clutched at her skirt, begging her not to leave me. She turned around and grabbed my forearm, half dragging me back up to the room.

She reprimanded me for making such a scene in the street. I apologized for embarrassing her. But could not bring up the feeling of shame she said I should have. We ate the food she fixed on the electric plate. The episode was not mentioned again, but I remember it clearly to this day. I never ate another snow cone without feeling guilty for spending good money on such empty calories.

Chapter 28

One day Judy took me to the Neighborhood House to enroll me in a one weekday camp for underprivileged children. There were craft things to do that involved coloring with crayons (a new experience for me), musical circle games and best of all a shallow swimming pool, to use the pool required a bathing suit, and I did not have one.

Judy offered to make me one on her sewing machine if we gave her the material. I had an outgrown skirt that was just enough fabric and Judy set to work on it. Somehow, she got busy in the store and didn't have time to finish the bathing suit by the next morning as promised. I was very disappointed and began to cry. I remember being unreasonably angry with this kind lady and tried to hide it, but it must have shown on my face and she promised to have the bathing suit ready the next day. It was hard to watch the other kids splash around in the pool that day. But the next day the suit was done, and I was so very grateful and told Judy in my broken English and we both had tears in our eyes.

After the week of Day Camp I had learned a few more words and had many questions about my new life. When I asked my black friends if they wanted to come to the Neighborhood House Day Camp, they just looked at me and shook their heads. It was then that I became aware there were no black children at the day camp. In fact, I was the darkest child there with my jet-black hair and dark tan.

After the culture shock of living on the chicken farm in Maryland, we were relieved to be back in a city with sidewalks, traffic lights, stores and cultural sites. Mutti worked in Arlington five days a week and most of the buildings were closed on Sunday. So on Saturdays we explored this beautiful city. We found that it was a short walk to the Capital Mall with its memorials and museums and visited a different one every Saturday

One Saturday we went to the Smithsonian Institute which was housed in just one building in those days. I was awed by the dinosaurs and many life like animal exhibits, but the glass cases in the basement were the main attraction. In one section there were whole Indian villages (teepees, dark people dressed in leather, skinning small animals, cooking food and weaving baskets). I never got tired of looking at all the little details: the cooking utensils, the animal bones that were used for combs, needles, weapons, and how the babies were strapped on their mothers' backs.

In another section there were several huge glass cases with the life size mannequins displaying the gowns worn by the wives of presidents at their inaugural balls. The gowns resembled the dresses my mother described in the fairy stories she told me. I fantasized about wearing those bejeweled gowns, the satin slippers, the diamond tiaras. I pictured the splendor of the ballrooms and the couples whirling to the music. I also read the names of the presidents and began to memorize them.

The National Museum of Art had a grand opening in 1940 and Judy suggested we take advantage of the free admission. (Did she know that all National museums and monuments were free to the public?). One Saturday we explored this impressive new building. There were several floors with paintings on every wall. Mutti was disappointed. "There are only pictures in this museum," she said. "I had hoped to see other artwork in such a famous place. Well, it's not Vienna" She added with a deep sigh. (I can only guess how much she missed her old life).

Later that summer we walked along the Capital Mall, enjoying the breeze from the Potomac River and the open space of the wide lawns flanked by the famous Japanese cherry trees Our plan was to visit the Washington Monument at the other end of the Mall.

We walked up the 898 steps to the very top where Mutti lifted me up so I could see out the window. I had never been up that high before. The people on the ground looked like ants. My knees felt weak and I got dizzy. Just before I thought I was about to throw up my lunch, we found the stairs for our descent.

Mutti had been studying about George Washington. While climbing down those endless steps she told me, in mixed German and English, the history of the great man who was called the father of this country and the first elected leader.

Sunday was devoted to laundry and general cleaning. A small laundry room with a huge tub and washboard was located a few steps down behind the grocery store. Mutti heated water on the hotplate in our room and carried pan after pan down to the tub until there was enough hot water to wash our heavy linens, (the top and bottom sheets, two pillowcases and the feather bed cover which consisted of two sheets sewn together, like a huge pillowcase). Each piece was scrubbed on the washboard, swirled around in the hot water and rung out by hand. Then I helped carry the load to the short clothesline in the small backyard. After hanging the linens we rinsed them with a hose attached to the faucet on the side of the building. Usually they were dry enough by evening to put back on the bed but sometimes Mutti had to iron them dry. Small garments were washed in the bathroom sink and hung around the bedroom to dry.

One Monday morning as Mutti was getting ready to leave for the day, Judy came up to our room and told us that Sunday was not a suitable day for doing laundry. She explained that people just did not wash clothes on Sunday in America. Mutti didn't answer, just nodded her head. We continued washing linens on Sundays. I thought maybe Mutti didn't understand what Judy meant, but I didn't say anything because it wasn't worth antagonizing her.

Mutti's English was improving, and we tried to speak only English to each other. The only reading material we had in English was the newspapers and the history book that Judy gave us to use. My mother's British-English/German dictionary was helpful, but confusing. My vocabulary was increasing, and I picked up new words and idioms every day and learned how to interpret the varied inflections of the word "really."

Mutti was reading a pamphlet about becoming an American Citizen. Besides all the instructions on how to apply for citizenship, there were several pages that listed the personal and civil rights all people had in this "free" country.[27]

One Sunday, when Judy and David were at the store taking inventory and we were hanging clothes up on the clothesline, Judy came out from the back door of the store and reminded us again about the unsuitability of hanging out washing on Sundays, Mutti answered her with a question. "Is America free country?" Judy didn't reply or mention the subject again.

---

[27] Soon I learned that those rights did not apply to people of color in those days

Chapter 29

Mutti came home from work one day and told me that we were going to stay in Arlington, Virginia while the parents of the boys she was tending went on a short vacation. The day we arrived at the townhouse apartment, the parents of the three and five-year old boys were already packed and ready to leave. Quickly the lady of the house gave my mother instructions about the food in the freezer and the pantry, showed her the bedroom we were to use, kissed the boys good-by and fled down the steps to where her husband waited by the taxi.

Mutti and I stood in the middle of the sparkling kitchen and looked at each other helplessly as the boys began to run around the serving table yelling, "We want shin shale." We asked them over and over what it was they wanted, and they kept yelling louder and louder, "shin shale."[28]

Finally, the older boy went to the refrigerator, pointed to a tall green bottle and said the strange word. Mutti poured some of the yellow sparkling water into a small glass and the boys were delighted. I tasted it and gagged. The boys thought this was funny and laughing they tossed some of the liquid from their glasses at me, I didn't laugh, but I didn't cry either. There had been some mean kids at the day camp who laughed at me when I didn't understand something that everyone else seemed to know. Sometimes I cried and they would laugh even harder and point their fingers at me calling me dummy. I had decided that I wasn't going to cry anymore just to spite these bullies.

---

28 Ginger Ale. A totally unknown drink to us.

My English and understanding of American culture were not developed to a point where I could judge the boys fairly. Perhaps they were not spoiled brats. Maybe in this culture yelling, screaming at the top of one's lungs, throwing food, beating up on girls, hitting the housekeeper and generally not doing what they were told to do was considered a natural outlet for their high spirits as their mother had explained to us. All I knew was that I hated them. The older boy took every opportunity to make my life miserable. He hit me unexpectedly while I was trying to read or grabbed my food when Mutti wasn't looking. When I fought back, hitting him with my fist or kicked him in the shins, he ran to my mother for protection, full of accusations that were corroborated by the younger brother.

There were moments of respite from the little demons. The older boy went to a day camp four mornings a week and the younger one took a nap around noon. Since many of the younger children in this apartment complex went to the day camp, the streets were deserted for several hours. I took this opportunity to ride one of the many tricycles that were left outside by the front doors. No one seemed to mind, and I always returned the tricycle to its place. One morning when I was about to ride one of the tricycles a woman came dashing out of her door, grabbed my arm in a bone crushing grip and screamed into my startled face. "Now I've caught you, you thief!!"

I had no idea what she was talking about. In my mind I had done nothing wrong and couldn't understand her words or her anger. She dragged me down the street, continuing her diatribe about me being a thief.

By the time we reached the door where my mother had come out to see what all the screaming was about, we had several more women following us. Calling this assemblage of housewives, toddlers, and a few dogs, a lynch mob might not be too much of an exaggeration. I didn't have enough English to defend myself. What were they going to do with me? I was terrified.

Mutti and I weren't sure what it was all about, but I began to suspect it had something to do with the sacred tricycles. Not knowing what the women wanted, Mutti started to scold me in German and broken English. What the women wanted was to see me cry, but when that didn't happen, they gradually walked away.

I was sent to bed without dinner that night and without knowing what the punishment was for. Even during the worst times in Vienna, when food was scarce, did I feel as hungry as I did that night. Eventually the feeling of frustration and anger drove out the hunger pangs. My only thoughts were about how much longer I would have to endure those boys?

One of the neighbors had shown Mutti the way to a nearby park. One Saturday with the courage of ignorance we walked the few blocks to the tree shaded area. There were swings and a manual merry-go-round. In a matter of minutes the two boys were a dusty, bleeding heap of rags. Mutti yelled at them in English and German and dragged them homeward.

I was reluctant to leave the park, and Mutti promised to bring me back on Sunday, when the boy's aunt would take them along for a family outing.

Sunday Mutti and I strolled through the park. Carefully staying on the gravel path and admiring the vast expanse of bright green lawn. The benches beside the paths had white signs that said, "NO COLORED" in big black letters. We speculated as to what this sign might mean. I could read a little by then and the word, "colored" made me think of crayons and coloring. We guessed that it warned people not to color on the benches.

After dinner, their aunt brought the boys back and in the conversation that followed, Mutti asked her, "What means "no colored" on the park seats?"

The aunt explained (in a mixture of English and Yiddish) that this was to keep black people from sitting on the benches and to discourage them from entering the park.

"We don't want Niggers in the park, do we?" She said, clearly expecting us to agree with her.

I understood what this woman had just said and remembered that in Austria, Jews were not to sit on public benches. It was a shock to think that such things could happen in America. Somehow Mutti got the courage and found the words to mention that we had seen a black lady sitting on a bench. I wondered if she would be arrested.

The aunt countered with a question. "Was this woman alone?"

"Well, no." Mutti replied "She was rocking a baby in a carriage."

"The nannies can sit on the benches while they are tending a white baby." The aunt explained. "They can even sit in the white section of the bus in that case."

Mutti and I nodded, because we could tell that this was expected after such a detailed explanation. But we didn't understand and never would.

When the parents came back, they brought presents for the boys. There were two beautifully wrapped boxes for each boy and as they tore off the wide satin ribbons and threw open the boxes I wondered if there would be a present for me. It soon became clear that there was no box for me, and I retreated to our room. I remember hoping the lump in my throat was not the onset of tonsillitis.

Much later Mutti came into our room. She was rolling the red and blue ribbons around her finger. "Look what I have for your hair." She spoke softly, patting my cheek but I could tell she was as angry and hurt as I was.

While we were packing up our things to go back to Washington, D.C., the boys' mother came into our room, took Mutti's hand and told her that arrangements had been made to send me to a camp for underprivileged and orphaned children.

The woman obviously expected me to be delighted at the prospect. I felt a variety of emotions, but delight was not one of them. How could she think to send me to a camp for orphans? I was not an orphan; my parents were alive.

Chapter 30

When we returned to Washington, D.C., Judy helped to get me ready for the camp. I didn't have the required sleeping bag (we had no idea what that was) so a blanket was wrapped around my down feather bed and pillow with a change of one sheet and fastened with a rope. Some underwear, my bathing suit, a couple of cotton blouses, a skirt and a sweater were stuffed into a pillowcase along with my toothbrush, comb, socks and a nightgown. Mutti tied the pillowcase with another piece of rope and I was ready for camp.

We walked over to the Neighborhood House where I got on a bus with about 35 other girls my age. The stench in the bus was overwhelming. Some of these kids had not had a bath in a long time and this was the middle of summer in humid Washington, D.C.

The bus ride was endless and very noisy. I didn't understand what the girls were saying. These children spoke a different English than Judy, David or even the black girls from the street.

We arrived starved, thirsty and tired. The first thing we did was march to our respective cabins that were scattered throughout the wooded area of the camp. We were assigned cabins but got to choose our bunks. I opted for a lower bunk for two reasons. I noticed that there were no rubber pads over the straw mattresses, and I knew I would most likely wet the bed. It did happen a few times, but by evening the sheet I had brought was dry and since I slept in a nightshirt, which I kept wound around my waist at night; I managed to keep my bedwetting a secret.

The girl in the upper bunk tried to talk to me. I couldn't understand what she was saying and every so often she would sigh and say, "Oh, brother." I knew the word "brother." I asked her if she had a brother who spoke German. She turned away exclaiming, "Oh, brother!" We never spoke again.

The food was tasteless, the counselors were mean, the cabin windows had no glass, and a chilly wind blew in during the night. The other campers were even colder than I was because I had my featherbed, which caused a problem. To pass the daily cabin inspection the beds had to be perfectly smooth and my featherbed was always lumpy, until one day I remembered how Mitzi smoothed the featherbeds each morning. She rolled a broom handle across the tops. I tried this and it worked. The other five girls watched in wonder and I saw friendly smiles for the first time.

Each morning we went to a wide spot in a cold, brown river where we were given swimming lessons. I was terrified of the dark, murky water and never went in past my knees. No amount of coaxing could make me go in further. I pretended I didn't understand when I was afraid or didn't want to do something, so the counselors ignored me most of the time. But the swimming lessons caused me to totally panic. When two counselors tried to carry me into the water, I began to scream, and they left me alone after that.

One morning while in the washroom, where we brushed our teeth and took showers, I saw a metal bracelet lying beside the sink. Since I was going to the mess hall for breakfast, I picked up the bracelet with the intention to find the owner there. Before I even got out of the washroom, a girl came in and started to yell at me. I didn't understand her at the time, but she was accusing me of stealing the bracelet. The counselor who was with her grabbed my arm and dragged me to the camp director's office.

There was more talk with raised voices. I had no idea what they were talking about and, although I wanted to cry, I had sworn to never cry again, and I intended to keep that promise. Eventually the camp nurse came in. She spoke German and explained to me what I was being accused of and translated my denial to the camp director who in turn told me to apologize for stealing the bracelet. Again I heard the words that I should be "ashamed of myself" when I had no such feeling. The director ordered me back to my cabin and told me to stay there until lunch time. Besides being very hungry—since I had not had breakfast—I was outraged at the injustice, but it was an incentive to learn English.

The second week of camp we were told that we were going to put on a play for some visitors. The play was "Peter Pan" and one night a counselor read us the story, of which I didn't understand a word. Everyone was to be in the play. I had no idea what the play was about, but I did understand that I was to be a "lost boy. "I did not want to be a boy.

The rehearsals were at night after dinner, so I just sneaked back to the cabin while the other girls participated in the play. Ten years later I finally learned about "Peter Pan" but never understood why anyone would want to make a play about such an inane story.

Every two days we wrote mandatory postcards to be sent home. I only wrote about how miserable I was, never mentioning the fun things we did, like hiking in the woods, toasting marshmallows over the campfire, doing craft projects that taught us skills like braiding and carving wood. Instead I complained about the food, the other campers, the counselors, the camp director and the stupid nurse who thought she knew German.

On one card, that my mother kept and is still among my paperwork, I wrote "If you don't come to pick me up right away, I will kill myself." (Since I wrote in German all that grousing got past the censors.)

When Mutti came to pick me up at the Neighborhood House upon my return from Camp, the first words out of her mouth were a scolding about how miserable that card made her feel. "How could you send such a card?" She screamed at me. I was surprised at her outburst. I thought she had not received it. I was sure that, if she had received it, she would have come to get me—if she still wanted me.

Chapter 31

The black girls were glad to have me back. They had been at a vacation bible school and were eager to tell me about it. They had colored beautiful pictures of Jesus. They asked if I wanted to have one for my room.

When I declined their kind offer and told them we were Jewish, (a word they connected with evil people and store owners) they looked surprised, but not hostile. We continued being friends. I didn't notice any difference in their attitude.

One of the older girls warned me to stay at least an arm's length away from the man who ran the liquor store next to the grocery store. He sat on a chair in front of his store, his white shirt sleeves rolled up, showing tattoos on both his forearms. Even before my friend's warning I walked by the liquor store as fast as possible. The men who went into that store looked disheveled and dirty and I didn't want them to come near me.

Also the stench coming from the owner's cigar was repulsive. Every time he saw me, he called me little darling, offering candy or Coca Cola. I didn't even turn my head, staying near the curb until I was well past the store. I don't know where it came from but, I had an innate fear of adult men that may have saved me from harm on more than one occasion.

During that hot summer in Washington, D.C. letters arrived from my father in Sweden, and usually included a few lines from Uncle Hugo. Mutti had obviously been writing about how miserable and lonely she felt among hostile strangers. She blamed herself for our situation, feeling that we all should have left Austria much sooner.

That she wrote them about my stubborn, rude, disobedient and childish behavior was obvious from the advice both Vati and Uncle Hugo wrote back to her. Most of what Vati wrote was tongue-in-cheek and in rhyme. He printed his letters to me in capitals not knowing I could read cursive by then. Through all his terrible ordeals he kept his wry sense of humor. Herewith I include one of his letters which rhymes in German (Austrian slang included). The English translation is awkward, but the meaning and humor come through.

***SWEDEN JULY 26th 1940

MY DEAREST TILDE AND RUTI

I CONFIRM RECEIVING YOUR LETTER AND WHEN I READ IT, I GOT A CHILL.

I REALLY DO BELIEVE EVERYTHING YOU WROTE ABOUT YOUR DIRE POVERTY, LONELINESS AND LONGING FOR A TIME GONE BY IS TRUE.

ALWAYS REMEMBER YOU ARE NOT ALONE WITH THIS FATE AND THIS BURDEN THAT YOU MUST ENDURE.

AFTER THESE TRYING DAYS THERE WILL COME A TIME WHEN WE WILL SAY TO OURSELVES, "LET'S FORGET THIS SORROWFUL TIME, ALL IS WELL AGAIN AND WE ARE TOGETHER."

OF COURSE ONE SOON LOOSES PATIENCE, BUT NEITHER OF US IS TO BLAME, DEAR TILDE, SO DON'T DESPAIR. ALWAYS SHOW A CHEERFUL FACE. REFRAIN FROM CRYING, YOUR TEARS HAVE VALUE, DO NOT WASTE THEM. MOST OF ALL LEAVE OFF YEARNING FOR VIENNA. JUST YEARN FOR ME AS I YEARN FOR YOU. PULL YOUR MOUTH INTO A LAUGHING POSITION.

SO OUR OFFSPRING IS NAUGHTY, DISOBEDIENT, FRIGHTENS HER MAMA AND MAKES HER NERVOUS. SOMETIMES SHE IS DUMB AND SOMETIMES SHE IS SMART.

BUT IT IS MY BELIEF THAT IT WOULD BE DUMB NOT TO FORGIVE HER THESE FAULTS VERY SOON. I ALWAYS

BELIEVE THAT FROM THIS BRAT WILL DEVELOP A
QUIET AND OBEDIENT ANGEL.

ONE THING I PROMISE HER, IN ANY CASE, WHEN I
ARRIVE THERE WITH YOU, I'LL SALT DOWN HER POPO
AND SHE WON'T BE ABLE TO SIT FOR SIX WEEKS.

I MUST KEEP MY PROMISE. I ALWAYS HAVE. YES,
YES, DEAR RUTI, YOU DON'T' NEED TO LAUGH BECAUSE
IT IS THE FIRST THING I AM GOING TO DO. INSTEAD
OF GREETING YOU WITH A KISS I'LL ASK TO SEE YOUR
BEHIND FIRST.

BUT IN THE MEANTIME YOUR MOTHER WILL GIVE
YOU SOME SPANKS IN ADVANCE SO I CAN ELIMINATE
THEM FROM THE 10,000 THAT I HAVE BEEN SAVING FOR
YOU.

An important letter arrived from my father. This was not
one of his long, rambling letters about how he liked milking
the thirty-two cows twice a day, or how he rode a bicycle to
the farm where his brother, my Uncle Hugo, worked or about
their one-day visit to Goetteberg (the big city nearby). This
letter needed to be answered immediately. The next morning, before leaving for work Mutti handed me a letter and
told me to go mail it at the post office.

I was not sure I heard her right. The post office was across
Constitution Avenue, which had a traffic light that allowed
pedestrians to cross the eight lanes of traffic, if they hurried. I
had been across this street with my mother several times but
never by myself. Walking to the Capital from where we lived
was one thing, it did not require crossing any wide and busy
streets, but I was feeling queasy about crossing the busiest
street in Washington, D.C. alone. I told Mutti I was afraid. She
frowned at me and said, "You are a brave girl. You can do it."
Then she got on the bus to Arlingron.

Heart in my throat, teeth clenched, head held high, I
marched across the eight lanes, with my eyes glued to the
green light in front of me. After dropping the letter in the mail
slot marked "FOREIGN" I started down the marble steps of

the post office. Suddenly I needed to find a toilet. Waiting until I got home was not an option. I had never used a public toilet before. My mother said they were full of diseases and even in our dingy room in Vienna she made me use the chamber pot instead of the common facility in the hallway.

Then I remembered the Smithsonian Museum was only a block away and on the same side of Constitution Avenue as the post office. Not needing to cross that street would help my situation. With the help of a kind lady, also visiting the Smithsonian, who knew the word "toilet" I found the right door just in time.

The toilets were in the basement, so I was already in my favorite place in the Museum. I took the opportunity to wander around the marvelous glass cases without interference. I just looked and looked to my heart's content. I even read some of the names and dates on the ball gown displays.

I was just starting to look at the case displaying an Indian village when I heard the loud ringing of a bell. Not knowing what it meant, I kept on examining the case in front of me. Suddenly the lights went dim. (It was at that moment that I realized I was very hungry)

Deathly afraid of the dark I ran for the stairs. The lights were almost all out by the time I got to the huge entry door. I pulled on the door handle and found it was locked. I rattled the handle with all my might and began to yell "Help!"— interspersed with *"hilfe!"* just in case the English word was not clear. I was terrified. (A locked door can still produce a panic attack in me.)

At last a guard came. He peeled my fingers from the handle, unlocked the door and pushed me outside. He said something to me in a gruff tone, but I was already down the stairs and on the sidewalk. It was still daylight, but the sun was sinking. The walk back to 4th Avenue is a blur in my mind. I only felt relief that I had escaped from that dark museum.

When I arrived at the grocery store, Judy was closing the store, Mutti was up in our room preparing food. No one had noticed my absence. That night I dreamt of dancing at an inaugural ball in a pink satin gown, with a tiara in my blonde hair.

Chapter 32

Towards the end of August Mutti told me I would soon be going to a Jewish Day school in which Great Aunt had arranged my enrollment.

Judy brought me English books and helped me read them. Soon I was reading on my own. The books were about life in America. The children had parents, a car, a dog, a room of their own, and many toys. They lived in a house surrounded by trees, they rode bicycles down these shady streets, lined with houses just like theirs. The fathers gave them money to buy treats at candy stores, and the family went to soda fountains and ate ice cream, visited zoos where they saw animals from exotic places. In the summer they went to fairs where they rode merry-go-rounds with real looking horses and ate pink cotton made from sugar.

None of this looked like the dirty streets of Washington, D.C. where people lived in tiny rooms with no heat in winter and hot in the summer. I knew that the girls I played with on these streets never went to a zoo or an amusement park. They didn't even go to the Neighborhood House.

The neighborhood where Old Aunt lived looked a little like the places in the children's books. There were trees and clean streets and some people had cars. But I never saw any children there. In Arlington there were children, but they lived in apartments. I wondered if there really were places like that in America.

Judy offered to make me a dress to wear to school if we bought the material. Since I had outgrown my two dresses, I was really excited about the prospect of a new dress, but there was no money for material. Finally, I got a couple of dresses from the donations at the Neighborhood House and they just needed a little shortening. So now I was ready for school.

After Labor Day (A holiday explained to us by the patient Judy)[29] I went to a nearby Jewish Day School. Old Aunt had insisted that I get a Jewish education and even offered to pay part of the tuition. In the morning we learned to write, read, and do simple addition problems. In Vienna I had already learned cursive writing, complex addition, subtraction, short division and the lower multiplication tables. I was bored most of the time. It might have been more interesting if I could have helped the other students with the mathematics, but my spoken English was not fluent enough for that.

English is a confusing language to learn because one never knows how a word will be pronounced. In German (and most other languages I have encountered) each letter is pronounced the same way, each time it is written, and silent letters are rare. In English there are many silent letters, and each word must be memorized because even the few rules have numerous exceptions.

I struggled with spelling until I learned to pronounce each letter in my head in German. Eventually I became a good speller, but the first year was very discouraging. I learned most of my English from reading and I pronounced the words in my head, trying to use rules that made sense to me. For example: "gh" is pronounced "F" in many words so I said cough=coff, laugh=laff but then there was bright= brift, night=nift. The ow sound was also confusing. There were words like "now, cow, bow" that sound like "out." Other words that end in ow make an oh sound. I did not know this, so I said snau, blau, lau, when I meant snow, blow, low. No wonder people did not understand me and often laffed at me.

In the afternoons we studied Hebrew, which made a lot

---

[29] In Europe May 1st is the day to honor wage earners with parades and speeches.

more sense than English. The Hebrew teacher looked at my low secular grades and tried to talk to me about the discrepancy. I couldn't explain it.

Even though the other girls in the class ignored me, I liked school and enjoyed the long walk home along the tree lined streets near Old Aunt's house.

During a heat wave in early September, our room was so hot that it was impossible to sleep. Like so many people in Washington, D.C. at that time, we didn't have air conditioning or even an electric fan. Judy told us that it was cooler near the river, so we took a blanket and walked to the banks of the Potomac River where we spent several nights along with hundreds of other people on their blankets. It was difficult to sleep with all the noise around us, but the breeze from the river allowed us to breath. Two weeks later it was so cool that there was talk about where and how to get a winter coat.

There were tense conversations during those autumn months about the upcoming presidential elections. Mutti, Judy and David were fervently hoping that President Roosevelt would be re-elected. I heard David say that if his opponent, Wendel Wilke, won the election he would cut back on immigration. No one had to explain to me this meant Vati might not get to America after all. Then one day the election was over. "Roosevelt won." David told us, with a sigh of relief, and I could feel the tension easing around me.

One afternoon on my way home from Hebrew School it began to snow. I danced around with my hands spread out, enjoying the feel of the flakes as they settled on my hands. Then I saw Mutti running towards me. She was waving a piece of paper. "Your Vati is on his way to America!" She called out to me.

We went upstairs to read and re-read the letter which explained his long, complicated journey to a place called Seattle, (which we pronounced 'Sit lee'). He would fly from Stockholm to Moscow. From Moscow he would get on the Trans-Siberian Railroad for a two-week trip across Russia to the port of Novosibirsk.

Then board a ship to Yokohama, Japan, where he was to stay with a Jewish family who took in European refugees while they waited for a ship to take them across the Pacific Ocean. Two days later the family would get him aboard the Hyan Maru for the three-week trip to that place called "Sit Lee" which happened to be in a place called Washington. (We thought he was coming to Washington, D.C., until Judy explained about the states in the United States) From there he was to take a train to a place called Portland which was in another state called Oregon. From the start in Sweden to Portland would take six weeks, so by now he was on his way.

He said he would send a telegram from Portland when he arrived. At that time we should take a train (a five-day trip) and meet him in Portland. In the meantime he would arrange, with the help of the local refugee committee, to get an apartment and a job.

We went to see Old Aunt, to tell her of our plans. She began to yell at Mutti that she had never heard of a place called Sit Lee and that Oregon was a wild territory (not even a state) with Indians, and gun slingers. "No one is going to take a Jewish child from this family out there if I can help it." She said emphatically "Thilde, believe me there is no culture, or even a decent school out there. Ask Leo to come here where we are civilized." She tried to reason with my mother, who was adamant about doing what her husband asked her to do.

When Mutti asked her for a loan of $300 for the train fare, she vigorously pounded her cane on the floor and screamed "No, and I will not allow anyone else in this family to give you that money."

As we were leaving the Old Aunt's house, cousin Gussie came running after us. Mutti was crying so loud that we almost didn't hear her call us to stop. She tried to calm Mutti then told us she would help us get the money for the train fare. Later that day, cousin Gussie helped Mutti write a letter to HIAS (Hebrew Immigration Aid Society) and they loaned her the $300 to be repaid when she had an income. (Mutti repaid the loan at $5.00 per month for the next five years. Among her papers I found the sixty receipts, a letter with "paid in full" stamped at the top and a handwritten thank-you from the administrator who mentioned that she was the first person, to his knowledge, who had paid them back in full).

Cousin Gussie gave us a big, leather suitcase and assured us that she would pack up our belongings that we couldn't take and send them along as soon as we had an address. I had always liked cousin Gussie, but now I felt real love for this "old maid" with a good heart. (Along with pity that she lived with Old Aunt).

Deciding what to take along to the "wilderness" and what to leave behind took several visits to Old Aunt's house, but I never saw her again. With the hope that eventually all the contents of the wooden crate would be sent to us, Mutti packed a few necessities into my small suitcase, some of her clothes and her other pair of shoes into the large case. Somewhere Mutti had found space for a small, cloth covered picture album and a cookbook, which had been her grandmother's.

By the time the telegram came, we were packed and ready to leave. David drove us to the huge Union Station, helped us check our biggest suitcase with an agent that assured us it would arrive in Portland, Oregon with us. We spent a long time looking for the westbound train and found the right track just in time. Since we were traveling second class coach we needed to stow our bags on the shelf above our seats. My mother is barely five feet tall and getting her heavy suitcase up that high was not possible. She left it in the aisle and several people stepped over it. A black man in a uniform offered to stow the suitcase for us. But first, he thoughtfully asked if we wanted to take anything out before he put it on the upper shelf. Mutti took out the things we would need for the next few days, then we settled back into the velvet covered seats and shortly we were rolling past the outskirts of the city.

After we ate a quick meal in the dining car, Mutti made

me comfortable in the well upholstered coach seat. She took off my dress, slipped on my night shirt, housecoat and soft slippers in place of my high-topped shoes. For herself, Mutti had a warm robe and fuzzy, pink slippers (Gifts from Gussie) that flopped loudly when she walked to the toilet. She carefully laid our outer clothing on the lower rack, just above our seats so they would not wrinkle. I curled up on the seat and fell asleep.

I was shaken awake by a frantic Mutti. We had arrived in Chicago and the conductor told us we needed to change trains to continue our journey to Oregon. Someone had probably told us about this, but Mutti was totally surprised. With the help of the kind black man, we gathered our things. Wearing the robes and floppy slippers, dragging our hastily packed suitcases we got off the train.

We must have been a comical sight, trudging around the immense, crowded train station. Some kind person guided us to the "Travelers' Aid" kiosk where a German speaking woman came out from behind the counter and walked us to the Portland bound train. The Travelers' Aid lady talked with the conductor, who smiled at us as he punched out tickets. We made our way through the crowded car to our new seats, that looked just like the ones on the last train. Still sleepy, I climbed into the window seat, and watched as another black man (called "Porter") stowed our suitcases on the high ledge above our seat. While Mutti carefully laid our clothes on the lower shelf, I fell asleep.

Chapter 33

The Wild West 1940-1941

When I awoke it was daylight and the landscape had totally changed. Mutti carefully dressed me and we went to the toilet at the end of the car to wash up in preparation to go to breakfast. In those days, meals were included in the train fare.

For the next five nights we slept in those blue, velvet seats. Mutti read me stories from the small books she had thought to bring, and we wrote letters to all the relatives. I didn't know that the letters to Austria (which was now called Ostmark) would not be delivered.

The scenery was changing constantly, and we saw strange structures near the barns which were close to the houses. We later learned that the bomb like structures were called "silos" and used for storing grain. For two more days we passed grazing animals and snow-covered fields that stretched to the horizon, reminding me of the ocean. The farm compounds were miles apart and far away from the towns where the train stopped.

On the third day the train started to climb into snow covered forests. Then through mountain passes with majestic peaks on all sides. I sat glued to the window absolutely dazzled. My mother was less impressed by the Rocky Mountains, after all she had been hiking in the much higher Austrian Alps. We rode over high trestles that spanned rushing rivers far below us. There were long, seemingly endless, tunnels. With a pounding heart I waited for the dark to end.

One morning we traveled along a wide river with high

bluffs on either side. It was all so beautiful, like moving through a painting. Soon the train was pulling into Union Station, in Portland, Oregon. The rain was pouring down in sheets and the cold November wind chilled us to the bone.

The man and woman who met us on the platform knew who we were and introduced themselves. They told us that my father was waiting at the apartment for us because he preferred to meet us in a private place. I could tell Mutti was disappointed, but I was relieved to put off the meeting with this man who was planning to spank me before he did anything else. Mutti had told me he was just joking, but I didn't believe her because I knew I deserved a thrashing since over the last two years I had caused my mother much anxiety and anger.

The ride in the car was fun, but the rain was splashing against the windows so I could not see much of the city. Mutti asked if it rained like this often. The man said it only rained thirteen months a year here in Portland. Mutti and I were shocked to hear that Portland had thirteen months.

It was a short ride to South West Corbett Street and we soon pulled up in front of a two-story Victorian style house. The Wexlers helped us out of the car. We were all drenched as we climbed the stairs to the second floor and there, in the middle of the living room, stood Vati. I didn't really recognize him, but I knew it was Vati because my mother had said his name. Would he really spank me? My mother walked into the room without a word to me or the couple who had escorted us to the apartment. They set down the suitcases then turned to leave, closing the door behind them.

I took a quick look around the spacious room, taking in the wide, bay windows to my left and a hallway to the right. My parents were oblivious to anything but each other. They had seated themselves on the couch, tightly holding hands and just gazing at each other, laughing softly. I watched for a few minutes as they began to touch each other. Finally, they were weeping and hugging.

By now I needed a bathroom, so I walked along the hallway to my right, past a small kitchen and a bedroom and found the bathroom at the end of the hall. A full-length mirror hung on the inside of the door and a smaller mirror was above the sink. For the first time in my life I could see myself top to bottom, back and front. My dress was much too long, and my coat was short and looked very tight. I giggled at the strange sight.

When I returned to the living room, Vati was ready to greet me. He tried to hug me, and I was relieved when he decided I was too heavy to lift. He bent over and placed a shy kiss on my forehead and asked. "You speak English, yes?" He didn't wait for me to answer but continued to chat to us in German. It was decided we would go out to lunch. Vati told us about a great place he had found the day before where they served a sandwich called a "hamburger" and something even better, called a "milkshake."

The rain had let up into a fine drizzle and we walked to the soda fountain. I had my first taste of an American hamburger. It was a strange combination of meat, vegetables, bread and mayonnaise (which I loved) and surprisingly tasty. As Vati had said, the milkshake was more than enough for the three of us. He poured each of us a glass out of the huge metal container. It was delicious and one glass was totally satisfying. Astonishingly, the milkshake only cost eleven cents.

On the way back to the apartment we stopped at a small grocery store, which looked a lot like Oma's store. I hadn't thought much about Oma since we left Wopfing that fateful day. When my parents started talking about the people we had left behind in Europe, I knew they were also reminded of Oma's store too.

Mutti started to find her way around the kitchen. There were dishes and pots, but she kept wishing for her own things that were still in the wooden crate in Washington, D.C. While she prepared a cold supper, Vati and I sat down on the couch to practice our English. After that day we rarely spoke German.

My parents were alarmed by the fact that I had missed over a week of school already and decided I should enroll in the neighborhood school the very next day. The next morning, after a somewhat comfortable night on the sofa that would be my bed during this stay in Portland, Mutti gave me a cup of warm milk and a strangely, spongy roll for breakfast. Walking in the drizzly rain we set off for Failing School. We had seen the playground from the apartment window on S.W. Corbett St., but we wandered around the building for a while until we found the front door.

The people in the principal's office were very busy and we waited for about an hour until someone asked what we wanted. Mutti had been rehearsing how to say, "I want to enroll my daughter in the school." However, filling out the paperwork proved to be difficult. I had no records of previous schooling or a birth certificate. My name was on my mother's passport and they took her word for my birthdate.

Eventually a lady took me down a wide hall to a room marked 2nd GRADE. The teacher was not pleased with the interruption, but took a moment to look at me, and without a word pointed to a vacant desk in the back of the room. Then she resumed with her lessons. I didn't understand much of what she was saying.

The other children turned to look at me with, what I felt were, hostile faces. I was beginning to be afraid. At recess everyone went out to the playground. The girls divided into several groups and I went from one to the other hoping to get a friendly hello or at least a pleasant smile. They totally ignored me. When we returned to the classroom, the teacher introduced me as the new student, then quickly went into the afternoon lessons.

While the other children worked on the papers in front of them, the teacher came over to my desk and gave me a piece of paper and a pencil. I understood that she wanted me to make a list of the school supplies I would need. I could not follow her rapid English. She talked louder and louder and I still didn't understand most of what she said. When I started to write in cursive, she seemed to get angry. Finally, she grabbed the paper and printed a long list of things that I recognized and, fortunately, already had at home.

Over the next two weeks I learned that second graders in America were just beginning to learn lower case letters and would not be writing cursive until the end of that year. This caused some friction between the teacher and me especially with spelling tests. When a word was misspelled, I often argued about a letter. An open "o" or a badly made "a" can look like a "u" etc. Relearning how to print was good practice and made me a better speller in the long run.

In Arithmetic the class was learning addition of double-digit numbers with a method I had never seen. The numbers were placed on top of each other instead of side by side, as I had been taught. (i.e. 23+17 = 40). I quickly learned to use the concept of carrying numbers and liked it.

Going back to printing was more difficult. I had not had much practice in printing since we began writing in cursive almost immediately upon entering school in Austria. I tried to print, but the letters kept running together and my grades for penmanship and neatness were barely passing for the rest of my school years.

My days at Failing School were not pleasant and mercifully lasted only about two weeks. I have no good memories of the teacher or students. There was a group of three or four boys that made it their business to make my life miserable. They followed me around the playground at recess (for lunch I stayed inside the lunchroom, eating my sandwich very slowly), taking turns at pushing my shoulder from behind or punching me in the back. Several times they almost knocked me down. Finally, one of the bigger boys in this group had the nerve to confront me. "You dirty Nazi," He hissed and punched my shoulder. I made a fist with my right hand and punched him on the side of his head. He was not expecting me to react that way (What they wanted was to make me cry) and lost his balance. As he fell over, he began to scream looking around to see if anyone was coming. A teacher came up to us. gripped my arm and with her free hand helped the bully to his feet.

She marched both of us to the principal's office. A "DO NOT DISTURB" sign hung on the closed door. The bell rang for the end of recess, so the teacher told us to sit down on the bench outside the office door and wait until the principal had time to see us. I stole a look at the bully. His eye was beginning to swell up. I was not sure how I felt about hitting him. I do know I was not sorry. I had never hit anyone before, and I sincerely hoped I would not need to hit anyone again.

The principal, a tall man whom I can't describe because I never saw his face, took one look at the bully's eye and began to yell at me. "In this country we do not hit other people." Then he told me I should be ashamed. (why should I be ashamed?) In my short life I had lost all respect for authority, no longer had any faith in justice, and had become an accomplished liar. I knew there were kind, compassionate, generous people (and I loved them) but the world seemed to belong to the mean, callous, greedy and aggressive bullies. To survive I learned to fight back.

As it happened, in a few days I was playing with the boys, which seemed to annoy the girls. As I went from school to school, I made friends with girls, but more often I found that playing with the boys was more fun.

Chapter 34

Just before the holiday of Thanksgiving and two weeks after starting at Failing school, my father got a job on a dairy farm in a place called Happy Valley, an hour's drive from Boise, Idaho. The nearest town was called Nampa and hardly worth the half-hour drive from the farm. The mailbox was on the main road about a mile from the house and picking up the mail was a daily chore for the farm hands. Vati learned to drive a car on these outings.

The Ansons had about thirty cows that were milked by hand twice a day, plus several pigs, a flock of chickens, and—this being a few days before Thanksgiving—a numerous flock of turkeys.

The house was a rambling structure which seemed to have been built in stages. The living room took up the front of the house. Across the room from the front door, a long hallway went to the kitchen where a back door led to a screened in porch that overlooked the poultry yard. Beside the kitchen was a small room for my parents with a window looking out to the porch where I was to sleep on a narrow cot, just below the window. The only light in this area was from a naked light bulb hanging from the ceiling in my parents' bedroom. I assume there were bedrooms and maybe even a bathroom on the other side of the house, but I never went into that area. Our sanitary facilities consisted of a wash bowl and ewer on a stand in my parent's bedroom and an outhouse (latrine) beyond the kitchen garden.

Mutti woke me up before full daylight on the first

morning after our arrival. She brushed the thin sheet of ice off the top layer of the several blankets that covered me and wrapped me in one of them, then took me to the warm kitchen to get dressed. "You are going to school today." She told me in English. I had mixed feelings about that news, but it wasn't as if I had a choice.

After washing up and eating breakfast, we set out to find the school. It was almost a two mile walk, but we arrived before the start of the school day. The school was a square, red brick building set in the middle of a muddy field. There was a bell tower on the roof with a huge bell that announced the beginning of the school day and also called the children to come inside from lunch and recess. There was a double door outhouse at the edge of the muddy playground. (one side for boys and one for girls).

Inside the schoolhouse there were two rooms. First, second and third grade students were in one room while fourth, fifth and sixth graders were in another room across the hall. An attractive young woman with dark brown hair and soft, dark eyes met us in the hallway and led us to the schoolroom. There were a few desks, a long, low table surrounded by little chairs, a blackboard on one wall, colorful pictures covered the other two walls and high, narrow windows ran along the fourth wall. A wood stove and wood box took up one corner. Keeping the wood box full was a chore for the boys and the girls wiped the blackboard.

The teacher, speaking slowly, asked Mutti some questions and helped fill out a form. Then took me by the hand and with a friendly, but firm, voice told Mutti that she would make sure I got back to the Anson farm after school. "Ruthie, I am Miss Blake," the teacher said to me and showed me where to put my coat and the lunch bag that Mutti had packed for me. Then she led me to one of the desks. She explained that the first graders used the low table while the second graders used the desks which had inkwells. Would we really be using ink like I had been doing in Vienna, instead of the pencils used by second graders in the Portland School?

In the few minutes before the other kids arrived, Miss Blake asked me about my math skills and gave me a book to read. "You will need extra help." She told me. "Today you go home with the other children, but tomorrow we work after school."

The next day and every school day after that, Miss Blake stayed with me for over an hour, teaching me English, traditional songs, (e.g., "Row, Row, Row Your Boat," "Jingle Bells"), the Pledge of Allegiance, the words to "America" (also known as "My Country 'Tis Of Thee") and bits of American history.

When the other eight children began to come into the classroom that first day, they looked at me with curiosity. With relief I saw no hostility. There were two second graders, three first graders and three third graders and they all wanted to talk to me after Miss Blake had introduced me.

The name "Ruth"—or "Ruthie," as Miss Blake called me, because she had heard my mother call me that—was not a common name in that area. During recess one of the boys called me Baby Ruth and the girls giggled, but not in a mean way. There was no playground equipment, so we played tag with the boys. After we ate our lunches at our desks, we went back outside and played circle games with the older girls. (i.e. Farmer in the Dell, London Bridge is Falling Down.) The kids all addressed me as "Baby Ruth." I tried not to let it bother me, but I was puzzled.

Miss Blake witnessed this and took me aside during a lunch hour and explained that they were referring to a popular candy bar, which was named after a famous baseball player. Later, during class, she asked what the students knew about Babe Ruth. Only one of the boys knew that the candy bar was named after the esteemed ball player. Miss Blake then went on to explain more about "The Babe" as he was known and showed us pictures and articles out of the newspapers. After that day, the boys still called me Baby Ruth, and I still didn't like it. One day after school the third graders asked me to go to the grocery store with them. I didn't know about a store in the vicinity and was really curious. Miss Blake must have overheard the conversation because she told me it was a good idea to show me the store.

So I went with the two boys and the girl from third grade, who told me the store was just down the road. It turned out to be a long walk down hill to a cluster of houses. I was fascinated to see signs of civilization.

The store reminded me of Omama's store. Everything was behind the counter or in a glass case, except the candy bars. They were in boxes on one side of the counter, propped up at an angle so the various names could be read, even by a seven-year-old. Sure enough there was a candy bar, wrapped in white paper with big red letters: Baby Ruth. I didn't have any money, or I would have bought one. (Four years later, in another town, I finally bought a Baby Ruth).

The third graders were headed in the opposite direction, so I had to find my way back to the school. There was really no way to get lost, but it was uphill on the way back and by the time I reached the schoolhouse it was beginning to get dark. I ran the rest of the way home, arriving exhausted with a painful stitch in my side. Mutti was setting the table for supper. She didn't say anything about my being later than usual, just told me to go wash my hands before I came to the table.

For the next few weeks I continued to stay after school. Since I had not told anyone about the extra time Miss Blake was spending with me, Mutti probably thought school didn't get out until four o'clock.

After-school Miss Blake taught me grammar and spent much time explaining the complexities of English spelling, with so many silent letters. There were myriad rules and just as many exceptions. i.e. "I before E except after C or when sounded like A, like in neighbor and way." (or weigh, which I had pronounced, "wife" because I thought all "gh" sounded like F and "ei" made an "I" sound.

Miss Blake told me about Thanksgiving, the Pilgrims and the reason we were going to eat some of those turkeys

I had been feeding. The things I learned in that two room schoolhouse served me well for the rest of my life.

One of the chores I was asked to do was feed the chickens and the turkeys. The chickens were a docile group and all I had to do was throw the grain out into the side yard where they spent their time. I also helped Mutti collect eggs from the nests in the chicken coops. It was a pleasure to feel their warmth in my hands on those cold mornings.

Feeding the turkeys was an altogether different experience. I was supposed to stand just outside the kitchen door with a bag of turkey food and throw handfuls of the grain to the turkeys. It looked simple enough and at first it was fun. Then the turkeys got bigger and came closer and closer. Some of them were taller than I was. They began to peck at my hands as I threw the food. One day they were pecking at my arms and getting near my head. I screamed and backed up into the kitchen. Mrs. Anson took the bag from me with an angry look and pushed me aside. She yelled something at me, but I was crying hysterically by then and didn't understand a word of what she said. In any case I didn't feed turkeys again and have no compunction about eating the mean and ugly birds.

Mr. and Mrs. Anson were a few years older than my parents and had a grown daughter who came to visit several times during our stay at the farm. Ginger was married but had no children. She spent hours teaching me to crochet a zigzag pattern for afghans and told me stories about growing up on the farm. In a hushed tone she told me that she never liked farming or the dirt and smells that came with it. When she was my age there was no electricity, running water or indoor plumbing. It sounded just like the situation in my grandmother's village. The big difference, in America, was that the houses were miles apart and I was told that everyone had a gun in their house. After listening to me while I told her about being torn away from my home and family, she became very serious and said, "It's a family secret, but I had a Jewish grandmother."

The Thanksgiving dinner was a grand affair. Ginger, and I set the table in the dining room while Mutti helped Mrs. Anson in the kitchen. I learned where to put the silverware, glasses and napkins. (always under the fork on the left of the plate). Then the food was put on the table, prayers were said, and Mr. Anson carved up the huge turkey.

Much of what was served was strange to us. The only thing I had eaten before were the green peas. For dessert we had pie that looked like chocolate. I took one bite and gagged. It was pumpkin pie and probably very good, like everything else on that table. But the disappointment of not tasting chocolate turned me off pumpkin pie for many years.

After dinner we gathered in the living room. I had never heard Mrs. Anson get involved in a conversation, but Mr. Anson liked to talk with my father. He asked questions about the dairy farm in Sweden and sometimes about his life in Austria. That night, after hearing what had happened to us in Austria and to many other Jews in Germany, Mr. Anson became very agitated. He grabbed his rifle, that hung over the fireplace, and pointed it around the room.

He began to yell about what cowards these Jews were, and, if anyone came to the door and wanted to take his property, he would grab his rifle and shoot them. It was clear to us that he had no notion of the situation in Europe. There was no way to explain how impossible his ideas were. Since laws had been put in place that took all rights (even the right to life) away from all Jews, whatever was being done to them was now legal. After that night we didn't speak to any American born person about what had happened to us. They would never fully comprehend what it was like to be declared sub-human with no legal rights, no better than livestock.

Chapter 35

After Thanksgiving we spent much of the school day decorating the school room. We spent hours making red and green paper chains, drawing and coloring Christmas trees to hang on the walls and making a gift for our parents. This was a piece of burlap with a drawing of a castle, which might have been a lighthouse, surrounded by very high ocean waves. We used chalk to color in the different numbered areas. After applying the chalk, we rubbed it around with our fingers to a desired shade, so each picture turned out a little differently. I thought my version was one of the best with a deep blue, white capped waves, a castle on a cliff above the sea, with a red roof against a light blue sky. The sky was darkened around the edge of the picture, to show a coming storm and I used yellow with a touch of orange to depict a light glowing from the windows.

I worked on the picture every day for two weeks. When it was finally finished, Miss Blake sprayed it with a glaze. It took two more days to dry, then I rolled it up and tied it with a satin ribbon. I carried it home and proudly handed it to my mother. She unrolled it on her bed and took a quick look at it. "So this is what you do in school instead of learning." She said and rolled it up. I never saw it again.

In early December, the whole school became involved in a Christmas play and the learning of Christmas carols. The play was about a grandfather who told the grandchildren the poem "The Night Before Christmas. My part was to be a friend of the grandfather, who sat nearby as the story was told, smoking his pipe and adding an occasional word and nod to enhance the story. The part fell to me because my English was not good enough for a speaking part, plus I was the tallest girl in the class. This made me unsuitable to be one of the children and besides there were not enough boys to fill the male parts. I loved being an old man, smoking a pipe. When I walked around the kitchen with a soup spoon in my mouth and told my parents that I was practicing for a play, no one paid any attention. The Christmas play was being performed on a Friday night and we all went home a little early so we could get back in time for the play. After dinner that night Mutti and I were finishing the dish washing and drying when I reminded her about the play that night. I took it for granted that my parents would have made arrangements for us to get there.

"Stop this foolishness about a Christmas play." I was told in German. "No one is going out anywhere tonight. Go do your homework or work on your knitting and leave the grownups alone." I was devastated, sad, furious and worried about what Miss Blake would say to me on Monday. I cried myself to sleep that night and pouted for the next two days.

Mr. Anson noticed my bad mood and decided to cheer me up. He promised to give me the next newborn calf. I could raise it and exhibit it at the County Fair. Both my parents told me this was a wonderful present and I should be the happiest girl in the world. I was far from happy, I was terrified. I had been to the barn only once and the mud and stench repelled me to the point of nausea. Now I was to have my own calf.

My calf was born a day before Christmas vacation, which, I was told, was an opportune time. I could start taking charge of the animal on a full-time basis. There was no way out. I pulled the oversized, rubber boots over my high-top shoes, put on a milking coat and went down to the barn to meet my present.

She was about my height and as she poked her nose through the fence between us, I knew I was supposed to pet her snout. I did and it was warm and slimy. Mr. Anson handed me a huge bottle of milk with a nipple on one end. I handed it back to him and made my way through the mud and manure, back to the house. Later that day I was reprimanded as an ungrateful brat by my parents. The next day Mr. Anson tried to coax me back to the barn. "Your calf needs a name." he told me. I told him to call her Alice, if he wanted to, but I was never going back to the barn again and I didn't.

During that vacation time Mr. and Mrs. Anson, at Ginger's urging, drove us to Nampa to see a movie. The six of us squeezed into Mr. Anson's station wagon and drove the thirty miles to the small town. The roads were clear of snow, but there was always a chance of black ice and it took us over an hour to get to the movie.

The film was being shown in a large warehouse. Rows of wooden benches faced a white bed sheet hung from one wall. A projector was on a tall table at the back of the benches, which filled up quickly and we had to sit near the back. Several tall people were on the bench in front of me so, when the movie started, I went to stand on a bench in the last row. It was a Shirley Temple movie. I had seen it before in Vienna. To my great disappointment, Shirley spoke perfect English. When I learned that she did not, and never had, spoken German. I was very annoyed with her for fooling me. It was the last time I went to one of her movies while she was still a child star. The Ansons had made a special effort to take us to that movie to please me. Instead of acting delighted and making an effort to chat with Ginger about the movie, I sat looking morosely out of the window into the darkness while the car endlessly skidded and bumped along.

The first morning after vacation I set off for school in a dense fog. Usually such a fog lifted before I got to the end of the driveway, but that morning it stayed low, right down to the ground. I passed the mailbox and turned onto the main road where I could barely make out the fence post along the side. I walked and walked, not knowing where I was since I couldn't see any of the landmarks along the way. When the fence posts disappeared, I thought I must be near the school, but I couldn't see it anywhere. After all the stories I had been told how witches could make people disappear, make castles invisible, (like in Sleeping Beauty) it didn't seem impossible that the school had been spirited away while we were on Christmas vacation.

I walked back to the Anson farm and told Mutti that the school had disappeared. She looked out at the fog and back at me. The fog had lifted a little by then and I could see that she was ready to scold me and send me back out to get to school. I tried to suppress the hysterical screams that were rising in my throat, but they overwhelmed me. I cried and screamed "No! No!" until Mutti dragged me to her bedroom, threw me onto the bed and went out of the room, closing the door behind her.

The room was cold, and I began to shiver. My shoes, socks and skirt hem were wet. I pulled the bedspread over me and fell asleep. I woke up in my own bed, but I was still feeling cold. It was dark when Mutti came out to the porch with a sandwich and a glass of warm milk. She told me I had missed supper, and this was all the food I would get until morning.

Later that night I heard voices from my parent's room. I had seldom heard them argue or raise their voices. But that night I could hear every word through the closed window. Mutti was saying she could not tolerate staying here any longer. She was a city person and needed to be in a place with sidewalks, access to cultural and medical facilities. "This is not a place for an educated person, and we cannot raise the child here!" she screamed. (They always referred to me as *Das Kind* [the child]).

Vati tried to reason with her in a moderate voice then it rose, but Mutti just kept on talking over his raised voice. She was not listening, and she used similar words she had shouted at Tante Fanny when she was determined to leave the chicken ranch. I fell asleep with my pillow over my ears.

In the morning Mutti brushed the ice off my coverlet and

started me on the morning routine of washing and dressing. I didn't tell her my throat was scratchy, but by the time I got to school the pain in my throat made it hard to talk. I lasted out the day, but when I got home, I told Mutti about my sore throat. She shone a flashlight down my throat and after one look at my swollen tonsils she immediately put me to bed in her room. She took my temperature and ascertained that I had a high fever. In the days before antibiotics, people with infections just stayed in bed until they were well (or died).

Every few hours Mutti brought me hot tea with honey and lemon, each time telling me how expensive lemons were and how generous it was of Mrs. Anson to let her have some for me. Eventually I recovered but was too weak to go to school. Mutti made me read and write something every day and Vati drilled me on the single digit multiplication tables. When I was well, I did not go back to the two-room school. Instead, we packed up our few possessions and traveled back to Portland, where my father hoped to find a job.

Chapter 36

In Portland we moved into a basement apartment on North West Hoyt Street. It felt wonderful to be back in a place with sidewalks, a corner grocery store, huge shade trees, and stately houses surrounded by patches of well-groomed grass and rose bushes. Hoyt Street slanted steeply toward 23rd Avenue, where the terrain leveled off. Walking along 23rd Avenue, with all the stores and restaurants, was entertaining; Rose's Delicatessen was a real treat.

I was enrolled in Couch School, a walk of about ten blocks from the apartment. The principal put me into the second grade, even though I would be eight years old in a month. Real schoolhouse desks sat in this room with ink wells built into the right-hand upper corner of each desk. (Too bad if you were left-handed. Having to reach across the desk to fill your pen nib often meant ink blots on your paper.) The inkwells were a temptation for the boys. More than once I watched as an unlucky girl, who happened to be sitting in front of a mischievous boy, had the end of her braid dunked into the ink well on his desk.

My English was much better than it had been during my first encounter with Portland schools and a biased teacher. At recess, several girls clustered around me, curious about the "new girl," and I was able to answer their questions and ask a few of my own. By the end of the first day I had made friends. The school had no playground equipment, just a wide expanse of pavement that stretched out to a park with tall trees and gravel paths. (The park was off-limits during school hours.)

We had no organized games during outdoor time. We girls walked arm-in-arm around the perimeter of the paved area, jumped rope, and sometimes played tag with the boys. I taught several of the girls the skipping dance I had seen at the performance of *Hansel & Gretel* and taught them to sing the song in German. During lunch and recess we had quite an audience. More and more girls joined us, and it was the most fun I had ever had.

Some of my friends came to school on roller skates. It looked so easy to just roll along on little wheels. Of course, I asked for roller skates and was told, "We'll see."

One day Vati came home from a job-hunting expedition and said he had been hired as an apprentice electrician. It was the first time in weeks that I had seen him smile. After his first paycheck, we went out to get a milkshake to celebrate. A few days later Vati came home with a small radio. My parents hated modern music, especially the crooners like Bing Crosby and Rudy Vallée, so they were especially delighted when they discovered the opera presentations of *The Standard Hour* on Saturday mornings.

For two hours each Saturday morning, for many years to come, they were transported back to the best times of their young lives. My father, who knew much of the music, sang along with sheer delight. He had a beautiful operatic voice, which he inherited from his father who was a cantor. Some mornings, much to my embarrassment, he opened the door and our one window, turned the volume to its loudest position, flooding the neighborhood with the sound of the world's greatest tenors. "This is real music, you barbarians!" he would yell out the door. At my mother's pleading he would finally turn down the volume.[30]

To my delight and total surprise, on the morning of my eighth birthday, a pair of roller skates sat on the breakfast

---

[30] After my father acquired a car, he bought gasoline only from Standard Oil Service Stations in gratitude for *The Standard Hour*.

table and the skate key was alongside on a long rope. I immediately opened the clamps to fit my shoes. I had watched my
friends hurtling down the steep streets and rolling around
the paved parking lots in the area, skate key flying back and
forth on a silk rope, just like the one I was now wearing. I
could hardly wait to join them.

After hugging my parents, I ran outside, sat on the steps
that led down to our apartment, and clamped on the skates,
turned the key to tighten them to my high-topped shoes. I
used the railing to pull myself up to the walkway that led
to the sidewalk. It wasn't easy. Getting to the sidewalk was a
matter of rolling a few feet on level ground, but once I faced
the steep slope the skates took over and in a matter of seconds, I was rolling to the bottom of the hill without a clue on
how to stop.

Fortunately, there was a wide, grass border between the
street and the sidewalk, and I had the sense to plow into
the grass and fell to my knees. I was in shock. I had no idea it
would be so difficult to stop those little wheels from rolling.
Taking off the skates I assessed the damage. My knees were
a bloody mess. Blood had run into my socks and stained my
dress. A sleeve was torn and covered with grass stain. It was
a painful climb back up the hill.

I walked past the colonial pillars in front of our apartment, right up to where Hoyt Street ended at 25th Avenue.
I sat down on the grass border and clamped on my skates,
turning the key as hard as I could to assure a tight fit. This
extra length of sidewalk gave me more time to get my balance on the skates. I enjoyed the ride until I again landed on
the grass. I did this a few more times, then went inside to get
cleaned up and scolded.

Every day, for the next week I rolled down the hill, walked
back up, and rolled back down again—landing in a heap in
the grass border, which was turning into a patch of mud. It
wasn't until I got to Longview, Washington, where the terrain
was totally flat, that I acquired the skill of stopping on skates

while standing up.[31]

Near the end of March, Vati told us that his job as an electrician was over. The next day he planned to go to the Jewish Immigration Service to apply for another job. My parents seldom talked about money, but that night I could hear the stress in their voices as they counted out how much they had left for the rent that month. Mutti said we must cut back on every expenditure. "No more luxuries," she said. I looked around the apartment and the only luxury I could see was the radio. My father even bought loose tobacco and cigarette paper, rolling his own cigarettes to save money. It never occurred to him to stop smoking. I rarely saw him without a cigarette. I slept in the living room throughout my childhood and I found the smell of cigarette smoke on my pillow a reassuring sign that Vati was nearby.

One day I came home from school and saw Mutti packing our two suitcases. "We are moving to a town called Longview, in Washington, across the river," she told me. "Vati has a job in a lumber mill. He left this morning to go find us an apartment and start his new job. We are leaving as soon as I clean up the apartment and get your school records. A train leaves tomorrow around noon."

Since it was a furnished apartment, we had only unpacked a few of our clothes and a few dishes, so packing was done quickly, and by ten the next morning, we were on our way to the train station in Mrs. Wexler's car. I had not had time to say goodbye to my friends at school. Mrs. Wexler waited at the curb while we went to the principal's office to pick up my records.

The train ride to Longview, Washington, was about two hours, but I didn't see much of the scenery because my eyes were full of tears. I hated leaving Couch School. I had been happy there.

---

[31] This was 1941 and no one thought about knee pads or helmets. The damage to my knees could have been permanent, and I still have the scars.

In Longview, Vati met us at the station and we rode in a taxi for the short distance to the Columbia Apartments, located above the Columbia Movie Theater, where we again had a studio apartment.

Chapter 37

The next morning, long after my father had left for work, Mutti and I headed to Kessler School. We walked along Commerce Street, checking out the variety of stores. Toward the end of the commercial district, according to directions from the taxi driver the day before, we turned right onto a gravel path that led us to a field. We walked a long way between the tall grasses, until a big, white building appeared in front of us.

The school was a square, two-story structure with a wide lawn in front and a paved play area in the back. It had a long, narrow, roofed structure along the back wall, which I later learned was the bicycle shed. More than half the students rode bicycles to school.

We entered the wide, glass doors, walked down the hall, admiring the gleaming floors. Rows of lockers flanked the walls. We found the principal's office. First, the man looked down at my records, then at me. Without a smile or a greeting he told my mother that he was going to try me out in second grade. He walked toward the door, motioning me to follow him. Mutti and I looked at each other and, without a word, she left the building.

The second-grade teacher was not pleased to see me. After all, it was almost the end of the school year and here was this new student who, according to her records, could hardly read, and her handwriting looked like hen scratching. She pointed to a desk at the back of the room, and I sat there staring out the window until recess. I don't remember much about my first day at Kessler school. There were some mean boys who made fun of me, called me "bean pole" (I was taller than most of them) and pulled my hair at recess. I kicked their shins (I found some benefits to wearing high-topped shoes) and they left me alone. The girls didn't come near me and generally ignored my presence.

That first day, my mother came to get me, and I met her halfway through the grass-lined path. I am sure I was crying and telling her how I wanted to go back to Portland. I don't remember exactly what she said, but she made me understand that, no matter what else we did, "We never go back."

The second day of school I was walking along the path between the tall grasses when a boy came up beside me. He had blond hair and bright, blue eyes—the same color as the sky that day. He asked me if I was lost because he had never seen anyone else walk along this path after school. I had not seen him in school, and he was a bit shorter than I was, so I assumed he was a first grader. But he didn't talk like a first grader.

He told me his name was Jackie Tanzer and that his parents owned a store. Sure enough, just as we left the grass-lined path to step up to Commerce Street, I saw the sign I had missed the day before: "Tanzer Men's Clothing."

That evening at dinner I told my parents that I had met a cute boy at school. They asked his name and when I told them his name they smiled and told me that they knew the Tanzers. They were one of the five Jewish families living in Longview. Mr. Tanzer had provided some work clothes for my father that first day he had arrived in town.

The next day, Jackie took me into the store to meet his parents. They were enormously friendly. Joe Tanzer, Jackie's father, had kind, blue eyes and his mother, Fanny, had a warm, welcoming smile. They each shook hands with me, treating me like a grown-up. Mrs. Tanzer led Jackie and me to the little kitchen area behind the store and set out cookies and a glass of milk for us. We sat across from each other and I kept staring at Jackie because I had never seen a Jewish boy with such deep blue eyes. After that day, we always walked home together, and the cookies and milk were always a welcome treat.

The Tanzers treated us with respect. We attributed that to the fact that Mrs. Tanzer had been born in Russia. Those Jews we met who were born in America had little concept of the immigrant experience. Just because we were not fluent in their language, they assumed we were not intelligent or competent. The Tanzers always spoke to us as equals and earned my father's loyalty. When he needed to buy a piece of clothing, he always went to Tanzer's.[32]

After a few weeks, my parents told me we were moving to another town, called West Kelso, and I would need to change schools. This time I didn't mind leaving that school. But I was going to miss Jackie. We met again only once a year for the Jewish High Holidays services held in the Longview Masonic lodge. Jackie and I would sit on the marble steps inside the lodge and talk about our favorite episodes from popular

Leo & Thilde Kelso, 1941.

radio shows (i.e., *The Lone Ranger* and *Red Ryder*). After the war started, we also listened to Hop Harrigan, Ace of the Airways. He was the best.

We moved into an unfurnished apartment across from a high, wide dike that ran along the Cowlitz River. The large Victorian house had been divided into two apartments. The

---

[32] Jacob (Jackie) Tanzer became an important part of the Oregon judiciary. His brother, Hershel, who was among the soldiers who liberated some Nazi concentration camps, and his wife Shirley, became a driving force for establishing the Holocaust Resource Center in Portland.

living room faced First Street with a view of the dike, which, at that time of year, was covered with a blanket of golden California poppies. The kitchen was a spacious room with a huge, black wood stove (just like my Oma's in Wopfing). A porch ran alongside the kitchen and ended in an ell-shaped area. A ringer-type washing machine and a laundry sink took up all that space. Beyond the washroom, surrounded by rough boards—like an afterthought—was a toilet and a shower. For handwashing, we used the kitchen sink.

House in West Kelso. Kohn apartment on the right, 1941.

Finally, it was time to send for the rest of our belongings from the wooden crate in Old Aunt's basement. Gussie said it might take a few weeks, but she would take care of everything. In the meantime, we had to buy furniture from the Goldberg Furniture store, which was owned by one of the other Jewish families in Longview. I had seen their daughter, who was a year older, at school, but just like the other two Jewish girls, she never acknowledged me.

Mr. Goldberg gave us a "good" deal by allowing my father to pay off the purchases over six months with no interest (ninety days being the usual time allotted for interest-free credit). He kept saying how much we should appreciate his generosity and how he would not do that for just anyone. "But your being refugees and all, it was the least I could do." (Later we found out that he had boosted the prices to make up for the lost interest.) It was the first time, and probably the last time, my parents had bought anything on credit.

I slept in the living room on a fold-out couch that I used for the next ten years. (In Longview, then in Portland where I finally had my own room for about a year, but I still slept on that couch with the crack in the middle.) For the first time in their married life my parents slept in a double bed (like Americans) that barely fit into the tiny bedroom on the other side of the kitchen. When our featherbeds and eider down pillows arrived, we finally felt like we were living in our own space.

Chapter 38

Catlin Grade School in West Kelso, Washington, was my eighth school. It was a two-story brick building with windows all around. The desks were the same, old-fashioned type with the seat attached to the desk behind it. Ink wells were at the top right-hand corner of each desk, and we were now ready to begin writing cursive with real, straight-nib pens, which needed constant dunking into the ink wells. If students were left-handed, the teacher admonished them to use their right hands to write, no matter how difficult it might be.

The playground had an extremely high slide; six swings with wooden boards for seats attached to thick, iron-link chains; and several teeter-totters (seesaws) with muddy gravel under the seats. A set of monkey bars was set firmly onto a slab of cement. Most days someone went to the nurse's office with blood somewhere on their body from being hit by the wooden swings or falling off the monkey bars. Iodine took care of most wounds, and nobody thought to call a parent since few people even had a telephone.

At the very edge of the playground, at a distance from the school building, stood an old, gnarled tree. In the trunk, some holes were deep enough for a child my size to hide inside. The branches spread out to cover almost half the playground, and the root system spread to all parts of that muddy field, ready to trip an unaware, running child. Those branches were made for climbing and that tree became my first friend at that school. It seemed like something out of a fairy tale, and I called it my "Golden Oak."

The second day, at recess, I was walking toward the side door that led to the playground when I noticed a frightfully thin girl in front of me. She had a brace on her left leg, which she was dragging along behind her as she slowly made her way to the outside door. (Later, I learned her name was Louise and she had survived polio.) I walked by Louise that morning, trying not to stare at her leg, but that brace was an interesting contraption. It had two steel rods, held together by square pieces of leather on each side of her leg. Leather straps were buckled around her upper thigh and around her ankles to hold the rods in place.

From the way she was struggling to move ahead, the brace must have been very heavy. Her long, brown braids swung from side to side with her effort to walk. I passed by her as we were going out the door, and after a few steps, I heard a muffled scream behind me. I turned around to see a circle of boys and girls around Louise, laughing and pointing as she struggled to get back on her feet. I could hardly believe that one of those kids had knocked her down, but it was obvious from their giggles that one of them had done just that. I pushed through the circle of giggling children and helped her to stand. Her round, little face was red with effort and completely serious as she pushed me away, saying "I'm okay, I'm okay."

A tall, thin and pale girl came up beside us. Louise linked her arm into Veronica's and the two of them walked away without another word to me. A few days later I learned that Veronica had a heart condition. She was not allowed to run or play any games with other children, so she and Louise became best friends.

I didn't become friends with Louise, as I had enough problems without being teased for playing with "the cripple." However, on one occasion I knocked down a boy who was teasing her. He tore a hole in my skirt; I pulled a handful of dirty, blond hair from his scalp. We wound up in the principal's office, but no one teased or knocked down Louise for the rest of the school year.

Walking to school meant passing a row of small, dilapidated cottages with dirt patches in front and clutter on each side. The next block had brick apartments, and nearer the school were two blocks of nicely-painted houses with well-kept lawns, similar to the pictures in the *Dick and Jane* stories.

The first few days I walked to school and back alone. One day, as I walked by the scruffy cottages, a girl came out and started to walk the same route. I said, "Hello," and she just looked at me with big, brown eyes. I kept walking waiting for her to say something.

"What's your name?" she asked as she wiped her runny nose on her sweater sleeve. I noticed that her sweater was torn and dirty, as was her dress. Her light-brown hair was plastered to her head like a helmet. She came up beside me and I was aware of a bad smell coming from her body. I told her my name and walked a little faster to keep a distance between us.

She told me her name was Margie, and that the girl coming up behind us was her twin sister named Nancy. They did not look alike at all. Nancy was very thin, her hair was so light it looked white, as did her eyebrows and lashes. Margie had a round, plump face with a turned-up nose. I thought she was cute and would have liked to look like her.

The twins' personalities were totally different. Margie was full of energy and we made a good team. We invented games and got others to join in. Our games were rough and required physical strength and courage. Lots of running, wrestling, and tree climbing to steal fruit (King of the Hill and Boys Catch the Girls, etc.).

My mother took pride in sending me off to school in clean, ironed dresses or skirts every morning. She had hand sown my skirts, and the waistbands ripped easily when pulled on; she spent many hours resewing them. I changed into play clothes when I got home from school, but even these faded and partially-outgrown garments needed washing and mending daily.

On the corner, just before crossing to the school, was a greengrocer. A colorful display of vegetables and fruit was already out in front of the store by the time I walked by each morning. Inside, I could see barrels of grain and nuts, and behind the counter were shelves of sundries, such as toothpaste, candy and soap. The proprietors were a young Japanese couple. Their daughter, Miko, sometimes walked across to the school with me. On the way home, Miko's mother treated us to a few grapes, an apple or a plum. On sunny afternoons, we sat on a box in the back of the store for a few minutes while we ate the fruit. Miko didn't have time to play; she had to help in the store and in the apartment upstairs.

Miko was the only other person in that school who had jet-black hair like mine, and from the back, we looked like sisters. She liked to read the same books I liked, and I often brought her books when I started going to the library. We never had much time to talk. She did tell me that she was still in the first grade because she was short, and that she was almost eight years old. At school she was called Mary, but at home her family called her Miko. She told me her parents could not say "R."

During the last week of school Miko, told me she always spent the summer at her grandmother's berry farm to help with the harvest. I told her about my summers at my grandmother's house. Miko told me she called her grandmother "Oba-a." It sounded a lot like Oma-ma, which is what I called my grandmother. It turned out that our grandmothers had much in common. They were in business, were extremely strict, and in spite of the fact that they often scolded us for running around in the woods and climbing trees, we loved them very much. (It didn't occur to me that I would never see Oma-ma again.)

A celebration was planned for the end of the school year. Each grade performed a skit or a dance. The second grade learned how to square dance. At first it was confusing to follow the caller, but little by little I caught on, and it was great fun. By the end of the week, I knew all the calls—and I still remember them.

Chapter 39

Summer of 1941

Now we lived in a totally flat landscape, and I could finally skate along the sidewalk for miles. A few days after school was out, I started to skate along First Street in the direction of Main Street. When I got to the corner of Main and First Street I turned right and just kept going. I breezed along the flat, even sidewalks until suddenly the façade of the Columbia Theater rose in front of me.

I was surprised that I had skated all the way to Longview. Now I had to find my way back. It had taken me about an hour to get to the Columbia Theater. I had hardly noticed that the terrain made a slight downward slope from West Kelso to Longview. Going back would take a lot longer. By the time I arrived back at our apartment the sun was setting. My parents were in hysterics, and I was exhausted.

My father spewed a tirade at me about how I had worried my mother. I had never seen him so enraged. He threatened to beat me to death if I ever did such a thing again, and he used a lot of other words, mostly in German, which I didn't understand. My mother tried, in vain, to calm him down. This was the first time I had seen him so out of control. But sadly, it was not the last time. He took my skates away; I never saw them again.

(Much later I learned about his bouts of unreasonable anger and his horrible nightmares. He would scream, twisting in agony among sweat soaked sheets. These were the result of the trauma he suffered in Dachau).

Early that summer I worked up the courage to cross the high bridge that spanned the Cowlitz River to find the county library our teacher had told us about. After hurrying across the bridge (taking quick looks at the rushing water underneath), I walked to the next corner, turned right as I had been told to do, then walked along the quiet, tree-lined street for what seemed like forever. I was beginning to think I was lost, when suddenly I saw the big black letters over the doors of a low, white building: Cowlitz County Public Library.

I ran up the four steps, walked up to the raised desk, opened my sweaty palm, and put the quarter I had been clutching onto the counter. The lady behind the desk asked if I wanted a library card. When I said "yes," she handed me a file card to fill in with my name, address and a parent's signature. She pushed the quarter back toward me and said to bring it back with the card filled out.

I was not about to walk the mile back home, over that long, scary bridge, without a book to show for it. Besides, it had been a tiring argument with my mother to get that quarter, which she might want back; she wasn't sure that the library was worth such an investment.

I walked back to the commercial street and went into the restaurant on the next corner, borrowed a pencil from the waitress, and filled out the card, signing my father's name. (It was the shorter of the two.) My library adventures had begun.

Since it rained all of June and often throughout the whole summer, I spent many hours at the library, discovering *Raggedy Ann & Andy* and *Little Nemo* (not the fish, but a boy who had many adventures). I found *The Adventures of Tom Sawyer* late that summer, and by third grade, I was reading the unabridged fairytales of the Grimm Brothers (gruesome stories that my mother had edited for my benefit). I loved *Paul Bunyan* and his blue ox called Babe, and I learned about lumberjacks and what my father was doing at Weyerhaeuser Lumber Mill.

On Saturday afternoons I walked across the bridge to the

movies and fell in love with those singing cowboys, alternating between Gene Autry and Roy Rogers (who was just too cute for my taste). After the movies, the library wasn't far. I stopped in to find books to take home in a brown paper bag, which needed replacing almost every week. (Why didn't I use the leather backpack that I had used for books in Vienna? Because no one in America used such a bag, and I never used it again. It was the most useless thing my mother brought along).

On sunny days I spent most of the day outside, running around, pretending to be a cowboy fighting imaginary Indians. After seeing several *Tarzan* movies, I began climbing the many trees around the yard (the area used to be an orchard), pretending to be "Jane," Tarzan's mate, and fighting off invading armies of one type or another.

Some days I went to explore the dike across the street. (Thankfully, my mother never knew how often I nearly fell into the Cowlitz River.) The willow trees and myriad bushes became the ideal place to pretend to be "Naomi of the Jungle," the lead character in a short serial drama shown between double features. She became my role model—brave, clever, strong, fighting for the rights of decent people, and outsmarting the evil men who tried to stop her.

Most of my friends were boys, who were rather interchangeable. We played cowboys and Indians, rustlers or outlaw gangs among the apple trees in our yard or across the street on the dike. I never invited the boys to my house because I knew my mother would think them rude and dirty. One at a time, boys could be good company, but when two or more of them were together they were capable of perpetrating mindless brutality. To be friends with a group of boys, I had to show I was as tough or tougher than they were.

The Catlin swimming pool was about a ten-minute walk from my house, and once I had discovered it, I went there every day (rain or shine). I taught myself how to stay above the water by going to the three-foot end of the kiddy pool where I could hardly keep my head above water. Flailing my arms, I made my way to the two-foot-deep end. Doing this over and over I eventually trusted the water enough to slow my strokes. I convinced my mother to spend the money for swimming lessons. Before the end of the summer I had learned to swim three different strokes and how to dive off the lower board. The pool featured several boards of varying height, and by the next summer I was the only girl to dive from the fifteen-foot board. By the time I was ten, I could jack knife and back flip. From the thirty-foot board I only did cannonballs, often touching the bottom of the ten-foot-deep pool.

The children from my immediate neighborhood didn't go to the pool, which cost ten cents, or to a movie, which cost eleven cents. Their parents said they could not afford the twenty-five cents for an annual library card or the eleven cents for a comic book. I had been sheltered from dire poverty. I never went without clean clothes, or (even in Vienna) without nourishing food. Now I met children who rarely ate a full meal, who wore the same dirty clothes day after day. The twins sometimes had to take turns going to school because, for a short time, they only had one pair of shoes between them.

I was surprised, disappointed, and fearful to find such dire poverty and ignorance in *America*. My fears only grew deeper when I encountered vile racism and anti-Semitism in every place I lived and in all the fourteen schools I attended.

The birthday of America was approaching. We had learned a little bit about the Declaration of Independence just before school was out. But I had no idea what the Fourth of July meant or what would happen on that day. That morning I was on my way to Rita's house (she lived in an apartment above one of the many taverns on Main Street) when the whole world seemed to explode around me. I stood still, frozen with fear, trying not to scream. Was that gunfire? Were they going to shoot me?

The explosions kept coming up from the front yards of the houses that were a few feet lower than the sidewalk. I saw some boys hiding along the retaining wall just below me. They ran out and started throwing explosive objects onto the sidewalk right beside my feet. I heard them laugh. Helpless to stop myself, I started screaming, and the louder I screamed, the more they laughed.

Finally, my mind cleared enough to run home. Sobbing, I collapsed on the bed couch in the living room. It was our neighbor, Laura Jean (she and her husband shared the other side of the old house), who came over and explained the fireworks. She had seen me run home and heard the explosions. Leaning heavily on her crutch (her right leg was much shorter and almost useless due to having polio as a young child), she pulled herself into the living room. She sat down on the couch, took me into her arms, held me for a little while and then began to talk in her soft, southern drawl, explaining the meaning of the Fourth of July and how Americans tended to celebrate this holiday.

Laura Jean was a slight, pretty girl, with long brown hair which she tied back with a ribbon, which always matched her dress. She was kind and thoughtful. She helped my mother navigate the neighborhood and showed her how to prepare food on a wood stove. She baked cookies, which she shared with us, and often told us stories about her life in Tennessee. I am not proud of the fact that I felt a bit uneasy around her because she had been afflicted with polio. We knew it was a highly contagious disease, and no one knew exactly how it was contracted. Her husband, who worked at the other mill (Long Bell), never said a word to us; if he came home and found Laura Jean talking to any of us, he took her arm and pulled her inside their apartment.

Crystal Pool, Kelso, WA 1942.

It was Laura Jean who told us about the public park with a swimming hole called Crystal Pool. Almost every Sunday during that summer of 1941, my parents and I walked the three miles along the river, then uphill for two miles on a forest trail road that was barely wide enough for one car. My dad (I had started calling my parents "Mom" and "Dad" by then) would carry the backpack from his hikes in Austria, filled with snacks and drinks. My mom and I carried towels and bathing suits. All three of us would stop and hold our breath when a car went by, kicking up huge clouds of dust. Sometimes a car would stop, and we were offered a ride. People began to recognize us, and this happened more often.

It was worth the ordeal of climbing over that dusty hill to the lush meadow. It was surrounded by tall trees that climbed up a steep hill on both sides of a narrow river. The park had picnic tables, a latrine, and a faucet for drinking water. The terrain reminded us of Austria.

I had learned to swim well enough to get across the river to the rope that was tied to a tree branch. The rope allowed swimmers to swing out over the murky water and drop down several feet into the deep pool in the middle of the river. My mother told me that she watched with raw nerves as I flew out over the river, and she held her breath until I came to the surface.

Chapter 40

Third grade was my most memorable school year. I liked my teacher, and she taught my favorite subjects—history and geography. Most of the time I read ahead of the class assignments and expanded my knowledge with books recommended by the librarian at the Kelso library.

That year I learned the skills and gained the knowledge useful for the rest of my life. Miss Davis, a wise and patient young woman (who reminded me of Mitzi), shared her pleasure of learning about the world. She made Columbus, Magellan, Sir Francis Drake, Vasco de Gama, De Soto, and Captains Gray, Cook and Cabot come alive. She kept a huge world map on the wall where we could visualize what we were reading and follow the explorers around the globe.

Our studies took us across the prairie and over snow-covered mountain passes. We forded rivers with Lewis & Clark. I could visualize this better than most in the class because I had traveled across those same plains, rivers, and snow-covered mountains.

Since my father also loved history and geography, we spent most evenings talking about these subjects, looking at maps and researching the culture, climate, and religion of the countries on each continent. No one else I knew seemed interested in these subjects. Even the teacher was less than eager to answer any questions beyond what she was teaching.

In the fall I experienced my first Halloween; it was great fun. Margie explained about dressing up in costumes and going from door to door to ask for treats. She also explained about the "trick" part. We found some old rags in the back of Margie's house and cut holes for eyes. I am not sure what we decided to be, but we were either witches or pirates. We had swords made of sticks we found in the yard and a broom from my house; Margie's mother didn't have one.

We took brown paper bags from my mother's collection and a bar of soap from the bathroom, then we joined other "trick or treat" groups in ringing doorbells (or knocking if there was no bell). Mostly we got homemade cookies, fudge bars, or popcorn balls. If there was no answer, or if people didn't give us a treat, we soaped their windows, which was almost as much fun as getting a treat. (Did we soap windows even if we were given a treat? Sometimes.) For us naughty eight- and nine-year-olds, watching people clean their windows the next day was also fun.

During the year of 1941, I had become friends with Rita, who lived above one of the many taverns along Main Street in West Kelso. Rita's father, like Margie's father, worked in a sawmill, drank up his paycheck every Friday, and spent the weekend in bed. I only met Margie's mother once, as was the case with Rita's mother. Both these women looked like witches with long hair covering most of their faces. (Later, I learned this hairdo was meant to hide the bruises.) I was uncomfortable inside their living rooms, which were identically cluttered and smelled like garbage.

A well-groomed girl lived in a large house next door along First Avenue. One day we walked home from school together, and I invited her in for a snack. We ate cookies, drank a glass of milk, and then I went with her to see where she lived. Her house was set way back from the street. The lawn was like a green carpet, and the house looked well cared for, just like she did. Her name was Betty Davidson, and I remember it because it reminded me of the famous actress, Bette Davis.

Betty and I played together with paper dolls, who had adventures with fairies and witches. While Margie was my outdoor friend (I didn't dare bring her home), Betty and I played in the living room or on the wide, front porch. She never invited me to her house. One day, while walking home from school, she told me that she couldn't play with me anymore. When I asked why, she said, in a matter-of-fact tone, "Because you're Jewish."

I wanted to ask Betty who had told her we were Jewish, since I had never mentioned it, and why that was considered a reason not to play with me. But the words wouldn't come out. The knot of fear, which I had hardly noticed for several months now, seemed to grow again and sent chills throughout my body.

My mother could tell something was wrong when I came into the kitchen. She asked me if I felt all right. I lied and told her I was "okay" (an American expression we had learned), drank my milk, and went into the living room to find a book. After that day, Betty and I often walked home from Catlin School together, but always parted before we came to my door.

For the rest of my school years, I had only non-Jewish friends. Most of them were good friends; we enjoyed each other's company. But I avoided telling anyone that I was Jewish. Even then, I was always on my guard for that anti-Semitic word, phrase, or comment that would indicate how they really felt. Sometimes when I told a friend—even a longtime friend—that I was Jewish, something changed in their eyes, and sadly, I knew where I stood.

An example of this was when Margie and Nancy borrowed some comic books that I had bought with my weekly allowance of eleven cents. Months later, when I asked them to return the comic books, Margie said, "I know about Jews. You're greedy and stingy." I was shocked and asked where she had heard those things. "My mother told me!" she screamed, and she ran home. I realized then that we were not safe in America after all. (Not safe on this earth, to be honest. Why?)

Margie and I didn't play together for a couple of days, but eventually made up. I didn't get my comic books back, but I learned an important lesson: "Neither a borrower nor a lender be." Shakespeare's words are always relevant.

On Sunday morning, December 7th the broadcast of *The Scandinavian Hour,* which was one of my father's favorites because he always sang along with the Swedish songs he knew, was interrupted by a newsflash: "The Unites States Naval Base at Pearl Harbor, on the Hawaiian island of Oahu, has been attacked by Japanese bombers."

They played no more music on the radio that morning, only talk of what would happen next. The president gave a speech, and then a lot of other men talked and talked. My parents and I sat in stunned silence. It was hard to understand exactly what the reporters were saying, partly because they talked fast and partly because we didn't want to believe what was being said. Our young neighbor, Laura Jean, came over later that day and in her slow drawl explained what had happened.

The immediate result of the declaration of war on the Axis powers was that our family was now considered "enemy aliens" since we had German passports. My father, as the head of such a household, had to register with the authorities once a month to let them know his whereabouts. Ironically, he also had to register for the draft because he was under thirty-five years old. Fortunately, he was classified 4E because he was working for the lumber mill, which was regarded as an "essential industry." It was a dangerous and confusing time. The very idea of reporting to an authority— for anything—aroused feelings ranging from worry to abject terror in all three of us.

The next few weeks went by without much change in our lives, but one day it was announced on the radio that there would be an evacuation of Japanese people. Since we were not Japanese, we didn't pay much attention.

On my way to school a few days after my ninth birthday, I noticed that Miko's grocery store was closed. I never saw her again. Her disappearance reminded me of how my friends had disappeared from school in Vienna. The knot of fear that began on February 15, 1938 (which had begun to subside) began to expand in my belly. In school that day I learned that "those dirty Japs have been evacuated." I was filled with dread. Would we be next?

Gasoline and many other commodities were rationed, and the buses ran only twice a day. To get to work my father bought a bicycle. Every weekday morning, he rode the ten miles to the mill and back again, often in the rain, sometimes in the snow, and likewise in the summer heat. He had to leave at five o'clock in the morning to get to his green-chain position by seven.

New employees in the Weyerhaeuser lumber mill usually began by working on the green chain. The job consists of dragging waterlogged timber from the river with huge grappling hooks and maneuvering the heavy logs to the first set of saws that take off the bark. Only large, strong men can do this type of work, and due to the deafening screeching of the saws, they can only work there for a few weeks at a time. My father, five foot six and weighing 145 pounds, was there for more than a year. Eventually, "The Jew Boy" (which is what they called my father) was promoted to working in the lumber yard, stacking boards, which he did for another five years, in all kinds of weather. In the summers, the men had to take salt pills to keep from fainting; in the winter, they were drenched in the continuous rain.

During this time, while I was in the third grade and my father was working on the green chain, the school offered music lessons. My mother decided I should learn the violin. We rented an instrument from the music store in Longview, and I learned to read music and play songs. My favorite was "London Bridge Is Falling Down." I began to enjoy playing, though I hated to practice the scales.

This presented one serious problem. The only time I had for practicing was after school, which was near the time my father came home from the mill. He endured the screeching noise of a beginner violinist for a couple of months. One day he said, "She makes sounds like the saws in the mill. This has to stop." My violin lessons were over.

I had really wanted to play the guitar like my friend Jean, who was a couple of years older and lived in a nice little house around the block. I enjoyed hearing her play. According to my mother, this was a low-class instrument only played by uncivilized cowboys who sang with an irritating nasal twang.

Chapter 41

In January of 1942 we learned about the "smelt run" in the Cowlitz River across the street. One morning the sky was covered with seagulls and it was advisable to take an umbrella when going outdoors.

Laura Jean came to our door carrying a bucket and asked my mother if she wanted to get some smelt from the river. She explained that these tiny fish came swimming into the river for about a week every winter. "We can just scoop them up in a bucket and take them home."

We went with her across the street and over the dike, carrying our own bucket. The river was teeming, from bank to bank, with little, silvery fish. We watched Laura Jean scoop up a bucket and then she helped us do the same.

My mother had no idea of how to cook the tiny silvery fish. She boiled them in a pot of water which resulted in a flavorless, fishy mush. She dumped the mess under a rose bush that grew beside the house next door.

In the spring everyone marveled at the magnificent size, fragrance and deep color of the pink roses that bloomed on that bush.

The war news was frightening. The Japanese were conquering Island after island, heading eastward across the Pacific Ocean, and the Germans were crushing country after country in Europe under their black boots.

At school we said the Pledge of Allegiance every morning (without the inclusion of "under God," which was added in 1956) and sang patriotic songs. "God Bless America" and

"America the Beautiful" were favorites. I taught them to my parents by waving my hands to indicate the ocean, the prairie, mountains, etc. We sang these songs over and over with deep feelings of love and gratitude for this wonderful country. The words gave us courage, lifted our spirits, and expanded our hope for a better future.[33]

What did we do during those rainy days and evenings? (No television, no phonograph; just our little radio.) After school, when it was raining and I couldn't go out to play, I listened to the radio. My favorite shows were *The Lone Ranger* with his faithful companion, Tonto; *Red Ryder* and Little Beaver, his little Indian sidekick. *Hop Harrigan*, Ace of the Airways, became my favorite after the war started. I imagined myself in each story as a friend and sidekick of my heroes, but my hands were never idle. I crocheted, knitted and embroidered my way through all the adventures.

During the next two winters, my dad and I spent our evenings playing a marble game he had invented. The kitchen floor slanted steeply, which made rolling marbles a good game. He also played endless Old Maid card games with me. To this day, I admire his patience. My mother still told me stories at bedtime, but she never played any games and preferred reading the newspaper when her endless chores were done.

The Texaco oil company printed a colorful pamphlet that had a page for each of the forty-eight states. With this little book my Dad and I learned the name, configuration, location, capital, state flower, bird and major product of each state. When we had memorized everything in that pamphlet, he taught me the multiplication tables. We drilled for hours until I was flawless up to 12x12.

Mrs. Jensen, our landlady, came by each month to collect the rent. We were probably her only tenants who always had all the rent ready for her. My parents never asked for an extension or made a partial payment, like some of her other

---

33 "The White Cliffs of Dover" was another favorite that still brings tears to my eyes.

tenants from the shacks where Margie and Nancy lived.

One day she remarked, as my mother handed her the rent, "You Jews always have money." She made it clear that in her opinion the Jews were to blame for the war. When my father asked her why she thought that, her answer was, "The Jews always make a profit from any war."

Once a month during 1942, my parents walked to the Safeway store in Longview to buy groceries. The Piggly Wiggly in Kelso was closer, but everything cost a few cents more. West Kelso had no grocery stores, only taverns lined the streets on both sides for four blocks. Now that the Japanese greengrocer was gone, fresh fruit and vegetables were only available in the supermarkets.

Sometimes I went with them on a Saturday morning (if I was not going to the movies because I had bought a comic book instead). My father carried the backpack he had used during his hiking days in Austria; my mother carried her purse and a tote bag. When I came along, I brought a pillowcase to help carry whatever didn't fit into the bags and backpack.

The Safeway store was like no other store we had ever seen. People walked around pushing metal carts and picking whatever they wanted from the well-stocked shelves on every side. (We were accustomed to clerks handing us our purchases from behind a counter.) The variety of products made us dizzy. Yet, I often heard my mother lament the many foods that were not available in a small American town, like rye bread, fresh baked crusty rolls, pickled herring, and the stinky cheeses we used to eat for our cold suppers. Mom would sigh and say, "I'm sure they have those things in America"—by which, she meant New York. Fresh produce was expensive, so we bought mostly canned goods and got produce at the greengrocer.

Due to my mother's frugality (one-fourth of each paycheck went into the bank), in late summer of 1942 my Dad was able to buy a 1935 Chevrolet from a man who had been drafted. The seller of the car gave Dad a short driving lesson and handed him the car keys, title, and a warning to register the car as soon as possible. We didn't know if this might present a problem, since "enemy aliens" were not allowed to own or drive cars. However, everything went smoothly at the DMV since Dad was employed in a "vital to the war effort" job.

I inherited the man-sized bicycle. The seat was much too high for me to sit on even at the lowest setting, but I insisted on learning to ride immediately. Each day after work, tired as he must have been, Dad went out to the street with me to teach me how to ride that monstrous bicycle. For three afternoons he ran along beside me, holding the back fender and giving instructions. The fourth afternoon he let go and I was riding on my own. The sensation of freedom was thrilling!

Usually I rode the bicycle on the backstreets going towards Catlin School, but one time I rode out onto First Street, where I occasionally encountered a car. I admit I had one close call, when a car had to swerve around me. As luck would have it, Mrs. Jensen witnessed the incident. She told my weeping mother that I was a nuisance, an out-of-control delinquent, and worse, that I should be in reform school. I was relieved when Mom agreed not to tell my father about the incident. I was very afraid he would take the bicycle away as he had done with the skates.

Just as school was out, I came down with the measles. I had to stay in bed, in a darkened room. The doctor said I could go blind if I were exposed to too much light. I spent much of those two weeks in bed, fantasizing myself into my favorite radio program. Alternately I was a spy behind enemy lines or a war correspondent for the local newspaper. I had many close calls and even was captured by the Germans one time. Of course I escaped by outwitting my guards. I had almost as much fun as going to the movies. When I finally was able to get up, I was very weak and had to learn to ride the bicycle all over again.

Before school started, we drove to Portland, Oregon, to buy some school clothes. In those days it was a nerve-wracking journey of two hours on a winding road. Mom fell asleep in the backseat. When we came to a somewhat-straight stretch of road, Dad sped up the car to over thirty miles per hour. I gasped when I saw the speedometer. "Don't tell your mother," he admonished me.

In Portland we went to Meier & Frank Department Store, where I got new shoes and a pullover sweater to wear with the two skirts my mother had made for me. We stayed overnight with my parents' friends, Jack and Blanka Klinger, and their daughter, Ruthie, who was a bit younger than I was. Blanka and my mother had known each other from Vienna.

The Klingers had lived in Longview for a few months. During that time they came to visit us in West Kelso, always mentioning what a bad neighborhood it was and what true friends they were to come to visit us. I was always ordered to "play nicely with little Ruthie," whom I disliked. It pains me to reveal the following incident, but it had a lifelong impact on me.

Margie and I were playing Jacks with Ruthie, who cried each time she lost a round. Margie said she knew a game we could play. She told Ruthie to lie down on the ground, face-up. Then I took her wrists and Margie her ankles and we swung her back and forth, a little like a jump rope. At first Ruthie was scared but soon she was giggling. That's when Margie and I decided to drop her on her back. Ruthie was, fortunately, not badly hurt. Mostly, she was frightened and of course ran to tell her mother. It was a mean thing to do, and even before Ruthie hit the ground, I felt shame. It was an extremely uncomfortable feeling and I never wanted to feel it again.

In Portland, the Klingers lived in the neighborhood where we had lived on Corbett Street and near Failing School. I overheard conversations about how the Klingers couldn't stand living in a mill town like Longview. My mother agreed it was dismal. Even Portland was such a low brow city compared to Vienna, but any place was better than West Kelso.

Jack berated my father for doing all that manual labor. My father retorted that he was paid well and considered vital for the war effort. Jack had worked at the mill for a about a month and soon was eligible for unemployment.

The trips to Portland were always exciting, but I resented having to play with Ruthie Klinger. She was a real girl's girl, playing with dolls, dressing in her mom's clothes, having pretend tea parties, crying at the least provocation. Mealtimes were a stressful affair. Instead of putting a plate of food in front of her, as my mother did for me, Ruthie's mother asked her what she wanted and cooked special food just for her, which made me jealous. We always stayed overnight, which meant sharing a bed with Ruthie—one more ordeal to endure.

I could tell that my parents were always a little nervous about traveling into another state. As enemy aliens, we had many restrictions to consider. It still seems strange to me that my thirty-four-year-old father was considered eligible for the draft *and* had to go to a federal office to report his whereabouts. What made this demeaning exercise so ironic was that the U.S. government didn't consider his German passport for immigration status[34] because he was born in an area the U.S. government recognized as Czechoslovakia. On the other hand, the government recognized the German passport for designating him an Enemy Alien. Either way, he was left out of the military draft. But he was frozen to the job at the lumber mill for the duration.

---

[34] At that time, a quota system was established for immigration based on how many people from a certain country were already here. The population included many Germans, but few Czechs. This meant that if someone were considered German, they had a better chance of getting into the U.S.A. Austrians were now considered German.

Chapter 42

In the fourth grade we doubled down on long division, complex multiplication, and a few (supposedly) simple fractions. Nothing about fractions was simple until our teacher, Miss Holt, drew a pie chart, and then it all fell into place.

Miss Holt was a young woman with dark, short curls and a pretty, round face that was marred by the fact that she had only one eye. She seemed to be winking at us, even during her sternest admonitions to "Be quiet!"

Compared to third grade, this school year was boring, but we were taught some important information. One of the subjects was about the structure of the government, how each of the three branches worked to provide checks and balances so that no singular person—not even one branch—could control the whole country. Making charts about how a bill is introduced in congress then travels through the system until it becomes law was not as exciting as discovering new lands with the navigators. However, that information is vital if someone wants to be a good citizen—and that was certainly a priority in our family.

Fourth graders were expected to form a glee club and learn how to read music. After Thanksgiving, Miss Holt spent hours writing Christmas Carols on the blackboard. We copied them into our school notebooks. Two weeks before Christmas the class began to sing the songs every day, over and over. No one asked me if I wanted to sing about the adoration of a figure I didn't believe in or care about. It was an uncomfortable few weeks. I liked the music and singing in general, but even at ten years old, I felt it was demeaning to an important religion to force children in a public school to utter words they did not believe.

Catlin School, West Kelso. Ruth: 2nd row, 3rd student from the left. Louise: front row, 2nd from right, 1943.

In the summer of 1943, while the war raged in Europe and in the Pacific war zone and the Americans and Australians were regaining some islands from Japan, my life went on much as it had the summer before. Some of that time was spent recovering from chickenpox, which was shorter but fiercer than the measles. The itching was unbearable. I was warned that scratching would cause the pock marks that marred the skin of so many people in those days. I was lucky to have only one pock mark on my left temple (which had almost disappeared, as predicted, by the time I was married eight years later).

During that summer we heard that Miss Davis was getting married in the fall. I really loved her and wanted to give her a wedding present. Having crocheted several sets of anti-macassars that looked good on our sofa (my fold-out bed) and overstuffed chair, I sent for a pattern out of the newspaper.

(Patterns were featured once a week in the Ladies Section of the Longview Daily News.) It was a complicated pineapple pattern, but I worked on it every day during the afternoon radio serials.

Moving into the next room for fifth grade was a depressing experience. This room had the same number of windows as the other rooms, but huge trees kept the light out. The teacher was a man who ignored the girls. He made it clear to us that educating the boys was his priority. If the girls learned something in the process, it was mere coincidence.

One example of this man's lack of empathy was the time I fainted from a tuberculosis test injection. When I started getting dizzy after getting back into the classroom from the nurse's office, I put my head down on my desk in a momentary blackout. Mr. teacher (I never did bother to learn his name) began to yell at me to sit up. I heard him; I wanted to comply, but then he pulled me up by the hair. Did he notice that I was sweating, short of breath? Not at all. The note that was sent home showed a positive result for having had tuberculosis. It was possible, of course, but it must have been an extremely light case because no doctor ever found a trace of it in my lungs.

That fall of 1943 was memorable. First, I started to get terrible cramps in my lower abdomen every school morning. Then I noticed a sore feeling in my breast area. Wrestling with the boys was no longer a fun game because some of them punched me in the chest just to hear me scream. They knew what they were doing, but I had no idea what was happening to my body. No one had ever spoken to me about "puberty" and that I should expect changes in my body. It was all a complete surprise to me.

One morning I noticed hair in my pubic area. Since my mother and I never talked about any matter that concerned "down there," I put on my clothes as usual and walked to school, trying to ignore the cramps, as I had been told to do.

A few months earlier, Laura Jean had shown me how to

curl my hair by rolling strands into strips of cloth dipped in sugar water. When the cloth was dry and removed, my hair was still totally straight. It was a waste of rationed sugar. Ironically, a week after discovering the pubic hair the hair on my head began to get kinky and fuzzy. My mother tried to braid it, but it was still too short.

Thilde trying to curl Ruth's hair. Outside kitchen in West Kelso, 1943.

On Sunday afternoons during the early fall of 1943, my friends from the neighborhood gathered on the dike to play among the trees and shrubs. We pretended to be outlaws escaping from the law or the posse that was pursuing the cattle rustlers. One of us might pretend to see a German submarine in the river and we would throw rocks (torpedoes) to sink it.

I thought of two boys—one in sixth grade and one in my class—as my boyfriends. We had played together since the second grade. Sometimes one or the other would walk me home (just across the street), or we would sit under a bush and talk about what we wanted to be when we were grown up.

The last time I spoke to this group of friends was a shocking surprise. It was a Sunday afternoon, and five of the youngsters, whom I thought were my friends, were sitting in a circle around a pile of rocks. They were pretending to have a campfire. I walked up to them along a narrow trail lined with thistles, careful not to brush against the clinging balls.

"There's the Jew girl!" one of the boys yelled out.

"Hey, dirty Jew brat, go away!" Margie barked. Then they all began to shout insults and call me names I had never heard.[35]

All five of them got up and began to throw thistles into my thick, black, very fuzzy hair. I just stood there in shock. I didn't want to get into a physical fight. There was a time when I might have done just that, but I was too sad. I knew they wanted me to cry, to run away, but I kept standing there. Then I told them that thistles were actually good for the hair and they might as well cover my head with them. They kept throwing thistles, which soon covered most of my hair.

Eventually they lost interest in the game and walked away. I went home. It took hours to wash and comb the thistles out of my thick hair. My mother kept asking why I would do

---

[35] Every Sunday morning Father Coughlin, a Catholic Priest from Boston, had a popular radio show. My friends had probably heard him speak about evil Jews.

such a stupid thing. I said what most children say when they can't explain their feelings, even to themselves: "I don't know."

Thilde, Ruth & Leo, West Kelso, 1943.

Feelings were becoming more and more important in my life—both physical and mental. A major event that had lifelong effects occurred one Saturday at a movie that would probably have been R-rated in later years because of the violence. During the film, a Nazi cell of spies in an American city kidnapped a young man who worked for the federal printing office, where he was involved with printing paper money. The Nazis offered him money to print counterfeit bills. (He had a wife and several children and lived in a modest apartment.) He refused. The kidnappers stripped him and whipped him for hours until he was a bloody, sweaty mess.

My ten-year-old brain began to absorb this horror. The stress was overwhelming. Suddenly I felt a strange—but not unpleasant—feeling rise from my groin and travel through my spine into my whole body. As the beating continued, the victim screamed in agony. I became engulfed in a feeling of pleasure. The movie had a happy ending. The young man was reunited with his wife and children, and I almost forgot about the episode of losing control of my body.

However, it came back whenever I was stressed or afraid, and eventually I found the area between my legs that could reproduce a faint replica of that sensation. Six years later I learned that this had been my first orgasm. As a result, terror and sexual pleasure were permanently linked in my brain. It's an example of the permanent damage caused by sexual abuse of a child.

My short-lived exposure to the Girl Scouts happened one afternoon when I accompanied a friend to a meeting. Several girls my age were gathered in a room at the local community center. Immediately I noticed they were dressed in brown uniforms. I stayed for a few more minutes, hoping the knot of fear in my stomach would subside, but when two older girls dressed in military-looking, green uniforms came into the room I made a hurried exit. With my heart pounding and my stomach churning, I ran all the way home. I have never lost my aversion to uniforms to this day.

Chapter 43

In November of 1943, Mrs. Jensen offered to reduce the rent for us if my father would do some of the yardwork around the two buildings that sat side by side on the lot, surrounded by apple trees. The house next to ours had a huge rosebush on one side and large hydrangeas below the front porch. My father trimmed the rose bush and cut the hydrangeas to half their original size. It was November, so none of these shrubs had leaves.

When Mrs. Jensen saw the hydrangeas she began to scream at my father, "You dirty Jew! You deliberately killed my beautiful bushes! I want you out of your apartment within thirty days or I will have you arrested for destroying my property." As an afterthought she added, "Maybe you are even German spies."

We were stunned by the hostility and anti-Semitism. Did everyone in America feel this way? How long before they came to kill us? So many people in that area owned guns. They hung rifles over their fireplaces or on a wall near the front door. At school I heard the boys brag about the handguns their fathers had, and how they went out to the rock quarry to target shoot.

Once again, Laura Jean gave us valuable information. When she heard that we were moving, she came by one morning during Christmas Vacation. Our things were ready for the moving van, so my mother, Laura Jean and I sat on one of the packing boxes, while Laura Jean told us about the sermons of Father Coughlin.[36] Her husband had told her that the mill he worked for, Long-Bell, would never hire a Jew like Weyerhaeuser had done. He had heard that even one of the accountants there was Jewish. (We knew Mr. Voremberg, who was also a refugee from Vienna.) Laura Jean gave me a hug, told me she would miss me, and then she was gone.

My father arrived home from the mill when the moving truck arrived. My mother and I rode with the movers in their big truck (which was almost empty since we didn't have much furniture), to give directions. Dad brought the car and a few grocery bags.

The one–bedroom apartment my mother had found in Longview was in a four-plex just at the edge of town. No more sidewalks beyond the corner of Hemlock Street. We now had a real bathroom with a bathtub; a living room, where I was to sleep on the fold-out sofa again; and a Franklin stove in one corner, next to my favorite and only armchair. The apartment had a dining nook with space for a small table and four chairs. The kitchen, a tiny space with room for one person at a time, had a "modern" wood stove and an ice box that held a twenty-five-pound block of ice. (The iceman came once a week.)

Laura Jean had told my parents about a used furniture store in Kelso where they bought a sturdy table and four chairs (made at Doernbecher Furniture Manufacturing Company in Portland, Oregon), which they delivered that evening. (The set is still in use by our family after seventy-five years . . . on its way to becoming a genuine antique.)

I spent Christmas vacation helping my mother arrange things in the apartment. We had plenty of cupboard space, and we spent days lining every shelf and drawer with newspaper. She explained that newspaper keeps the cockroaches away; when it turns yellow, you know it's time to change the paper.

---

[36] Father Coughlin was a popular Catholic Priest who spouted anti-Semitism to his congregation every Sunday morning, which was broadcast nationwide. His magazine carried articles defaming Jews and other refugees.

Mathilde & Leo Kohn. Longview, Washington 1944.

On Monday, January 3, 1944, my mother and I walked the mile to St. Helens Grade School to enroll me. The principal must have noticed that, according to my transcript, this was my seventh school in the United States. He raised his eyebrows but made no comment. After my mother filled out the required forms—with considerable help from me—the principal took me to one of the fifth-grade classes. It was a big school with two classes for each grade. Mrs. Bell, a tall, gray-haired lady, adjusted her gold-rimmed glasses and gave me a stern look. She assigned me a seat toward the front of the room, one row over from the tall windows that took up one whole wall. I was relieved to find a well-groomed girl at the window-row desk next to me. In fact, as I looked around the room the students all looked clean and tidy.

The class seemed to be a bit ahead of Catlin's fifth grade in arithmetic and reading material. Mrs. Bell gave me an outline of the curriculum. Among the subjects were literature, poetry and music. This looked like it would be fun. She spent the time before recess going over the material the class had covered to date.

Recess was awkward and lonely. The girls walked arm-in-arm in small groups, circling the large, cement slab that was the playground. (The school had no play equipment.) The boys played ball games. I stood in the doorway of the side door, shivering in the cold wind, and much relieved when the bell rang.

Lunch was eaten at our desks; after a toilet break, we went outside. The wind had died down, and the sun shone brightly in a deep blue sky. I looked around at the landscape. It was totally flat except for the hills of Kelso far in the distance. One of the teachers, monitoring the playground, stopped a group of four girls and introduced me. I linked arms with one of the girls on the end of the row. She didn't say anything, but her nod indicated that it was okay to walk with them. They kept on chatting with each other, totally ignoring me.

I walked home alone that day, as most of the students lived in the opposite direction. The next day while walking home—feeling alone but enjoying the unseasonably warm sun on my back—I noticed a small girl walking ahead of me. As I got nearer, she stopped and waited for me to catch up with her. For a few moments we stood looking at each other. On that day, she was still much shorter than I was, barely coming up to my shoulder. I envied her smooth blonde hair, pure white skin, and gray-green eyes. (For years I had been praying each night that I would wake up in the morning with that coloring.)

She said, "Hi."

I said, "Hi."

We started walking side by side on the narrow, dusty trail that ran parallel to 30th Avenue. A grassy field edged with blackberry bushes stretched out to our right. We talked all the way to where I lived on the corner of Hemlock Street and 30th Avenue. She lived about two blocks further along 30th Avenue, which was a designated "rural" area.

I don't remember what Shirley Jo Rimkus and I talked about that afternoon. We did agree that we didn't like Mrs. Bell, we liked to ride bicycles, and were very curious about each other.

Gradually, I learned that Shirley's father and mother both worked at a lumber mill (Long-Bell) and that, at the ripe, old age of ten, she was set on being a nurse and believed in Santa Claus. I told her we had moved to Longview from West Kelso, where I had played with some very rough kids. We agreed that we didn't like bullies and would rather be friends with everyone at school.

Several boys and one girl obviously resented my presence at their school. Every day, one of the boys or the "tough girl" would start picking a fight with me. Since my only friend was Shirley, who barely came up to my shoulder and had a reputation for timidity, I was alone and an easy target. Most days I spent my lunch hour fighting with one or the other of the playground bullies. They would come up behind me, pull my braids (long and very thick), kick my butt and call me names. "Nigger" was a popular one, as my hair was jet black and fuzzy. They knew I came from West Kelso and kept yelling I should go back there.

Eventually I beat up each bully in turn. The "tough girl" got some scratches in her face and clumps of hair pulled out of her head until I was able to knock her down and sit on top of her. With my knees holding down her arms, I twisted her nose with one hand until she cried "Uncle" (meaning "I give up"). After that fight, the bullies left me alone, and "tough girl" and I became allies—but not really friends. I found out she was not allowed to play with Jews.

For the rest of the school year, Shirley and I rode our bikes to school, waiting for each other when we had to fix a flat tire. (During the war, rubber was a rare product, and our tires were full of patches.) Mrs. Bell tried her best to separate us. She scolded us when we came in late together, and she admonished Shirley that she had always been on time before I came along. She never listened to our excuses about flat tires, but she kept me after school on several occasions so that we each had to get home alone.

Chapter 44

On the Sunday morning just before my eleventh birthday, I developed a stomachache. The stabbing pain came in waves and got more severe with each incident. My father decided it must be constipation and gave me castor oil to take. When the second dose didn't help and the pain was getting unbearable, my mother went to the manager's apartment, two doors away, to use the telephone to call a doctor. (In those days, doctors made house calls, even on Sunday.)

The doctor diagnosed acute appendicitis and ordered my father to drive me to the hospital at once. "If the appendix bursts, she could die of blood poisoning," he said. He also told my anxious parents that a laxative was the worst thing one could give a person with that condition.

The surgery was done at the last minute. The St. Joseph Hospital had no children's ward, and I was in a room with five other women who were recovering from hysterectomies, obstetrical problems, and the removal of several other organs. I heard all the conversations with the nurses (who were nuns in full white habits) and doctors (all old men). It was an education in anatomy.

Due to the wartime shortage of sutures, my incision was not sewn but clamped with metal clips. They were very painful and left a deep scar. The anesthetic used was ether; even a whiff of ether now still makes me dizzy and faint.

During my ten-day hospital stay, Marcia Cohen came to see me. Mrs. Cohen, a divorced woman about my mother's age (a rare case in those days), lived at the Monticello Hotel, the tallest and most elegant building in Longview. She sold real estate (a rare occupation for a woman). She had a son who was a star athlete at R.A. Long High School. Marcia taught Bible classes to several of us Jewish youngsters every Sunday.

She brought me a book, *The Story of Doctor Wassel*, to read while in the hospital. It was not suitable for most eleven-year-old girls. But I read it cover-to-cover at least twice and looked up words I didn't understand. (Gary Cooper played Dr. Wassel in the movie version. He was perfect for the part.)

It was about that time when I began to fantasize about being an important spy, working with Hop Harrigan, Ace of the Airways, who in my mind looked a lot like Gary Cooper. Together, we were helping the Allies win the war. In my fantasy, my name was Genevieve and I was related to General Eisenhower. The book helped me fill in some details about war I would never had known.

Since we didn't have a telephone, I'm not sure how my parents communicated with the school. But they let Mrs. Bell know that I would not be coming to school for the next two weeks and to send homework along with Shirley, who knew where I lived. Shirley had never actually come into our apartment. (I had been to her house a time or two during that first month we knew each other.)

For the next two weeks, Shirley stopped by to bring me assignments from Mrs. Bell and pick up my finished ones to take back to school. We drank Ovaltine, which I hated and she liked; we munched on cookies; and we chatted a bit with my mother. Shirley didn't seem to notice the hesitant, accented English with which my mother questioned her about her family. Shirley didn't ask about our origins, and I never told her we were Jewish.

When I got back to school, things had not changed. The girls still walked around, arm-in-arm, at recess and lunch, and the boys played ball games or teased the girls. During one lunch hour, a boy came up behind me and tore the ribbons off my braids. My hair would have draped down past my shoulders if it had been normal hair, but it was very thick, curly and stuck straight out from my head when it was loose. It was a strange and frightening sight. When I went to class after lunch Mrs. Bell sent me to the principal's office and he sent me home. He told me that I was a distraction. I didn't have my bicycle that day, so it took a half hour to walk home; I had no reason to go back to school. It was my first unexcused absent mark—and my last.

On a Saturday morning in late March of 1944, I woke up to find blood stains all over my sheet, and on my nightgown. I thought my appendix operation had opened and I was bleeding to death. I screamed "Mom!" at the top of my lungs, and when she saw the mess, she turned around and disappeared into the bedroom, leaving me to sob alone. When she came back, she took me to the bathroom, cleaned me up, put a garter belt on me, and attached a pad that came from a box marked "Sanitary Napkins" (I had seen these boxes at the grocery store and thought they were especially clean, table napkins.) Then she handed me a little book that had information about menstruation. Mom did not offer to answer questions, nor would she ever talk to me about the subject again.

Approximately a month later I began to get excruciating cramps. At first, I thought my appendix had grown back. When I woke up with these cramps and told my mother that I couldn't go to school in such pain, she said, "It can't be that bad." When I reread the little book about menstruation, I learned that some women suffer terrible, debilitating cramps. The suggestion was a hot water bottle on the abdomen and alternately rest and mild exercise, like walking. When I asked my mother about the continuing cramps, I got impatient answers like, "It can't be that bad." "I never had such cramps." "You started this much too early"—as if I had any control of that function.

One afternoon, just before school was out, I began to get a cramp that just kept getting worse and worse. I began to dig my fingernails into the wooden desk. I heard the teacher drone on and on, and then I heard the bell ring for the end of the school day. The cramps began to subside, so I tried to get up, but my fingernails were stuck in the desk. It took me several minutes to pull them out and the marks were visible on that desk for the rest of that school year. (For the next 27 years I endured a week of agony every month, except while pregnant.)

Sometime during that spring, I took my babysitting money, went uptown to a photographer, and had a picture taken of me with my braids. Then I went next door to a beauty shop and had my hair cut short. When I got home, Mom had a screaming fit. One would think I had cut off my nose. Having the picture placated her a bit, but she kept moaning about why had I not told her, as she would have wanted to save those beautiful braids.

Braids before haircut, 1944.

Shirley had little interest in my past. She did remark once about how I changed languages when my mother and I got into an argument. The fact that there were people who spoke another language was a new idea to her and to many people I met in the first few years in the United States.

One day, a reporter came to St. Helens school to talk to me. She had heard from someone that I was a refugee, and she asked if I would tell her something about my experiences. I told her where we came from, and what had happened to us in Vienna. She asked a lot of questions, and then she proposed we do an interview on the radio, telling something of what it was like to be Jewish in Europe. Then we would urge people to buy war bonds. One Saturday afternoon I went to the local radio station to what I thought would be a rehearsal, but it turned out to be the program.

I sat down in front of the microphone and talked about the nights we had to go shovel snow in the streets of Vienna.

As a result of that program, Shirley and my other friends found out we were Jewish. I knew that most of them didn't like Jews, so I had kept that part of my life a secret. Now everyone knew and I quickly found out who my real friends were.

Shirley had mixed feelings, but we stayed friends. She felt she had to tell me of an uncle who might have been Jewish because he was so stingy. She also explained that her parents avoided talking about religion because they had been disowned by their families when they married. (Her mother came from Swedish Lutherans, and her father from Catholic Lithuanians.) All that aside, Shirley believed in Santa Claus. This was hard for me to understand, and I must have said so. In December of 1944, at the age of eleven, Shirley found out the truth, cried for a week, and blamed me for her disillusionment.

Shirley Jo Rimkus had everything that I wanted out of life: She was blonde, petite,[37] with white skin, had a dog who loved her, played the piano, and had a room of her own and a big brother who gave her his outgrown jeans. She knew at the age of ten that she wanted to be a nurse, and had lived all of her life in one place, in a house her parents actually owned.

I knew they were not rich, not like the people who lived in grand houses around Lake Sacajawea in the middle of the town. But they were not poor like my family, who rented low-cost apartments and felt insecure at best and frightened of losing everything again at worst.

It's likely that Shirley envied my carefree existence. When I came home from school, I was met by a smiling mother with a cup of warm Ovaltine and cookies. I never had to make my bed (I slept on the living-room sofa) or do anything around

---

[37] She came up to my shoulder at that time. I was taller than most other students.

the house. Shirley's parents both worked at the lumber mill, so when she came home from school, she was met by a long list of chores which included feeding and milking the cow, feeding the chickens, and collecting eggs. Lastly, she had to practice the piano for at least a half-hour. I loved listening to her and her older brother, who played beautifully.

On June 7, 1944, the Allied troops landed in Normandy, France. The day would be commemorated as "D Day." I was in the middle of a bad case of the mumps with a high fever and terrible pain in my jaw and in my groin. The doctor said that having the mumps after puberty was dangerous. The fever lasted for ten days and my mother was frantic but could do nothing except put cold towels on my head. When I recovered enough to sit up and read, Mom gave me the newspapers about the invasion. My parents and I read and reread the stories about the brave men who took on the German war machine. The casualties were devastating, and everyone knew someone who was wounded or killed. But it gave us all hope that this nightmare might be over some day.

Shirley and Ruth, 1946.

Chapter 45

In the summer of 1944 Shirley and I had joined the Camp Fire Girls and started collecting cans and newspapers for the war effort. We were awarded beads for doing good deeds and learning new skills like cooking and canning. My mother bought a crate of peaches, and we went to the cannery with a neighbor to prepare them for canning. It was hot, smelly work, but the peaches were our dessert that winter.

When Shirley's parents went clamming at the beach, they would start out before daylight. The limit was twenty-four clams per person, so they invited me along a couple of times—not that Shirley and I helped dig for clams. We ran up and down the beach with Shirley's dog, made sandcastles, and poked the fire we had made to keep warm. We did help load the bags of clams into the trunk of the car.

On our drive back to Longview, we ate our peanut butter sandwiches. As soon as we arrived at the Rimkus house, Shirley's mother filled a huge laundry tub with hot water. Then the four of us sat around the tub opening the clams. There's a reason these mollusks are called "razor clams." Within a few minutes of trying to pry the shells apart and removing the clams, the water was a pool of blood. Even the experienced grown-ups had a few cuts. But Shirley and I had slashes all over our palms and fingers. Shirley's mother prepared the canning jars and soon there were dozens ready to store for winter dinners. (It took thirty years until I ate and liked a razor clam.)

With the money we earned picking berries and beans, we

were able to go to camp during the first two weeks of August. Every day was cold and miserable. It wasn't until the end of the second week that the weather cleared, and we could see Mount St. Helens towering over the crystal-clear waters of Spirit Lake. That was the day we knew we wanted to return the next year. For five more years, we returned to that awesome scenery.

Those were some of the best times in our lives. We swam in the icy waters, rowed across the turbulent lake, went on long hikes into the primal forest, and spent nights looking at the stars and scaring each other with stories of the legendary apes of Spirit Lake. Sitting around the nightly campfire, singing rowdy camp songs, putting on funny skits, and roasting the rationed marshmallows; we briefly forgot that many campers had fathers, brothers, and uncles fighting in the war that consumed the thoughts of our parents.

With all the news and radio programs being about war and destruction, children began to think that it was the way to do things. During a period when Shirley and I were not talking, I made friends with Barbara. We agreed we hated St. Helens school and all the stupid, mean kids in it. I made a diary entry on November 27, 1944, that outlined our plans to blow up the school. We didn't go through with it and never really meant to, but it was fun planning.

When the Germans surrendered in May of 1945, my mother started her years-long search for our family we had left in Europe. When there was no trace of my Omama, Tante Franzi, or the Tauber family, my father sunk into a deep depression. My mother was frantic. She alternately cajoled, whined, scolded, and tried to keep his spirits up. Eventually he recovered, but he was never quite the same again. He had lost his father in WWI, and now the rest of his family had all been murdered. Like so many other survivors, he questioned why God would allow such atrocities.

After the war was over the carnival came back to the small towns of America. Around Labor Day, just before school started, a carnival encamped in a field near our house. Shirley and I went one afternoon, and we had a great time playing games, riding the carousel (my favorite thing to do), and I bought cotton candy. I had brought two dollars from my berry-picking money, and by the end of the afternoon, I had a dime left. I had decided to keep it, but Shirley asked if I would buy her a cotton candy. I offered her some of mine, but she wanted her own.

"My Dad was right. You Jews are all alike, selfish and stingy!" she yelled at me. My free hand came up and connected with her face, where I was surprised to see a hand-sized, red blotch before she ran away. (The similar incident with Margie in West Kelso echoed in my head.) A few days later we made up, and we went on to have many more adventures together. We rode bicycles everywhere, even to the top of the Longview Bridge that spanned the Columbia River, and we dangled our feet over the river, one hundred feet below. During our ride home, we realized how dangerous that had been.

We were now sixth graders. Our teacher, Miss Hemphill, was stringent about homework and did her best to stuff our heads with the history and geography of Oregon. I remember her well because of her crooked shoulder. She told us that one of her shoulders was higher because she spent years carrying books in that arm. Maybe because of that drastically-sloped shoulder, Miss Hemphill was a stickler for good posture.[38] She picked on me and a girl named June. We were the tallest students in the school and tended to slouch to hide our budding breasts. June was also very plump. The boys made fun of her on the playground and even in the classroom, singing the first line of a popular song, "June is Busting Out All Over," until June, who had very white skin, blushed beet red. More than once she put her head down on her desk, sobbing helplessly.

---

[38] On weekend mornings my mother made me walk around the house with a broom stick behind my back, held up by my elbows, with a book on my head. Her theory was that you are how you walk.

This made me angry, but there was nothing I could do.

Gasoline was still rationed, so as soon as the weather got warmer, my dad started riding his bicycle to work to save up for a vacation in Long Beach. On the first of April, my Dad came home from work, walking up to the back door, and my mother told him that the dentist had called; his new teeth were ready. He had been waiting for a month for those teeth, and hearing the news, he hopped right back on his bicycle and headed for uptown Longview (about a two-mile ride). As Dad rode out of sight, my mother turned to me and began to cry. "I shouldn't have done that," she sobbed. "He is going to be terribly angry. How could I do such a thing to him? He worked hard all day, and now I've played an April Fool's joke on him." I was not at home when Dad came back, and Mom told him about her prank. I must have had dinner at Shirley's house, and things were a bit tense around our house for a few days.

Later that summer we left for Long Beach. We chugged along in the 1935 Chevrolet for two hours until we reached the isolated, little cottage, surrounded by tall pine trees and the sound of the crashing waves. I was excited to see the ocean again, but it turned out to be a long walk to the water. We were overwhelmed by the moldy smell that permeated the cottage, and my mother started a cleaning process immediately.

It was late in the day, so we just planned to have some food, clean up the kitchen, and go to bed. In the morning it was overcast, windy and cold, but we walked to the beach. The wind drove us back up to the cabin. The next day was a little warmer and a few patches of blue sky appeared, but no sun. After trying to walk on the beach while I played in the sand, my parents went back to the house. I mentioned to my parents that the kids at school had told me about a place called "Seaside" on the Oregon coast, where they had an amusement park, and I asked if we could go there instead of this desolate place. They said that Seaside was for frivolous people who didn't care about nature and just spent money on silly games and rides. No way were we ever going there.

That night we went to a movie in "Downtown" Long Beach. It was an old warehouse with rows of benches and a white sheet strung up on one wall. We had no idea what the movie was about, but it had a lot of sword fighting, and the couple kissed in the end.

A brochure provided information about the road that led to the beach where one could drive along the ocean, so we drove there the next day. Lots of cars were driving along the beach, and we joined them. Dad parked the car facing the ocean, and we sat there and marveled at how high the waves were and how they came closer and closer. Dad backed up the car to avoid the waves until we were stuck in the dry sand, and ours was the only car left on the beach. When the waves came up to the front bumper, my mom grabbed her purse and me, and then ran up the incline behind us. My dad reluctantly followed us, and we turned around and watched the waves take our car away.

Mathilde and Ruth next to 1935 Chevrolet that was lost in the ocean.

Some kind people gave us a ride back to the cabin and explained that the beach disappeared during high tide—as did our car. Someone called a tow truck, and Mom packed up our stuff. We took a Greyhound bus back to Longview. Dad stayed another day to arrange to get rid of the salt-soaked car. It was embarrassing to get off the bus near our house and explain to the neighbors what had happened to our car.

In August of 1945, we came back from YMCA camp to learn that the war was over. A peace treaty would be signed shortly. I had known war all my life, and the fact that it was over seemed impossible. Our lives didn't change much. In our family, we had not noticed the deprivation felt by many Americans. We had always lived as if everything were rationed, and we never bought a surplus of food or unnecessary products. Throwing away food was a serious crime, and replacing something that was not worn out or outgrown was unheard of.

With the end of the war came the hope that our family members might have survived. Slowly the news trickled out that, while most of the Jews of Europe had been murdered, some survived. The pictures of the concentration camp survivors in the newspapers and in *Life* magazine were unbelievable, but my father had been there; he knew they were real.

My parents never discussed their concerns about our family in front of me. It was as if they had never existed. I suppose, looking back, they wanted to spare me the horror and the grief that they were suffering. Dad (yes, I called him that, finally) went into a two-year depression which caused a lot of scolding, crying, and pleading from my mother. She threatened to leave him if his morose attitude continued. It was a frightening time for me. Miraculously, he recovered sufficiently to live a somewhat-normal life. Eventually, he was able make the three of us laugh at his jokes again.

My mother subscribed to *The Aufbau*, a German newspaper that catered to the refugee community, mostly for New York where the largest number of refugees lived. It published pages and pages of names of people who had survived and were now in Displaced Persons Camps (located in the very concentration camps from which The Allied troops has liberated them) or scattered around the globe.

For years, my mother spent hours every night huddled over the endless lists of names, but she didn't find one name she recognized. Except for the Schischas in the Bronx (who had told us about the *Aufbau*), my dear Uncle Hugo in Sweden, and my mother's brother in Italy, everyone had disappeared. (After fifty years we found out that they had been brutally murdered in the gas chambers of Auschwitz. We had no doubt, as the Germans kept meticulous records.)

Chapter 46

The next year we were teenagers, with all the upheavals that come with that time of life. I was extremely interested in boys; Shirley wasn't so much. A boy named Dale had moved into our apartment complex. His mother was the new manager. He had flaming red hair, faded blue eyes behind thick glasses, freckles all over him, and buck teeth that added to his goofy looks. He was also quite chubby, awkward, and a couple of inches shorter than I was.

Dale liked school, and we talked about world events. He wasn't into most sports and preferred reading to chasing a ball. I really liked him, and he was unattractive enough so that other girls would not compete for his attention. A new era was about to start in my life.

I imagined myself in love with Dale, but I was very aware from the very beginning of our relationship that it was a pre-view to what would be my "real life," which would entail marrying a Jewish man and having his children. (Before that happened, I wanted to become a foreign correspondent for a prestigious newspaper, travel all over the world, and win a Pulitzer Prize for my fascinating and relevant stories. In the process, I wanted to make the world a better place.)

All that altruism did not extend to our neighborhood. By October of 1945, I had organized a group of, mostly, boys and a couple of girls (including Shirley). We often played catch-baseball on Hemlock Street. We were probably noisy and trespassed on other people's yards.

When the ball went into the yard of an elderly woman

who prided herself on her flower beds, she would come out and confiscate the ball; we didn't dare ask her to return it. She called us hoodlums and worse names (which we probably deserved). So on Halloween, I outlined a plan. We climbed over her low, picket fence, found a ladder, and some of the boys carried her garbage can up to her roof. They dumped the garbage, leaving the can on the roof, and came back down.

We had done a mean thing to a person who was not nice to us, but the revenge did not feel good. In fact, it was the second time I had felt ashamed of myself. I hated the feeling and avoided doing anything out of sheer meanness from then on.

When I overheard the other culprits brag about that Halloween escapade to our other friends, I felt ashamed all over again. I never mentioned that it was my idea.

At some time before the end of 1945, my Dad bought a car with some of the insurance money from the lost Chevy. The new car was a DeSoto with a LaSalle motor and a very modern, streamlined body. Every Sunday Dad would wash the car and spend the morning reading the newspaper in the back seat.

In the summer we again drove up to Crystal Pool, and now we took along Shirley and my "boyfriend" Dale. Shirley and I would swim across the river to the rope swing and spent most of the day swinging, dropping into the water, and going back up for more. Dale spent the day sitting at the picnic table, reading and eating. It turned out he didn't know how to swim or own a bathing suit.

Before the end of that summer, I convinced my parents that we should go camping like so many of my friends did. They had been hikers and spent many nights in the little cabins along the hiking trails in Austria, but Americans took along their own tents. Dad borrowed a tent from a man at work. We gathered up blankets and packed some food and set out to find a campground.

By late afternoon, we were lost somewhere in a wooded area. Dad parked the car and we tried to set up the tent. It kept collapsing, and we finally gave up. We stuck it back in the car, ate some of the food, and laid out the blankets to sleep under the open sky. Before dawn, it started to rain. So Dad gathered the blankets, and we walked a few feet to a bridge and lay down again. Just as we began to doze off, we were awakened by a loud, pounding noise and the ground began to shake. We were under a railroad trestle.

This was our first and last camping trip.

Before the end of the seventh grade, Dale had learned to swim. He joined the swim team and spent much of his time in the pool. In the evening, we often walked around the lake. We found a weeping willow tree where we could hide while we stopped to hug. When the weather got cold and rainy, we sat on a bench in the attic drying space where we hugged and talked. Feeling his arms around me was pleasant and comforting. One night in late fall, he kissed me while we were in that attic. I saw stars, and it was a wonderful feeling to think that someone besides my mother loved me enough to kiss me. Hard to believe, but I never made a connection between sexual desire and kissing.

That evening turned out to be quite an adventure and our last tryst in that dark, quiet place. While we were discovering the pleasure of that first kiss, Dale's mother, in her capacity as the apartment manager, came to check to see if the door to the attic was locked. We heard her coming up the outside stairs. She stopped at the door and turned the latch to lock the door from the outside. We were trapped. We didn't dare tell her we were there. We weren't sure what would happen to us if we were discovered, but we knew it would be bad.

We waited until she went back down and tried to think of what to do. Dale remembered that there was a small trap door in his closet that opened to the attic. He found the door and squeezed into his closet. He nonchalantly went downstairs and out the kitchen door, and then he snuck up to the attic to let me out. I went over to our apartment, and no one said anything about my coming in after dark because my parents thought I had been over at Dale's playing cards, as we often did. Dale told me that his mother caught him coming back in and was surprised to see him, as she thought he had been up in his room. It was a close call.

That fall I started Junior High School at Kessler school. (No, I didn't see Jackie Tanzer there.) Dale made it clear that he would never take me to a dance or even a movie. He was not going to be seen with a girl.

After that I sensed that my social life was going nowhere with Dale. We stayed friends, but my interest began to include other boys. I was especially fond of Dick Clayton[39] who, like Dale, was a year older than me, played the clarinet in the high school band, and knew how to touch me in places that gave us both pleasure. We went to movies, took walks around the lake, and danced at the weekly Hi-Jacks dances at the YMCA. We corresponded for another year after I moved to Portland, Oregon. This relationship gave me an idea of what I wanted in a possible, far-in-the-future husband. I wanted someone who was a good dancer, told funny stories, enjoyed music, and knew what to say to make a girl feel she was loved. Yet, until I met Fred Lindemann, I was totally, unbelievably, innocent and ignorant about the process of sexual relations.

Ruth, Coburn brothers and Thilde, Summer 1946.

---

[39] Dick was killed in Korea during the Korean "Police Action," 1953.

A Modern Witch, Halloween 1946.

To get to Kessler Middle School, we had to cross Lake Sacajawea on a footbridge just wide enough for one bicycle. This meant that Shirley and I could not ride side-by-side with each other or with our current boyfriend. So for most of our time in Middle School, we walked, hoping that the most recent boyfriend would walk us home. Shirley was dating a boy named Bob Ruth (a coincidence). The two of them walked home most days, leaving me to walk alone. Although Shirley and I would walk to school together, she seemed to snub me the rest of the day and ignored me, even as she and Bob walked by me on the way home. I tried to figure out why she might be mad at me again. She had displayed this type of behavior more and more frequently, and by eighth grade, we were almost strangers.

One day in the spring of 1947, we happened to be riding our bikes to school. On the way home, we got to the entry of the bridge at the same time, so we couldn't ignore each other.

She finally said, "Hi," and I took that as an opening. I asked her why she had been avoiding me. She told me that Bob Ruth had asked her to the dance, and he told her she had to break off our friendship because he didn't want to be seen with a girl who was friends with a Jew.

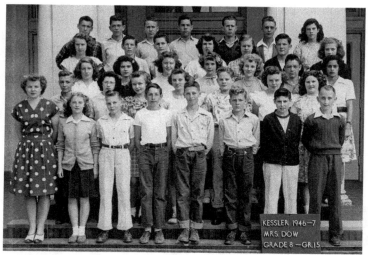

Kessler, 7th Grade 1946.

Perhaps Shirley saw how sad that news made me, or maybe her conscience began to come to the surface, but she said she was breaking up with Bob right after the dance. That made me feel a little better because I knew how important that dance was to all the eighth-grade girls. (Temporarily giving up a friend seemed like a small price to pay. Priorities are skewed at fourteen.)

Dick had to play in the band, so he couldn't take me to the dance we had all been so anxiously anticipating. He asked his friend, Burton, to take me, and I agreed in the hopes of having at least one dance with Dick. The night of the dance, Burton was an hour late. I had been pacing the floor, all dressed up, thinking he was not coming. He didn't apologize, just gave me a corsage of gardenias.

We walked to the high school. The dance was in full

swing. Burton immediately disappeared into the crowd of boys at one end of the gym and I didn't see him again until the dance was over. Dick came by my chair to say hello during intermission, but we never got to dance. As everyone was leaving, Burton appeared and walked me home. I had a miserable time. I've hated the scent of gardenias ever since—and the name Burton, which reminded me of the ungainly cad.

That was the year I learned how to sew. Home Economics was a required class for girls, and thankfully this teacher decided learning how to sew was more important than learning the names of all the kitchen implements, etc. I made a dress that I wore for many years.

The science class was another story. Mr. Hanley did not think it was necessary to have girls in his class, and he let us know it. When a boy broke a rule (passed a note, chewed gum, whispered to his friend) he was scolded, but if he caught a girl (which was rare because he hardly looked at the four girls in the class) he made a regular scene. One example was when he caught me chewing gum. I had been a minute or two late for class because of having gym class and needing a shower for the previous hour. Mr. Hale came up behind me, grabbed the neck of my sweater and pulled me up from my seat. In the process, my sweater rolled up over my breasts just under my throat. The boys began to giggle. I was mortified. Mr. Hale dragged me over to the waste basket and yelled, "Spit it out!" After he let go, I pulled down my sweater and left the room. I can't remember if I went back to that class; but if I did, I didn't learn much.

It was during my middle school years that the United Nations was being formed at the San Francisco Conference. The newspapers were full of coverage of this momentous event. I was filled with hope for a peaceful world. We had no idea what that would be like. My peers and I had only lived with the media (radio, newspapers, newsreels at the movies) showing images of war and the destruction caused by the bombings of European cities. Seeing all that rubble and suffering, how could sane men fight wars? Nobody was a real winner. Everyone would lose the best of their young men and valuable possessions.

I filled a thick scrapbook with the write-ups and pictures of that San Francisco Conference. I followed the development of the United Nations while the headquarters were built in New York. Until the recognition of the State of Israel, I was hopeful and optimistic about the success of this new organization that had so much promise. However, when there was no effort to keep the five biggest Arab nations from attacking the miniscule, new-yet-ancient state, I lost most of my hopes for a better world. Some disgruntled leader caller the U.N. a "toothless tiger," and that's the best description of its functions to date.

By the summer of 1947, Shirley and I were best friends again, and we got up before dawn to pick strawberries, raspberries, and green beans to earn money for camp and school clothes. On weekends we both found jobs babysitting. It was the most tedious way of earning money as young children tended to be unreasonable and silly. Perhaps I resented them since I didn't have a real childhood.

That summer, Shirley and I went to YMCA camp again. The beauty of the lake and Mt. St. Helens always quieted my soul while I spent hours just gazing at that lovely scene.

That year at camp, the food was better. We even had hamburgers and chicken dishes instead of potatoes, carrots, and hard-boiled eggs. One day on a hike, we discovered the Portland YMCA boys camp across the lake. Somehow, we persuaded the counselors and eventually the straitlaced director to organize some joint activities. The boys were encouraged to go fishing in the lake and in the brook behind our camps. Fish began to appear on our dinner tables. Fraternizing had its benefits.

In the morning, Spirit Lake was smooth like a sheet of glass, but by noon it was covered with white capped waves. One day, Shirley and I took out a rowboat after breakfast.

Maybe we had the idea that we would row across the lake to the boys' camp, but it took a long time to get to the middle of the lake and by then it was getting choppy. When the boat began to rock and water came over the gunnels, we were terribly frightened. We knew swimming in that water was impossible, and the boat could capsize any minute. We rowed hard and fast, knowing our lives depended on getting ashore.

By the time we approached the beach, all seventy campers, counselors, and the stony-faced, fire-eyed director were on the shore. Some were scolding, some were cheering, while Shirley and I were filled with relief to be alive. Our hands were blistered and raw for a week; we didn't go rowing again that year.

Dock at YMCA Camp at Sprit Lake, WA 1945.

Chapter 47

At the end of that summer we did our school shopping in Longview. I had enough money to buy saddle shoes, a pleated, plaid, wool skirt, a sweater, and a see-through blouse that needed a full slip. I felt very grown up when I was, finally, allowed to wear a brassiere and my first silk stockings (held up by a garter belt). Keeping the seams straight was a time-consuming chore.

I realized being a woman was going to be complicated. But it wouldn't be as complicated as it had been for our grand-mothers who'd had to wear corsets, petticoats, bloomers and high-topped shoes. In the 1940s & '50s, women were expected to wear dresses, full slips, and pumps, with stockings held up by garter belts or girdles. Going uptown meant putting on a hat and white gloves. We did not wear uniforms to school, but we all dressed the same: sweaters, skirts, bobby socks, saddle shoes.

During the morning of our first day we were taken on a tour of R.A. Long High School. Although Shirley and I had been using the indoor swimming pool for the last four sum-mers, we had never been inside the classroom area or seen the front of the building. We were dazzled by the colonial structure, elegant winding staircases, and the wide, marble halls that led to spacious, well-lit classrooms. That we would each have our own locker was a pleasant surprise.

The four months at R.A. Long High School were quite memorable. It was like starting a new and interesting adven-ture. Every day was full of challenges, and I especially enjoyed the mind expansion needed to understand Algebra. The subject intrigued me; it was like solving a mystery story. I could hardly wait to get to school each day, where I experienced the thrill of finding the answers to the puzzles on the board. When I got the right answer and understood the concept of the formula, I felt as if I had won an important competition.

Some of the challenges were more difficult than others. Finding out that there were no elevators to the second floor, after buying elevator tickets from smirking seniors, meant overcoming anger and embarrassment and going on with my life as if I didn't care that I was duped (like most other Freshman).

By this point, Dick and I were going steady. My feelings for him were not the same as they had been for Dale, but I really liked being with him. We walked around the lake, sat in quiet corners, "necked" (nothing dangerous, just touching and hugging, with an occasional kiss), went to the movies, talked about politics and laughed about our fellow classmates, teachers, and parents. We both had a sharp and wicked sense of humor.

Dick was still in the school band, and I happily sat through the practice sessions. He played an awesome clarinet, and he had a sense of rhythm that made him a great dancer. We danced at the teen dance, called "Hi Jacks," at the YMCA every Saturday, and we walked the mile or so to our homes. The popular girls had boys flocking around them, walking them home in a group, and the not-so-popular girls, like me, walked home holding hands with one boy who might kiss them goodnight at their door.

The school band played at the football games and, as a special friend of a band member, I always had a seat at the fifty-yard line. Since learning the rules of baseball, basketball and football was part of the gym class curriculum, I knew when to cheer and scream during the Friday night football games. That fall, I was hoarse every weekend and barely able to speak even by Monday. Being able to scream at the top of my lungs was the best part of the football games.

Shirley and I were getting along quite well during this time. We didn't have any classes together but usually walked to school and back. Longview was a fairly-safe place in those days. High School students walked to wherever they needed to go during the day or night. However, it must have been a relief for my mother to be able to see the school from our front door.

That fall Shirley and I tried out for the girls' swim team. We would have liked to organize a water ballet or synchronized swimming group. We had been emulating Esther Williams for hours on end during the last two summers. I loved being in the water; it gave me a sensation of freedom, peace and safety that I never felt on dry land. The swim coach was set on putting together a winning team, so we began to specialize. Shirley's expertise was in the back stroke. By then she was a head taller than I was, which was a benefit for being on a team.

I didn't qualify for any stroke competition. The coach said my strokes were almost perfect, but I was just too slow. I had never been competitive in sports or most contests; I mostly competed with myself. Every time I participated in a competition, I wanted to do better than my time before but didn't think much of doing better than another person. Shirley and I loved the Esther Williams movies, and we'd spent many hours over the last two years practicing the water ballet movements we saw on the screen. We never wore goggles, so after several hours in the pool we saw rainbow halos around every light bulb.

When I tried out for diving it was a different matter. My jack-knife was "almost perfect" (the coach's words), and my swan dive was "elegant." I had trouble with the back flip, so that was left off my list of dives.

Being in the water almost every day until our skin wrinkled didn't worry us, but the chlorine did strange things to our hair. Mine began to have a green sheen and became almost unmanageable unless it was wet. We used soap to wash our hair after swim practice. At home we had shampoo, but being on the swim team, we seldom used it. No one had heard of conditioner. The only thing to do was keep my fuzzy hair short; it usually looked like a worn-out dust mop. I thought I was ugly, awkward and unpopular, and my mother reminded me every day that I was right. The looks I got from the boys were a contradiction.

During Christmas vacation I went shopping for gifts with Shirley, and we joyfully spent our babysitting money on little gifts for friends, parents and teachers. I liked receiving presents but got just as much pleasure in the shopping and giving process. We wrapped the gifts in colored paper in Shirley's room, listening to Christmas carols on the radio. We knew all the words of every carol, as we'd learned them in school and later sang them in the choir.

That year it snowed, and it was a beautiful white Christmas. I knew we were not Christians, but the holiday totally enveloped the world I lived in. Being Jewish was a hidden side of my life; almost like being two different people. Truly, I *was* two different people. I was the Jewish refugee girl who lived with her slightly paranoid parents; they talked about the tragic loss of family and lived only for me and for each other. With my friends, I wanted very much to fit in and be a normal American girl. This was impossible because I looked different from the blonde, fair-skinned girls my age. Eventually I made peace with the real me who tended to be a leader and a daredevil with no respect for authority. Looking back, I was a bad influence on the acquiescent girls who tended to mind their parents and tried to conform to the expected submissive-female role.

It was during the time between Christmas and New Year that my parents told me they had entered a partnership with Jack Klinger and his wife Blanca to buy a grocery store, and we were moving to Portland. I was devastated. My mother told me how interesting it would be to live in a big city again and meet other Jews my age (hinting that I might find a husband there). She said, "You need a Jewish social life if you are ever going to get married."

I came close to having a tantrum. I tried to get out the door, but she blocked my way. "How dare you act this way?" she asked and began to raise her voice. "Your father has worked at the mill for *seven years* doing work that he is hardly able to do. He can't last there much longer; it will kill him. He is out there in the lumber yard right now, loading boards in this freezing cold. In the summer he needs to take salt pills in the heat so he won't collapse. Do you want him to die? "

I calmed down and started to think of how it would be to start over at a new school for the thirteenth time. Maybe this would be my lucky number. Trying to make friends with Jewish kids might make my life less complicated. If they snubbed me or excluded me from their circle of friends, it would be because they honestly didn't like me, not just because I was Jewish.

Another benefit of moving to Portland was the air was not filled with the stench of the paper mills. We hardly noticed the smell while we lived there, only when we had spent the day in Portland. Coming home we could tell we were getting near Longview by the pervasive stench. Also, Portland water was clear and tasty; the water around Longview had a chlorine taste. No one ever thought of buying bottled water in those days. My mother drank only hot tea.

Dick and Shirley both promised to write, and Shirley and I planned to go to YMCA camp for one last summer. It was just one more goodbye for me. Once again, I would be a stranger, needing to find friends. In high school, it was harder, as most people were in cliques with people they had known all their lives—or at least since first grade.

Chapter 48

The area around 102nd Ave. & Burnside was still a rural part of Portland and beyond the city limits. It had no sidewalks, stores, or nearby public transportation, nothing but barren fields for miles around. To me it looked utterly desolate. Burnside Street stretched for miles over a low incline with no end in sight. It reminded me of the first line from my favorite poem, "The Highwayman" by Alfred Noyes: "The road was a ribbon of moonlight over the purple moor."

I consoled myself that I now had my own room and could pin up pictures of my favorite movie stars (i.e., Van Johnson, Victor Mature, Guy Madison, and some others whose names have faded from my memory). Also, I had use of a telephone—although it was a block away in the grocery store where my parents spent all their time. It cost me a nickel to use the pay-phone, but my friends could call me from their homes, and when I called them, I let it ring twice, hung up, got my nickel back, and waited for them to call me back.

The house on 102nd Avenue was set back about a hundred feet from the road, surrounded by a large expanse of grass, in the middle of what had been a cherry orchard. It was a block from the Burnside Market where my parents spent twelve hours a day, seven days a week. (Jack and Blanka Klinger, the parents of little Ruthie, were supposed to share those hours but rarely showed up.)

Since it was still winter vacation, I was expected to come to the store and dust cans, make hamburgers and milk-shakes at the soda fountain, and restock the shelves. This was exhausting, and I soon kept forgetting to show up for work. My parents didn't reprimand me about this; in retrospect, they might have felt a bit of remorse for taking me to this wilderness. They hired a teenage boy to restock, dust, and even make deliveries. One of his jobs was to run over to our house and let me know if there was a telephone call for me. Sometimes people who called waited the eight minutes it took for the boy to get me and for me to reach the telephone; sometimes they hung up and I called them back with the two-ring signal.

Another benefit of moving was that we now had a gas stove and an electric refrigerator. My mother was terrified of the gas stove, and my father kept complaining about the cost of the electricity for the luxury appliances. We now had our own washing machine, but the clothes were still hung out to dry on a clothesline in the back yard with a vegetable garden and raspberry bushes that went all the way to the property line. My parents talked about growing things but never had the time.

During the first few days of 1948, my mother called Mrs. Wexler at the Jewish Welfare Association, who advised us to contact Washington High School and Gresham High School, as I had a choice of attending either school, living right on the border of the district. Although there were some Jewish students at Washington High School, it would cost about one dollar per day to get there and back, while Gresham High School had a school bus that didn't cost anything. I chose to go to Gresham High School. Once again, I was the only Jewish student in a school.

I don't remember the registration process, except that I know neither of my parents would have come to the school. I probably had to take some forms home to be filled out and signed by my parents, and they probably never saw those forms.

Gresham High School was a culture shock. The halls were so narrow that getting anywhere between classes was a physical struggle. The students had to share lockers. I was lucky that my locker mate, another Shirley, was a clean and tidy person, and we got along very well. We eventually became good friends and remained in touch for several years after school. (We met again at our fiftieth reunion and have had a locker mate get-together every year since.)

Signing up for classes was a revelation. I had my transcript from R.A. Long and wanted to continue those same classes. The school counselor informed me that girls did not take algebra at Gresham High School, but that ALL girls were required to take Home Economics. It was also advisable that I take typing and shorthand which would be beneficial in finding a job until I got married and had a chance to use those Home Economics skills.

Most of my friends got on the national honor role, but I didn't make it since I consistently got a "D" (barely passing) in Home Economics and a similar grade in typing (top speed of thirty words per minute). I earned a 120 words-per-minute pin in shorthand, which was soon an obsolete skill. I consistently received "A" or "A+" in all other subjects (English, History, Bookkeeping, and Latin). In Personal Finance, I was the only girl in the class. The teacher—who made it clear that he thought girls had no business learning about banking and should be learning to be secretaries instead of the stock market—ignored my presence in his classroom, but did give me a reluctant "A."

Boys were in my life during all my school years, but I never felt anything but a vague liking for them. They were children, after all, and I had never been a child. I enjoyed seeing admiration in the males I encountered, but I didn't want them to touch me. A kiss and hug felt good from the ones I really liked, but it never occurred to me to let them do anything else. My ignorance of what that "else" might be was astounding. Yet, I always kept in mind that I was not going to do anything that would make my parents ashamed of me.

Those first months at Gresham High School were confusing. The girls who befriended me were the ones who rode on the same bus and came from the low-income neighborhood that surrounded the Burnside Market. These girls were not interested in learning and often skipped school to go for joyrides with boys who drove dilapidated cars. They talked about sexual matters that I didn't understand and made me feel vaguely dirty. Although I did not join them in skipping school, I often went for car rides that were hair-raising at best and dangerous at worst. Eventually, I got bored by the empty-headed pursuits and spent my time reading and using my sewing skills. I was learning to make myself a blouse on the sewing machine that had been left in the rental house.

In March, I developed a severe cough that kept me from speaking. Whenever I opened my mouth, I began to cough. It got so bad that I had to stay home from school. The Klingers persuaded my father to take me to a doctor they knew who treated refugees. Driving to downtown Portland was a big undertaking. Finding a parking place and the doctor's office required planning to spend the whole day away from the store. Jack Klinger offered to stay in the store with my mother.[40]

Doctor Lawrence Cohen examined me and then told my father that I was a terribly sick girl and would need a treatment that could last for many months. When we got home my parents had a fight—as usual when my welfare was concerned. My father said the doctor was a quack, didn't know a thing about my condition, and just wanted our money. My mother said we should give him a chance to treat me. As their voices rose, I went upstairs to my room and coughed the rest of the night.

A boy I had met in the grocery store, Irvin Spangler, brought me homework from school and took my completed papers back to the teachers. He was a romantic seventeen-year-old and we talked about many things. I started to recite "The Highwayman" one afternoon as we were looking east

---

[40] That evening I overheard her tell my father that Jack had made inappropriate advances toward her in the storage room. "I know he's a pig," was my father's calm reply.

on Burnside, watching the moon come up. Although I had let him kiss me and ridden around with him in the wreckage he called a car, occasionally buying gas, I never invited him into the house. (He was poor, the youngest of ten children of an illiterate mother and a drunken father.) My parents were in the store all day and had warned me repeatedly to never be alone in the house with a boy.

Conversation was impossible because every time I started to speak, I began to cough. Eventually, I realized that it was his presence that exacerbated the coughing. Maybe it was an allergy to Irvin or something he was wearing that needed washing.

Irvin wrote songs and sang them while he played the guitar. He was quite good by high school standards. I went with him to several parties where he played and was generously applauded. I tried to like his songs but soon the nasal twang from the cowboy movies I had outgrown, the dour lyrics about the self-made troubles of ignorant people, got on my nerves.

In any case, I cut him out of my life when he said we should get married. I told him I was much too young at fifteen to think of such a thing, and besides, I was already promised to a cousin. He told me that his mother and grandmother had married at sixteen and some of his sisters had been married for years. I began to be afraid of him, as he sounded a bit crazy, and I told him to never come near me again. He stayed away, but even when I saw him at a distance at school or at a ball game, my skin would crawl and I began to cough.

Chapter 49

I went back to school in early May, and this time I concentrated on my studies and began a warmer relationship with my locker mate. However, my heart and mind were still in Longview. I exchanged many letters with Dick and Shirley, making plans to visit them. A visit would be complicated because of the flood that had devastated the area.

Shirley & Ruth, Longview visit, 1949.

When school was out, my cough disappeared, so we finalized my plans to visit Shirley in Longview. The town of Vanport had been destroyed and swept away after a railroad trestle collapsed due to the high water in the Columbia River. The area around Longview, which was below sea level, was still under several feet of water. My trip to Longview was delayed by two more weeks. I had to find the Multnomah County Health Department to get the several shots for cholera and other diseases, and I filled out the paperwork so I could be found in case I got sick.

I stayed with Shirley for a week but spent most of my time with Dick. I saw Dale once, from a distance, and couldn't believe I had been in love with him. Taking the bus back to Portland, I thought a lot about Dick. It was obvious that he had other girlfriends by then, and soon we stopped writing. I was going back to Longview in August to go to YMCA Camp, but I made no plans to see Dick.

The next few weeks, I got up at four o'clock every morning to go strawberry-picking in nearby fields to make money for the camp tuition. The farm truck brought the pickers (mostly younger than me) back home by noon. After washing off the layers of dirt, I usually slept until dinner time. The picking was hard work, but I preferred it to babysitting.

Dinner was usually after seven o'clock since my parents were in the store until six. Mom prepared dinner, while Dad sat at the table counting the money from that day's business and reading the newspaper. I was expected to do the dishes before I went out. I only dated boys who had a car. Nothing was within walking distance except the grocery

When the berry-picking season was finished, I had a little money left over after paying my camp tuition. So one morning, I decided to go to Downtown Portland. I asked Jean if she wanted to go, but she said no, so I went alone. The bus ride to the 82nd Street trolley car cost twenty cents, so I walked the mile to save my hard-earned money. I had a map of the downtown area and had marked where I wanted to go. The first place was Jolly Joan's restaurant on S.W. Broadway near Alder Street.

After a hamburger and a Coca-Cola at the fountain, I headed for the sixth floor of Meier & Frank Department Store where records and sheet music were sold. I must have spent two hours in that department, playing records in the little, glass booths. Finally, I picked "Nature Boy" by Nat King Cole. (Eventually, I wore it out.)

Clutching the bag with the record, I wandered around the streets looking at store windows. None of them were as elegant or lavish as the ones I remembered from Vienna. Having lived in the Longview/Kelso area for eight years, it was exciting to be among buildings of more than two stories. (Meier & Frank was the tallest building in Oregon at ten stories.) While I was walking, I realized that I was having fun; not in spite of being alone, but simply because I *was* alone. That sense of freedom was exhilarating.

A few days later, my mother asked me if I would go to downtown Portland again to buy some herring. She had found out from Blanca Klinger that the fish vendor at the Farmers' Market had fresh herring, and she wanted to pickle some. It had been years since we had tasted pickled herring and our mouths began to water just talking about it. Although we had looked for it in the markets, no one we talked to had heard of such a thing.

My mother found a recipe in her mother's cookbook, which she had brought from Vienna. She had all the ingredients at the store, as well as a few Mason jars, so all we needed were a couple of herrings. So one warm June day, I headed downtown and, following Blanca's directions, found the fish vendor. I bought three herrings, each about a foot long, which the fish monger wrapped up in newspaper. Clutching the bundle like I would a baby doll, I headed for the trolley car that would take me to the end of the line on 82nd street in Montavilla.

I found a seat on the trolley, ready for the forty-minute ride, and noticed that after a few minutes the passengers near me began to move to other seats. It wasn't long before I discovered the reason. Not only was the herring beginning to seep through the paper and stain my blouse and skirt, but it also wafted an odor through the whole car. To say I was embarrassed would be an understatement. I was mortified and would have liked to get off the trolley. When we finally got to Montavilla and I was able to escape from the trolley car, I began the mile-long walk to our house. I could have taken a bus, but I was not about to get on it.

When I got to the house and had put the herring in the refrigerator, I took off all my clothes and threw them into the garbage can, putting a couple of old magazines on top. I took a shower and washed my hair, but even after putting on a clean blouse and skirt, I had the sensation of smelling herring on me for several days. I told my mother about the humiliating experience, and she just laughed. I must admit that the herring was delicious when we finally got to eat it in early August, but I didn't buy another fish for many years.

I lived for the day I would leave for camp. That last year at camp was different since we were now the senior girls, most of us over fourteen years old and interested in boys. The Portland YMCA camp was across the lake, and we rowed over to visit on free mornings. The boys hiked around the lake to see us and often brought fresh trout. They were forbidden to enter our camp, but the cook was happy to get the fish. They provided a nice change from potatoes, hot dogs and bread.

The most memorable moments of that camp session happened one moonless night when the girls in our cabin decided to go skinny-dipping in the lake. It must have been near midnight when we snuck down to the dock, went around the boathouse (so as not to be seen from the other cabins), removed our clothes, and slid into the water. (Was I the instigator? Probably.) The water felt warmer than during the day. The sensation of swimming naked was exhilarating. We tried to be quiet, but suddenly there was a shout and a floodlight spread across the water. Dorothea, the camp director, screamed, "Get out at once!"

The boy who worked in the kitchen and the man who did repairs and handywork around the camp were standing next to the camp director, grinning widely. Instead of getting out, most of us girls ducked under water hoping they would all go away. Finally, we swam to the edge of the dock, but were not about to get out with the guys watching. I yelled that we were not getting out while the men were there; eventually they did leave, and we got out, put on our pajamas (a nightshirt in my case) over our wet bodies, and then trudged back to our cabin. I never forgot the sensation of being nude in the water; it felt like flying.

We finally convinced Dorothea (she hated it when we called her Dotty) that a dance with the Portland boys might be fun. On the last Saturday of camp, instead of going out to the usual campfire sing along after dinner, we decorated the mess hall with crepe paper; the tables were shoved against the wall. A counselor loaned us her phonograph with several records of dance music. The boys came trickling in and soon we were dancing and talking. Word got around that I was a Portland girl. Several boys asked for my telephone number (we still didn't have a telephone, but I told them the code to reach me). When I got back to Portland, at least two of them came all the way out to 102nd Avenue to take me to a movie. But it was obvious that these were just one date events.

At last my dear Uncle Hugo was coming to America. He had recently married a beautiful, much younger girl from Romania. She was a survivor of Auschwitz who had been sent to Sweden to recover her health. Their romance was a touching story, and eventually my new aunt (we called her Lucy, but her full name was Alicia) wrote about her experiences in Auschwitz. (It is a testimony to the reality of the Holocaust and the depth of depravity to which humans can sink. *Tapestry of Hope*, by Alice Kern, is in many libraries and being used to this day by teachers who want their students to know how this catastrophic era impacted a young, innocent person and her family.)

Uncle Hugo & Lucy Kohn, 1946.

At first, Hugo and Lucy lived with us in the third bedroom, which had been my sewing room. I gladly gave it up and welcomed Lucy not just as my aunt, but as the older sister I always wanted. She learned English quickly, and soon she and Hugo found jobs. Lucy could only work an hour or two at a time, and not every day, as her bones were not healing and she had to be in a full-body cast most of the day. How she endured this amazed me, but later when I found out about the brutality she had endured, I understood how strong she was, both mentally and physically. She was always cheerful, looking toward the future.

There was always a bit of tension between my mother

and Aunt Lucy. In the first place, they were total opposites in almost everything they thought and did. That was not surprising; although they both came from Europe, they came from totally different backgrounds. Aunt Lucy had a carefree childhood and was a teenager in an affluent family. Her attitude about money and possessions was they should be enjoyed without guilt or worry about the future. My mother, who had to earn her own living for most of her life, was extremely frugal and had strict rules about money: one-quarter of income goes to savings; and *never* buy anything on credit, or anything that is just decorative.

My mother had strict rules on how to live. Everyone who did not conduct their life the way she did was wrong. This had a lifelong influence on me, and I felt wicked when I deviated from the acceptable routine. I had not really experienced any other way before then, but I learned that my mother was missing out on some of the best experiences in life.

Chapter 50

In the fall, I went back to Gresham High School. I was a fifteen-year-old sophomore with no boyfriend. Several boys were my friends, but I didn't have a "special" boy in sight. My diary is filled with lamentations about this. My taste in friends had changed by then, and I stopped spending time with Jean and Madge. They weren't interested in school, politics or anything beyond their next date and, in Madge's case, her next drink. They were not interested in serious, moral relationships but clearly had chosen to be with a promiscuous group of boys.

It had taken me nine months to realize how frivolous and boring these people were, but I finally started paying attention to my locker mate (who was also named Shirley) and her friends. Soon Shirley Ellis, Zelma Mitchell, Lois Howk,[41] Ruth Lear, Donna Lingle, and I were good friends. I hadn't told them that I was from anywhere except Longview, Washington, but they repeatedly asked what church we attended, so I finally told them we were Jewish. I watched their eyes and facial expressions. Only one of them briefly revealed her changed feelings, but they never surfaced.

A required subject for sophomores was Biology. The teacher, a large round-faced woman, did a good job of teaching us about flora and fauna (dissecting worms, frogs and naming the body parts). One morning, she apologized to our

---

[41] We had many years of reunions, taking turns hosting in our separate locations (Seaside, Gresham, South Beach). Then we had health problems, and then one of us died, and then came the Corona virus.

class that she was not allowed to teach us about Darwin's theory of evolution. She told us that it was only a theory and refuted by religious teaching, but we could look it up in the public library if we were curious about it.

Telling students to explore a forbidden subject can have beneficial results. The next Saturday several of us went to the Multnomah County Library in downtown Portland (a lengthy trip by bus and trolley car) and looked up Charles Darwin. We tried to check out "On the Origin of the Species." It wasn't exactly a "banned" book, but the librarian was reluctant to let us take it out. She said something about restricted material, which made us twice as curious. To me, the theory made sense, but my religious friends had their doubts. So we never discussed it.

In October I started to be friends with a friend of Jean's boyfriend, who played the bass drum in the school band. Since Wally needed my help carrying the drum, stand, drumsticks and other equipment up the steep steps to the last row in the grandstand, I got in free to the games. Later, I would go down to the lower rows and join my friends, who had to pay to get in.

Wally was a tall redhead, easygoing, smart, and a quiet sense of humor. We were good friends even after Jean and his buddy broke up. It was a relief to be with a boy who was easy to talk with without needing to fend off double entendres, flirtatious remarks, and sexual overtures. We talked about school subjects, his family's nursery business, and movies we had seen. He didn't have a car, so we only saw each other at school or when he came to visit with me at the school store soda fountain, where I worked during lunch and after school.

The job at the soda fountain paid two dollars per week, and I could eat and drink whatever I liked. I had permission to leave class five minutes before the bell for lunch and at the end of the day. I didn't have much time for socializing with my friends, and it meant taking the second bus, which meant getting home after dark in the winter. (An early bus ran at

3:30, and a later bus at 4:45.) Since my parents didn't get home until after six o'clock no one missed me. I did most of my homework on the bus going to and from school.

Working at the soda fountain, I learned to make sandwiches, adding more and more mayonnaise as the tuna and hardboiled eggs ran low. Experimenting with the various fountain drinks was a lesson in chemistry. Some flavors just don't mix well, and a little bit more ice cream is sometimes too much.

Visiting teams played at our school about once a month. This was always a busy time at the soda fountain. Meeting new people was usually fun, but when the boys from Central Catholic came there was near chaos. They would order and forget to pay, or order what they called "Timber Floats" (a glass of water with a toothpick on top) which took time to fix and cost them nothing. Many teenage boys tend to be rowdy and rude, but these boys were especially wild. We dreaded their coming and were glad when they lost a game.

Uncle Hugo started working at Doernbecher Furniture Company in the refinishing department where he met other refugees who spoke German. They told him about the "Friendship Club" formed by a group of mostly-German refugees. Many of them were recent arrivals who had spent nine or more long years in Shanghai, China, waiting to come to America.

On the Saturday after Thanksgiving, Uncle Hugo and Lucy asked me to accompany them to the Friendship Club dance, which was held in the Neighborhood House. My parents never went to social events or anywhere else, but my father offered to drive them since it was on the west side of the Willamette river and would take hours to get there by bus and two different trolleys.

I was most reluctant to go to, what I considered, an old folks' event, but Hugo persuaded me that I should come along in case they needed to speak English. So I broke my date for that night, and we were off to the Neighborhood House. The route we took seemed convoluted as we crossed one of the bridges across the Willamette River, and then circled around in the narrow streets. I recognized Corbett Street where we had lived a few weeks before going to Idaho. I hoped that my Dad would find his way back to 102nd Avenue and then back to the Neighborhood House to pick us up. It was already eight o'clock, and Dad usually went to bed by nine.

"I'll be back at 10:30," my father said as we climbed out of the car. Slowly, I followed Lucy and Uncle Hugo up the stairs into the huge brick building, and so began the evening that would seal my fate.

I was still worrying about my Dad finding his way back as the three of us walked into the large room, where we saw several tables arranged around the wall leaving an open space for a dance floor. A raised platform like a stage was at one end of the room where a man was putting records into a portable phonograph. The people sitting at the tables all looked like my parents' age or older, and they were chattering away in various dialects of German and some other languages I didn't know.

I was certainly the youngest person there and the only female wearing bobbysocks and saddle shoes. A young woman came up to us as we stood in the doorway and introduced herself as Helga Lindemann. "You must be Mr. & Mrs. Kohn?" she chirped in English, with a heavy German accent that had a trace of British English (like my mother's).

Helga led us to the table where her parents were sitting with another couple. Hugo and Lucy sat down and began talking to the people around the table. Helga took my hand and pulled me over to another table where she was sitting with two other girls and introduced us. I could hardly hear her over the music, and I didn't get a good look at the girls because the lights were quite low in the room; I could barely make out the faces of anyone.

Hardly listening to the girls, I began to wonder when this ordeal would end. Ten-thirty seemed a long time away. Suddenly, a young man came up to me and asked me to dance.

He was wearing a suit and tie, like all the other men there, and he had an accent that wasn't German, which intrigued me. I said "okay" and he led me to the dance floor. He said his name was Lester Schonstal. He was a good dancer, and I was familiar with the song. When the music stopped, he took me back to the table and said he would be right back, and asked would I save the next dance for him? I said, "Yes, of course."

While I was waiting for Lester another man came up to me. He seemed older and his accent was the same as Helga's, but his English was a little better.

"Can you tango?" he asked me, without introduction or other comment.

"No, I've never danced to Latin music," I replied and turned away to look for Lester.

"I will show you how to tango," the older man said. It sounded like an order. Just then Lester came back.

"Sorry," I said, "I promised this next dance to Lester." Then I put my hand out to Lester and we tried to dance the tango. Lester was having trouble with the steps and the rhythm. I was relieved when the "older" man asked to cut in. Just then the song was over. We walked over to the phono-graph. On the way he told me his name was Fred and that he was Helga's brother, and he mentioned that he brought the music each month for the dancing.

The music started, and Fred placed my left arm across his upper shoulder, took me firmly into his arms, and under his expert guidance we moved along as one. It was heady stuff; I was thrilled. Of course I didn't expect this man to ask me for another dance, but if he did, I wouldn't say no. He changed the record for another tango ("Besame Mucho"), making sure I didn't leave his side. While I stood there waiting, several other men had come near us, but Fred waved them off, and I didn't get to dance with anyone else the rest of the evening.

I liked each new song more than the last one. The whole evening was a voyage of discovery into sheer pleasure. The songs—"La Comparsita," "Perfidia," "Jealousy," and of course our first one, "Besame Mucho"— still haunt me.

We talked a little. Again, he told me he always brought the music for the dances. He asked me what music I liked. I mentioned that lately I had bought a recording of "Nature Boy" by Nat King Cole. He asked me how old I thought he was. I guessed he must be at least thirty (twice my age), but I said, "Twenty-seven," since I thought it would make him feel better. (Thirty seemed ancient.) He laughed and then said he was going to be twenty-one next Sunday.

I saw Uncle Hugo and Lucy dancing, but promptly at 10:15 they beckoned to me that it was time to leave. Hugo was already holding my coat. Helga asked for my telephone number. Uncle Hugo said her father had the number. I explained about the telephone procedure at the store and that she could wait on the phone until I got there, or I could call her back and hang up after two rings to let her know I was there to answer the phone. Then she could call me back.

When we got to the street, my Dad had the car waiting at the curb. It was raining and awfully cold, and we hurried to get into the car. Just as I was closing the door from the backseat, Fred came up and held it open. He thrust a card into my hand and said, "Here is my business card. My personal telephone number is on the back. Call me if you ever get lonely." He stepped back and I quickly closed the door. I put the card in my pocket and didn't give it, or him, another thought.

Chapter 51

At around ten o'clock the next morning, Tommy, the boy who worked at Burnside Market on weekends, came knocking on our door. I had just gotten up and was eating my cereal. My parents had left for the store about a half-hour ago. Tommy was breathless from running the block to our house. "There is a telephone call for you," he announced. He caught his breath and ran back to the store.

Tommy didn't tell me who it was, or if they were waiting on the line, or if they would call me back per arranged method. I got dressed and went to the store. Tommy had thoughtfully written the number on a piece of paper and left it on the shelf under the payphone. I got a nickel out of the cash register, called the number, let it ring twice, hung up and returned the nickel to the register. A few minutes later the call came in. A woman was on the other end. I recognized the accent; it was Helga Lindemann. I listened while she made small talk about what a nice time she'd had last night. Then she said, "Some of the people from last night are planning to go to a movie this afternoon. We'd like you to come along, please."

I was surprised and didn't know what to say. She continued, "We will meet you downtown at one o'clock, on the corner of Broadway and Alder."

Helga seemed friendly, and I found myself wanting to go. I told my mother about this plan, and she didn't say anything against it. When I got back to Helga, who had been waiting on the telephone, I told her I would come. "I don't have stockings and high heels; I hope it is okay to wear saddle shoes and bobby-socks."

"Of course that's all right," she chirped. "I am so happy you are coming."

With butterflies in my stomach, I walked down to Stark Street and just caught the bus that only came once a day on Sundays. It cost thirty cents, but it went all the way downtown, so I didn't need to transfer to the streetcar in Montavilla on 82nd Street. By the time I arrived at the corner of S.W. Broadway and Alder Street, the butterflies had subsided, and I told myself that I had nothing to lose. Helga seemed quite friendly, and having an older friend could be a good thing.

Stepping down from the bus, I saw Helga's brother, but no Helga. He took my arm and helped me up the curb. "Where is Helga?" I asked, a bit taken aback.

"She had to run an errand and will join us at the movie," he said. His deep blue eyes were hypnotizing. "This is my friend, Stephen Katzan," he continued. "I think you met him last night." (I didn't remember anyone from last night except Lester, whom I had hoped would be there too.)

We started to walk to the Paramount Theater, while Stephen told me the movie was called "Scaramouch," and it was historical fiction about the French Revolution. Fred had put my hand into his elbow, but he had not said another word. When we arrived at the theater, Stephen stepped to the cashier and paid for his ticket. I started to get out my money when Fred said, "I buy the tickets for us."

The newsreel had started when we entered the dark theater. An usher showed us to seats that were much nearer the screen than I usually sat. I looked around for Stephen, but couldn't see him in the dark. When I took off my coat, Fred put it and his heavy, camelhair coat on his lap. I thought this was a gentlemanly gesture. No boy had ever done that before. He settled himself in the seat and started to slide his arm around the back of my seat. I must have flinched because he thought better of it and put his hand back on top of the coats.

Just about the time the movie started, Fred began to talk

to me about his job as repairman in a radio/appliance store. He had been hired over the telephone. Then he started to tell me how very lonesome he had been since he left Shanghai. I had not heard about the Jewish Europeans who had fled to Shanghai, China, and his story was a revelation.

He told me about the lovely, blonde girl he had left behind, and he asked me if I had any idea how devastating it was to leave someone you loved and know that you would probably never see them again. I mentioned that my parents went through that ordeal when my father escaped to Sweden. I think that was the last full sentence I spoke during the movie.

Fred had a soft voice with a strange accent that intrigued me, and he talked all through the movie. When it was over, I had no idea what the film had been about. The lights came on and I looked for Stephen, but he had disappeared; Helga had not shown up either. We went outside and Fred helped me with my coat (another charming gesture). Slowly we walked to the bus depot where we had to get the Gresham bus. This bus went up Glisan Street and would let us off on 102nd Avenue, with a lengthy walk to Burnside from there.

The bus ride took about forty minutes. It seemed much longer. I didn't know what to talk about to this definitely grown-up man. He wouldn't be interested in what I did at school, and we couldn't talk about the movie because neither of us watched it. I was thinking that I would probably never see him again because being with a teenager must be very boring.

To my surprise, he took my hand and asked, "Will you be my girl?" I didn't know what to say. I didn't even know what he meant exactly. I had no intention of going steady with anyone just yet, especially with someone I only met yesterday. "You are from Vienna?" he asked, but it really wasn't a question.

I answered "yes," being glad to have something to say. We sat in silence until 102nd Avenue. I thought he was annoyed that Helga hadn't shown up. He must be bored with what he might consider a babysitting job.

We got off the bus on Glisan Street, and as we walked along 102nd Avenue, Fred asked me about my family. Being an only child, I didn't have much to tell. "I want to meet your parents," he said.

The Burnside Market closed early on Sundays, so my parents were at home. I introduced him, hoping he would leave afterward. Instead, he began a conversation with my parents with a perfect Viennese accent, something I had not heard since I left Vienna eight years ago. (Hugo and my father spoke in Wopfing dialect when they conversed.)

Fred even told an off-color joke, which I was certain would shock my straitlaced parents. (we *never* mentioned anything that referred to a human activity below the waist.) They chuckled politely and he went on to tell another off-color story that referred to fecal matter. I was disgusted and embarrassed to have brought such a person into our house. He must have seen my expression because he began to make his good-byes immediately.

At the open door he held my hand, and once again I was mesmerized by those blue eyes. "So, you are my girl, yes?" he breathed. Not giving me a chance to answer he walked quickly down the gravel driveway. I watched until he got to the street, wondering if I wanted to see him again. When he turned to wave a kiss, I knew the answer.

The first week of December I came home from school, and a service truck was in the driveway. As I walked by the driver's window, Fred called out to me. I was extremely surprised. He got out of the truck and explained that he had a service call in the neighborhood and thought he would stop by to say hello.

He got out of the truck, leaving the door open. Seeing him in the fading daylight, he looked even more handsome than I remembered. He had the straight, blond hair I had always wanted, and his dazzling blue eyes sent warm ripples up and down my spine. A devilish smile played around his lips, and as his smile broadened, I could see his eye teeth were longer than the rest and gave the impression of being fangs. I found them charming.

"My family wants you to come and have Friday night dinner with us," he said in a matter-of-fact tone, quickly adding, "Helga wants to apologize for standing you up on Sunday." Suddenly, like a theater curtain being drawn aside, the whole scenario flashed through my mind. Fred had used Helga to get me to meet him on Sunday. She had never intended to go to a movie with me. Stephan had come along with Fred as a kind of support system but melted away at the opportune moment. I had fallen for his devious device. For a moment I was annoyed at myself for being so naïve, then I was flattered that Fred had gone to so much trouble to get me alone.

With one foot on the running board of the van and one hand on my shoulder he told me his plan for Friday night. He had to work until six o'clock, and he would be home by six-thirty. Could I please get to his house on my own? That way we would get there in time for a seven o'clock dinner. His parents would be so glad to see me again, and Helga was especially anxious to see me. He told me he had a younger sister named Inge. She was thirteen and needed a friend like me who was close in age, a refugee, and a good English-speaker.

Fred was very persuasive, and when I looked into those blue eyes, I could not say no. I must admit that I was also curious about the people who were present at the Friendship Club. They were mostly upper-class German, and I had not been around that culture before. It was like visiting a foreign country. I had noticed that all the adults addressed each other formally as Mr. or Mrs. or Miss (Herr, Frau, Fräulein), No one had ever called me Fräulein Ruth before. For the last ten years, I had been totally inundated in the American culture, hearing only English. The only people around with an accent were my parents. My dad sometimes spoke Viennese with the Klingers. It is a different-sounding language from German, and Austrians tend to be insultingly jocular when they talk to close, longtime friends.

Fred came prepared. He gave me a timetable for the bus to Montavilla, the streetcar to Northwest 21st Avenue and Northrup Street, and specific instructions on how to find the apartment. However, on Friday morning I was still trying to make up my mind if I was really going to go to the Lindemanns' that night. I certainly didn't learn much at school that day.

Chapter 52

Thursday night I told my parents that I had been invited to the Lindemanns' for Friday night dinner. My plan was to take the school bus, which went to S.E. 94th Avenue and Stark, and then walk the twelve blocks to the trolley line in Montavilla to catch the N.W. Portland streetcar.

"I assume Fred will bring you home," was the only thing my mother said. I assumed this also. Coming home alone to 102nd Avenue after dark was out of the question. I had no doubt that my father would come and get me, but I hoped it wouldn't be necessary.

It was dark by the time I arrived at the Washington Apartments on N.W. Northrup Street. I went up the steps to the entry hall, saw the "Lindemann" listing on the mailbox, and ascended the stairs to the second floor. Standing in front of the designated door, I heard loud voices speaking in a strange language. It sounded like two people having an argument. I thought I must have the wrong door, but it was the number on the mailbox and the one Fred had given me. I knocked.

A short, plump woman opened the door, and the tall, dark man standing behind her held out his hand. They both had a friendly smile and spoke my name. So I had the right door. Helga came up behind them and pulled me into the small living room. She made introductions and in a few minutes, her younger sister, Inge, a small dark-haired girl, came into the room.

Helga took my coat while introducing her parents, "Rosa"

and "Leo." I shook hands. Just then Fred came home. He apologized for being late, took my hand, looked into my eyes, and said, "So, you came." His smile made me warm all over.

Helga Lindemann, 1946.

In a few minutes, we were sitting around the dining room table. Leo and Fred put on black kippot (traditional brimless caps worn by Jewish men). Rosa lit the Shabbat candles (a ritual I had not seen for ten years; lighting candles on Friday evening to usher in Shabbat, or the Sabbath). Leo said kiddush (the prayer or blessing over the wine) and we each drank from the glass at our place (my first taste of wine). Rosa broke pieces from the perfect Challah (the braided bread) on the table, and everyone but me said the HaMotzi (traditional blessing). I couldn't remember that ritual at all, but it sounded familiar to me—and I became inexplicably sad (I still get a lump in my throat when I hear these rituals).

The soup was salty, the boiled chicken tasteless, the vegetable cooked to a pulp, the potatoes lumpy, and I began to appreciate what a good cook by mother had become. We had more wine and a piece of tasty cake for dessert. I did not make a good impression as I hardly ate anything. I tried to explain that I had worked at the school store for an hour after school; I had come here directly after that, and I was too tired to eat much.

It was obvious that the Lindemanns were not Austrian. I was curious where Fred had picked up the Viennese jargon with such accuracy that he had fooled my parents. He told me he had learned radio repairing at the ORT school in Shanghai, and then he had apprenticed with a radio repair shop owned by a man from Vienna. It seemed that Fred had a talent for languages; he had even learned Chinese and had Chinese friends.

Since I had not spoken German for several years, I decided not to try talking in German with the Lindemanns. They spoke German with each other but English with me, assuming I didn't speak German—a natural assumption since I didn't have an accent.

They were from a northern area called *Oberschlesiens* (Selesia was a part of Prussia), and they spoke a language called *Hochdeutsch* ("high German"). When they found out that I was from Vienna, something changed in their attitude. From the remarks they made to each other in German, I learned that the Lindemanns looked down on Austrians. I heard Rosa ask Fred if I was from *guten Hause*.[42] He avoided answering her. (Even though they owned a store now, in Europe, my parents were working class people, which meant I was not from *guten Hause*.)

Fred held my hand all the way back to my house. He must have noticed something was bothering me, but I could not explain it to him. I didn't want to admit that I understood much of what they said about me.

He started to talk about his parents. "My mother came from a very wealthy family. She lost everyone and lived in dire poverty for nine years. All they have left is their pride in who they were." Fred talked about his life in China, and in contrast to his parents, he had an egalitarian attitude about people from other cultures—including Austrians. I was beginning to like him and not just his blue eyes.

We stood at my front door for a long time while he kept talking about how someday he wanted to buy a car and be in business for himself, and suddenly he changed the subject.

"I have a lot of friends who are having a birthday party for me on Sunday afternoon around three o'clock. Will you come?" (Or was it more like, "You will come!") He also asked

---

[42] Presumably educated and/or prosperous; not working-class people.

if I could meet him downtown since it would take all day to come pick me up. "My friends are teasing me about having a girlfriend who lives halfway to Mt. Hood, when there are lots of Jewish girls who live nearby." He chuckled while waiting for my answer. When I agreed to come, he put his arms around me, pulled me closer than he had during the tango and kissed my lips.

I don't remember Fred ever telling me that he loved me, but his kiss said it all. The night was very cold, but we stood in the doorway for a long time feeling a newly-found warmth. From that moment, I couldn't imagine life without him and lived for that next kiss.

Fred's 21st birthday party, Northrup Street, 1948.

Fred's twenty-first birthday party was to start in the afternoon, since it was Sunday and nobody had to go to work. I don't remember whether Fred came "halfway to Mt. Hood" to get me, or if I traveled to his house alone, or if the weather was fair or rainy. I just remember being in the Lindemann's living room with a lot of people who were much older, who laughed a lot about things I didn't understand. I also remember being deeply embarrassed by Fred's attitude toward me and the other females at the party.

From the joke that Fred had told my parents, I knew that

he had a crude side and, since that was absolutely the opposite of my parents' straitlaced way of life, I was intrigued. Fred drank hard liquor, played poker regularly and won; he and Helga had frequented nightclubs where they often won dance contests.

Fred had known most of his friends since his Shanghai days and, as he introduced me, he joked, "Remember I call all my girls 'Trude.' That way I won't get in trouble for forgetting a name." (He called me "Trude" for many years then flipped to "Honey.")

Some of the men had brought dates who had not met Fred before. After they were introduced, he would seriously ask the girl, "Did you wet your hair this morning?" When she answered "No," he asked, "So you peed through a straw?" As the others laughed the new girl usually felt uncomfortable but might chuckle politely. He would tell unwitting girls how he knew how to repair radios and offered to make house calls to check out their tubes. This remark brought uproarious laughter from the men, and some of the girls blushed. Given my innocence and ignorance of sexual matters, most double entendres went right over my head. (Eventually, after hearing these same jokes over many years, I understood what was meant, but I never found them amusing.)

I was getting more and more uncomfortable and wished I had not come. After Fred's father offered me a jigger or two of the delicious Cherry Heering brandy (my first hard liquor), I began to relax. The rest of the party is a blur. On the bus ride home, I tried to remember what I had said or done, but I only remembered Fred's crude jokes and the taste of the cherry liqueur.

Fred Lindemann, 1949.

On Monday I showed my school friends the picture that Fred had given me, they all four said in unison, "Your uncle is a handsome man." When I explained that this was not the uncle who had recently arrived from Sweden but my new boyfriend, there was an ominous silence. He was wearing a tie and a well-tailored brown, pinstriped suit. This was an adult. What was I thinking?

Chapter 53

Several times during the next three weeks, Fred came by the house in the repair truck just as I was getting home from school. It seemed that, at times, he waited as much as a half-hour for me to get home. He questioned my late arrival, as he found out that some students came home much earlier. I explained that I worked at the school store's soda fountain for an hour after school and took the later bus home. The bus made two trips as too many students needed a ride, and the second bus was convenient for those who did after-school activities and athletes who had to stay for practice. We came close to an argument when Fred wanted to know who the boy was who was walking with me before I turned up our driveway.

Fred, 1950.

I did not like to be questioned, but I had nothing to hide. Again, I explained about the two buses and the second bus usually carried the boys who went to after-school sports practice sessions, and many of those boys were my friends. We would start talking on the bus and sometimes spend time standing at the bus stop to finish our conversation, or the boys would walk with me if they were going the same way.

I told Fred that it was unreasonable for him to be annoyed about waiting for me when I had no idea he was there. He obviously didn't like hearing this. He got into the truck and drove away. The next day he was there again after school, all smiles and plans for the next weekend (maybe a movie or dinner in a restaurant), as well as a party invitation for New Year's Eve. He asked if I might stay overnight because the party would last long after the last bus. I could sleep in Helga and Inga's room, where they had an extra cot. I told him I needed to ask my mother. To be honest, I was hoping she would say no to such a plan. However, she only asked if Fred's parents would be there and a little more detail about the sleeping arrangement. (Fred slept on a daybed in the living room, his parents in the other bedroom behind the kitchen.)

I had thought the New Year's Eve party was to be at the Friendship Club, but New Year's Eve was on a Friday and many members were observant Jews. Fred and some of the younger people were invited to a party given by the daughter of the man who owned the apartment building in which the Lindemanns, and several other refugee families, lived.

The Gross family had a mansion on Vista Blvd. Their twenty-one-year-old daughter, named Inez, was a friendly, warmhearted girl, but regrettably, in size and features, she resembled her stout father. The party was a sort of coming-out party for Inez. Her parents had invited every eligible young Jewish man around her age. Some of them, like Fred, brought dates along, and it became obvious that the girls who came (most of them refugees like me and Helga) were not especially welcome.

We had dancing to a live combo and lots of food and alcoholic drinks. The men all took turns dancing with Inez, who towered over many of them. When our dates came back to the couch where most of the girls were huddled together, they made insulting remarks of how big Inez would be without a girdle and how any man that married her would definitely be earning all that money the hard way. Fred's favorite saying was *"Inez ist besser wie keiness."*[43] Which rhymes in German, which got said every time she left the room or the group to go dance. Again, I was feeling uncomfortable by the level of crudeness.

Suddenly, it was midnight and 1949 had begun. Fred took me in his arms, and I forgot everything except the touch of his lips on mine as the heat flowed through my body. "It's a new year," he said in my ear, "and it's going to be our year." If I had any vague notions of being free again, they vanished in his arms.

We had obviously all had too much to drink, but this was the first, and last, time I saw Fred visibly drunk. We tumbled out of the taxi, stumbled up the stairs to the apartment. Fred's hand was shaking so badly that we stood in front of the door for a long time before he fit the key into the keyhole. Helga kept giggling and telling us to be quiet so as not wake Inge. Finally, we got into the apartment, took quick turns in the bathroom and got undressed. Fred knocked on the door. "Trude, come say good-night to me," he said softly.

"Goodnight," I whispered and got into the bed. Helga had fallen asleep immediately, but I lay awake a long time thinking of what might have happened if I had gone to Fred's bed to say goodnight.

The next morning I went out to the living room in my nightgown to say good morning to Fred. He was dressed and curtly told me to get dressed, and then he would accompany me home. I was surprised because the plan had been for me to spend New Year's Day with him and his family. It was

---

[43] "Inez is better than nothing."

Shabbat and his father had invited me to go to the Synagogue with him and Inge. (Rosa never went on Saturday.) Helga usually went to work at Lipman & Wolf on Saturday, where she did alterations. This was one Saturday she could sleep in, and she didn't plan to go out.

It was obvious that Fred was annoyed about something I had done—or not done. I started to ask why the change in plans, but he didn't answer me. I got dressed, trying to be quiet so as not to wake the sisters. On our way out, I didn't see Fred's parents, so perhaps they were still asleep.

To my surprise, Fred got on the street car with me and continued to my house on the bus. It was a quiet ride. He never told me why he was angry and only became quieter and colder when I asked him to tell me what the problem was. When we got to my house, he didn't say goodbye, just turned around and left. The rollercoaster had begun.

Sunday, I cried most of the day, thinking that my relationship with Fred was over. By evening, I was reconciled to the idea that it wasn't meant to be. Monday, I went back to school, my mind on how I was going to live the rest of my life without him. After all, I had plans to become a foreign correspondent for a news service like Associated Press and spend almost all my time traveling. Having a jealous, possessive man in my life would be complicated. By the time the bus arrived at school I had decided to enroll in the journalism class and get on the school newspaper staff.

The next two days went by calmly. I was sad about losing Fred, but as I often did when I fretted about a situation, I asked myself, *Can I do something to change the situation?* If the answer was yes, I started working on a solution; but if the answer was no, I needed to concentrate on my own life. So my mental state was shaken when, on Wednesday, upon my return from school, I was surprised to see the Ott's truck in our driveway

Fred acted like I should have expected him. He launched right into a plan for the coming weekend. He suggested I stay for two nights—Friday night dinner with his family, and then going out to a movie afterwards, Saturday we would sleep late, and then go to Joanna's for lunch. After lunch, we would spend the afternoon with friends; he wanted me to meet them and we would all go dancing at the Crystal Ballroom. (Minors accompanied by an adult could go because no alcohol was allowed.) Sunday, he would accompany back to my house.

My acquiescence was taken for granted. He pulled me into his arms, and I was flooded with relief. We stood beside the open door of the truck, kissing. "See you Friday," was all he said.

When I told my mother that I was going to the Lindemann's again for Friday night dinner, she only nodded as if she already knew about it. Her next words sounded like a warning: "Ruthie, Fred is a grown man. He will expect more than those boys from school."

Somewhere in the back of my mind, I knew this. After all, I had read a few banned books like *Forever Amber* and *Duchess Hotspur*. The love scenes in those books always ended with the couple in a "fierce embrace." Since I had practically no knowledge of the male anatomy, I thought love scenes just ended with kissing.

My familiarity with the female anatomy was also limited. That Friday night after we returned from the movie, Fred gave me a jigger of Cherry Heering brandy for a nightcap and invited me to sit in the living room for a while to talk about the movie and so forth. Fred changed the record on the phonograph. He had a box full of records. The store where he worked had a record department, and he bought a record almost every week. The apartment was always filled with music. His taste was eclectic. He listened to tangos, operas, Frank Sinatra, and The Ink Spots. He sang along with them while looking into my eyes. I was dazzled.

We sat on his daybed and we began to kiss. He started to touch me in places where I had not been touched before. His movements were not tentative like some of the boys I had dated. He was skilled and aware of the effect on me.

That night I learned about my own body and its function. Fred was gentle, patient, reassuring, and told me not to worry about losing my virginity. After all, he was a Kohan.[44] However, the next day I felt like I had done something shameful and bad, and—as I had read in several books that purported to help girls navigate their sexuality in relation to boys—"If you let a boy go too far, he will never respect you again. He will tell all his friends about you and they won't respect you either." Had I let him go too far by letting him put his fingers where I didn't even know that fingers could go?

I had allowed Dick to touch my breasts, but I was certain that he never told anyone else. I had known Dick for several years before we started necking, I trusted him. Did I trust Fred the same way? I had only known him for a few weeks. On our way to lunch at Joanna's, I naively told him that I was afraid he would not respect me after the things I had allowed him to do the night before. "That's crazy," he said. "You're my girl, and I respect you for that." I wasn't sure what he meant, but I didn't bring up the subject again.

We took a bus to the Falkensteins, who were friends from Shanghai. They lived in SW Portland, where most Jewish families lived in those days. The mother and father were home, but they drifted into the kitchen after introductions and left Fred and me to visit with their daughters, Ruth and Inge, and two other men. One of the men, Gary Becker, was from the Shanghai group, and Burt (obviously an American) had a car. We talked mostly nonsense and the men told jokes. Toward evening we had a snack and left in the car to pick up Stephen Katzan and his sister, Rochelle.

The Katzans were refugees who had escaped to Portugal and had recently arrived in Portland. Mr. Katzan had gone into the jewelry business and seemed to be doing quite well. Rochelle invited me, Ruth, and Inge into Rochelle's lovely

---

[44] The Kohanim are the priestly sect descendants of Aaron (the brother of Moses). They are required to marry only virgins, never go near a dead body, be the first to be called up to read the Torah, and lead the services if no Rabbi is present.

bedroom, ostensibly to "freshen up." They took this opportunity to find out that I was only fifteen years old. Then they
took turns warning me that Fred would take advantage of
me. "Be careful," said Rochelle, who had her eye on Fred for
herself. "He is too old and sophisticated for a child like you."
(I didn't tell her that I already knew that.)

For my sixteenth birthday, Fred gave me a set of amethyst
earrings and a pin/pendant, set in gold on a chain. It was
a beautiful, adult present. When I showed it to my parents,
they said nothing, but Lucy gasped and told me it was not an
appropriate present for a teenager, and she suggested I give it
back. Fred assured me that I deserved it, and he would take
me places where it was appropriate to wear.

In fact, he and Uncle Hugo had already made plans to take
me out to dinner and to the Crystal Ballroom for dancing. So
I wore low heels, a silky dress, nylon stockings, and the lovely
amethyst/rhinestone jewelry. I felt totally grown up.

By now I knew that it was best not to tell Fred what Lucy
had said about the jewelry. It was obvious that he was super-
sensitive. (When I finally grew up, fifty years later, I realized
that he was super insecure.) I kept getting the cold, silent
treatment often during our relationship. If I said anything
nice about another male or made a slightly critical comment
about anything he said or did, he went into a funk. I never
knew what it was I had said or done, only that his behavior
was my fault. When I asked him to tell me what it was I did—
so I could avoid doing it again—he always said, "You know
what you did." If I kept asking, he just got angrier. I learned
to wait it out. A few days later he would come home from
work and be his jolly, sweet self.

In March of 1949, Fred bought a 1939 Pontiac from Mr.
Falkenstein. This was quite an accomplishment after being
in the U.S.A. for only a year and a half. Regrettably, the car
needed work that Mr. Falkenstein had not told Fred about
when he bought the car. It happened to be several hundred
dollars, and for months most of the Lindemann conversation

was about the dishonesty of Mr. Falkenstein. However, Ruth, Gary, Burt, Stephen, Rochelle, Fred and I kept meeting at the Falkenstein apartment on occasional weekends, where we listened to music brought by Fred.

We often talked about the situation in Israel. Continuous fighting was going on, although a ceasefire had been declared. Fred told us about his friends who had left Shanghai for Israel and were now involved in the fighting. Some of them were pilots, and we were impressed to hear how they had originally trained with the famous "Flying Tigers" led by general Chenault. Although he had not learned to fly, Fred had worked on the radios for this American squadron, which had fought the Japanese army, flying out of Burma. When the Flying Tigers were stationed in Shanghai, Fred worked on the base. (He has a commendation by General Chenault for his valuable service.)

As the weather got warmer and a bit dryer, Fred and I often included Inge, Helga, and his parents on weekend outings. I usually had to navigate as we perused the maps to find the tourist attractions in the area. By summer, we knew our way around Oregon and found our way to Seaside. We all rode the Ferris wheel and the carousel in the amusement park. Fred, Helga and Inge liked the bumper cars (which I hated). We ate corndogs, walked the promenade, and waded in the ocean.

Fred's parents always dressed formally—Leo in a three-piece suit, tie, and Stetson hat; Rosa in low-heeled shoes with stockings, skirt, blouse, jacket, and a hat, even when we went to wilderness areas like Silver Creek Falls. Of course everyone dressed more formally in those days. Corduroy or linen slacks for the men, a cotton dress and sandals for the women were considered casual and women—seldom wore slacks except to go hiking, for which there were special hiking skirts.

(L to R) Louis, Rosa, Helga and Inge Lindemann, Ruth Kohn Lindemann
and Fred Lindemann, 1937 Pontiac in 1949.

Summer 1949.

Chapter 54

When school was out, I traveled across town to the Social Security Office and got a card and a work permit, which had to be signed by my father or other male guardian since I was a minor. Every day I spent the mornings looking through help-wanted ads in the newspaper, then walked the downtown streets the rest of the day, looking for help-wanted signs in the window. They were few and far between. I filled out many applications, but I didn't hear back from anyone.

One morning in June, I saw a help-wanted ad from Montgomery Ward, which was a huge department store and national mail-order house in Northwest Portland—just about as far as one could travel and still be in the city.

I took a bus to S.E. 82nd Street, the trolley to N. W. Portland and two hours later was walking into the enormous six-story building. In the employment office I filled out a form for part-time, summer employment. The personnel director asked if I had ever worked in retail. I said "yes" since I had spent a few hours working in the grocery store. She took me to the manager of the men's department who put me to work selling men's underwear.

I was in no position to decline working there, but I did express concern since I was totally inexperienced in that field and told the floor manager that men might be embarrassed to buy underwear from a sixteen-year-old girl.

She gave me an amused smile and said, "Look, honey, men do not buy their own underwear. You will see only wives and mothers in this department." And for the most part, she was right. Business was slow and I was tremendously bored.

One morning a grizzly, old man, who looked like the prospectors in western movies, came into the department and asked if he could talk to a salesman. When I told him I was the clerk in this department, he looked uncomfortable. He cleared his throat and softly asked if we had any long johns (a totally outdated one-piece, knitted, wool garment worn in the winter). This was July and if we had such a garment in stock it would not be on the floor. Luckily, I remembered my father wearing such a thing years ago when we were in Idaho. I told the gentleman (he was very polite) that I would look for it and went into the back room to find long johns. To my surprise, I found dusty boxes of them on a shelf just above my head. Triumphantly, I returned to the sales floor with three different sizes. The man chose one and I took his money, put the underwear in a bag, and handed him his change. He pressed two dollars (one hour's wage) into my hand, saying, "That's for you. Bless you, sweetheart." He was the only male customer I had all that summer.

Steve Katzan & Fred, 1949.

Fred Lindemann, Lake Oswego, 1949

Helga and Rochelle, 1949.

During that summer we finally got a telephone installed in the house. I could call my friends and get a weather report and the time of day. Most importantly, Fred and I could talk about our plans for the weekend every night.

As the weather got warmer, we drove to Blue Lake or Battleground Lake or one of my favorites, Lake Oswego. It was at Lake Oswego that I learned a bit more about Fred's feelings about women. The first time we went there with several of his friends, he rented a rowboat for the two of us. By the way he got into the boat, I could tell he was not an experienced rower. After watching him struggle with the oars for about half an hour I suggested he let me row for a while. "It doesn't look right for a woman to row a man around," he said.

"But I'm good at it, so let me row for a few minutes," I suggested. Finally, he gave in. We exchanged seats, and I rowed us back to the dock. Sure enough, we heard remarks from his friends about the kind of man who lets a girl row him around. That afternoon, I learned that he had to feel that he was in charge. Every time we were together, he found something about me that displeased him. One day he said his friends thought I was a snob. "You always talk like a book," he said. "It makes the rest of us feel dumb." If this was supposed to be an insult, I didn't take it as such. But I dumbed down my words after that.

During those outings I swam in the cold, freshwater lake, while Fred and his friends sat at tables and played cards. Helga was the only Lindemann who knew how to swim, and she often joined me in the water. Sometimes my parents came along and my mother, who was an excellent swimmer, spent hours at a time swimming in circles while I used the diving board. I dearly missed the pool in Longview.

I was happiest in the water and could not understand the reluctance of Fred and his friends to get wet. The exception was Helga, who was the daredevil of the family. Rosa told me that it was Helga who was always climbing the highest into a tree, wading the deepest in a creek, and riding her bicycle faster than any of the boys. Just being with her was fun and uplifting. Yet, a sadness was in her demeanor, especially around her parents. The tension between Helga and her father and Fred was palpable.

One day the mystery was solved when I overheard Fred, Rosa and Leo telling Helga that it was a sin to keep secrets from ones' parents. Seems she had met secretly with her one true love, who had stopped in Portland between trains to Detroit, Michigan. The family didn't approve of Hans Peter Rosenberg, as his father had been in show business in Berlin. Rosa explained to me that people in showbusiness, like menial workers, were not from *guten Haus* like her family. Obviously, my working-class background was not from *guten Haus* either, but Fred was a man and could marry down; girls were expected to marry up on the social scale.

Visiting Shirley, YMCA Camp, 1949.

The summer of 1949 passed quickly. I got to visit Shirley one time, and another time she came up to Portland to meet Fred. They were cordial, but it was plain they did not like each other. Shirley thought he was taking advantage of me, and Fred didn't trust Shirley. My mother had not trusted her either and I was aware of the undercurrent of Anti-Semitism but tried to subvert my feelings about that. My criterion for non-Jewish friends was this: "Would that person hide me from the Nazis?" If the answer were "no," we would not be friends. Only two or three times in my life was the answer "yes," and these were friends I could trust. In most cases the answer was "maybe," and the friendship was only on the surface and would not last. Shirley was a special case. Our friendship lasted over sixty years, but through all those years I fortunately didn't need to test it.

(L - R) Shirley, Fred and Ruth, YMCA Camp - Spirit Lake, WA 1949.

The owner of the house my parents were renting wanted to sell it for three thousand dollars. It was a good price for the location. The house was set back one hundred feet or more from 102nd Avenue, near East Burnside. The lot alone was worth half of that. My parents didn't have three thousand dollars, and when they approached a bank for a loan they were denied because they had no credit record. So we would need to move. By then, Hugo and Lucy had moved to a small rental unit attached to the Burnside Market. Hugo was working at the furniture factory and Lucy found a job sewing at the White Stag sporting goods factory.

Over the last year my parents had cultivated a friendship with Isidor Fox and his son, Louis. They owned a small grocery on the corner of 102nd and Hassalo Street, one block south of N.E. Halsey. They also owned a lot behind the store and offered to build a house and sell it to my parents on a contract. The little salt box on the bare lot would cost seven thousand dollars, and the loan could be for fifteen years at the going rate of interest.

Rather than move into another apartment, my parents decided to sign that deal. The house had two bedrooms, a small living room, a kitchen with eating space, a tiny bathroom between the bedrooms and a central floor heater. It had no garage or basement but a place for a wash machine near the back door and room for a clothesline in the back yard.

First house of Kohn family, 10125 NE Hassalo, Portland, OR 1949.

We moved to the new house on N.E. Hassalo, where I still had my own bedroom, but had to sleep on the hard, fold-out, sleeping couch that I had used for ten years in Kelso/ Longview. After sleeping in a real bed for over a year, the crack in the middle bothered me, but I got used to it again.

However, I was bigger now and couldn't just fit onto one side or the other of the crack. Instead of buying me a bed, my parents bought a small sofa and two chairs for the living room.

We had to apply for a telephone all over again. The payphone at the store was too far away to use, but after six weeks we finally had a telephone again. Fred had made a habit of coming over every day after work to eat dinner with me. My mother cooked a dinner the night before and set aside a portion for us. Years later, I learned that Fred thought I had cooked these meals, which were always tasty and nourishing. After we ate and sometimes did the dishes, we would go for a drive, find a place to park, and neck.

I started my junior year in high school wrapped up in thoughts of pleasing Fred and spending as much time as I could with him. I was totally exhausted from getting up at six o'clock to catch the school bus and not getting home until after five that evening because I took the later bus after working in the school soda fountain for another hour. There were only a few boys on this bus, so it was easier to do my homework. I seldom finished the assignments the night before they were due because I was just too tired. Fred usually brought me home around ten o'clock. I did homework for an hour, then he would call, and we talked for another hour. I seldom got to bed before midnight.

Just before winter break in late December, Fred complained that I was tired all the time and frequently irritable (especially around my period). He decided I must quit my job at the school store. It would mean I could take the early bus home and do some of my homework before he arrived. It made sense, even though I had to give up the two dollars per week.

That may not sound like a lot of money now, but in those days a nice dress could be bought at J.C. Penney for around six dollars, and a blouse or skirt for three dollars, so giving up the two dollars was a big decision for a teenage girl who, after a month of working, could buy herself a piece of clothing without asking her mother for the money. I was giving up some of my independence.

Before Fred took up all my spare time, I used to babysit for various couples in the neighborhood. I didn't like taking care of small children, but I did get a dollar or two each time and had opened a bank account. At that time I was saving money to use for a trip to Longview, so I wouldn't need to ask my parents for money. Fred seemed to sense my feelings because after I gave up my job, he often offered to give me money whenever I had plans to go downtown. "Buy yourself a dress," he would say, while giving me a twenty-dollar bill.

The winter of 1950–51 was bitter cold. The snow piled up along the streets several times. Portland had a snowplow— just in case— but had to rent a second one from Seattle for that winter.

One very wet, cold night, after midnight, Fred was driving me home when a car came out of a side street and plowed into my side of the car. The 1939 Pontiac was a sturdy car, and I wasn't hurt, but the door was totally broken. My lap was filled with glass. The other driver was visibly drunk, so we were not interrogated beyond our names and Fred's driver's license number.

We were nervous because there was a curfew for girls under eighteen; I was still about a year away from that age. Fred was twenty-three, and being out with an underage girl could mean being arrested and worse. A lot was at stake, mostly for him. I was terrified that the glass might have cut my face; I was aware that my future with Fred depended a lot on my looks. Would he want a wife with a scarred face?

Sometime in early spring of 1950, Helga asked her father to sign the release so she could take some money out of her savings account to pay for a visit with her sister Hannah in New York. Leo Lindemann gave her an unequivocal "no" for an answer. One day she didn't come home from her job in alterations at Lipman & Wolf department store. I'm not sure about what she told her parents, but the family thought she had gone out with a friend. When she didn't come home the next day Leo called Hannah who told him that Helga was on her way to visit her. "Didn't she tell you?" Hannah asked.

When Leo checked on Helga's bank account, he discovered it had been closed. At first, he accused Fred of forging his name on the release.[45] Finally, they found the letter that Helga left for the family explaining her actions and her plans.

Heinz and Hilde Jacob, good friends of the Lindemann's from their Shanghai days, had helped Helga make her escape. Heinz had forged Leo's name; Hilde had helped her pack and hide her suitcase. They had driven her to the train station where she boarded the train leaving for Detroit. By the time the Lindemanns read the letter she was arriving in Detroit and flinging herself into Hans Peter Rosenberg's arms. A few weeks later, with Hannah as a witness, they were married on May 28, 1950. Although Leo never spoke to Heinz and Hilda again, Fred and I were good friends with them over many years.

---

[45] In 1950 minors and married women had to have a male relative co-sign bank accounts, loans, and revolving charge accounts.

Chapter 55

In May of 1950, I started to write in my diary again, and it helped to put my thoughts down on paper. My conclusion was that I was trapped due to the fact that I was in love. I could not imagine a life without Fred.

One Sunday morning in early May 1950, Fred parked the brand new, light mint-green Studebaker in front of our house. It was the same shape in front as in the back. You couldn't tell if the car was coming or going. Fred was especially proud of the small propeller on the airplane-shaped grill in front. (It was stolen after a few months.)

New Studebaker, Salem, Oregon, 1950.

The other refugees in Fred's neighborhood on N.W. Northrup Street passed the word around that it was not suitable for a recent refugee to buy a brand-new car. Leo, who was sensitive to "what people will say," reprimanded Fred sharply, causing more friction between father and son. Being critical and abrasive with children seemed to be a European trait. I could never please my parents either; even a rare compliment was, usually, left-handed.

The exciting thing that spring was the junior prom. It would be my first formal dance, and I would be attending with the handsomest, best dancer in the world in a brand-new car.

Fred told me that I was the best-looking girl at the prom in my white dress (bought on sale in the basement at Meier & Frank Department Store), wearing the amethyst jewelry and a gold mesh bag that Fred had given me. We danced every dance, and I could see glances of admiration from my friends as well as students I hardly knew. The evening was a success.

Fred's older sister, Hanna, lived in Manhattan with her husband, Martin Henner, and worked for a firm that produced publicity photos. Martin was a tailor and worked for a clothing manufacturer in the cutting room. This made him a Polish, working-class person even though he was born in Berlin; his family had originated in Poland. I heard the family talk of how Hanna had married beneath her station (which would also be the case with Fred if he married me). The fact that Martin's parents

Hanna 1947.

had owned a successful grocery store in Shanghai and supplied all the food for Martin and Hanna's wedding had no bearing on his social status.

Hanna was coming to Portland to celebrate Rosa and Leo's twenty-fifth wedding anniversary. The afternoon of her arrival she was dressed in an elegant black suit with stylish hat to match. Everything about her, even her urbane language, indicated sophistication. Fred had warned me that any girl he married would need Hanna's approval because she was the wisest person in that family, and he trusted her judgment (even if she did marry a Polish, working-class man).

Fred, Summer 1950.

Hanna had a sweet smile, complete with the Lindemann fangs, which, on her as on Fred and Inge, looked charming. It was interesting to see how respectful Leo and Fred acted toward Hanna, in contrast to how they talked to Rosa and Helga.

It was during her visit that I learned more about the hardships the Lindemann family endured in Shanghai. The refugees spent hours every day waiting in line for food, the latrine, and a shower. In the Wayside Camp, the six of them lived in one small room, divided into three sections by a blanket on a clothesline. During the Japanese occupation, all the German Jewish refugees were herded into a ghetto in the Hongkew section. The curfew, cruelty, and punishment for breaking arbitrary laws were a constant threat. The Japanese built antiaircraft towers in the middle of the ghetto, which became a prime target for the nightly bombings by British and American bombers.

Fred finally broke his silence about his life in Shanghai and—with Hanna's encouragement—talked about lying under a picnic table watching the flares and bombs during those nights of terror. I became more tolerant of the idiosyncrasies of this family. What a shock for someone like Rosa, who had grown up in the lap of luxury, to find herself in a refugee camp.

Hanna's visit was a week of real fun and pleasant events. We took her to Blue Lake one Sunday, and she seemed to enjoy the primitive surroundings. On another Sunday afternoon, the family went to a tea dance at the Safari Club. Fred asked the band to play some waltzes. Watching my father and Hanna whirling in a Viennese waltz was an unforgettable pleasure. They looked almost professional and certainly happy.

The summer went by with weekends at Blue Lake or other picnic areas. More and more, Fred and I spent time alone. Once we went trout fishing on the Toutle River (a lovely area destroyed by the eruption of Mt. St. Helens in May 1980). At other times we drove to beaches along the Columbia river. Friday, I had Shabbat dinner with the Lindemanns and spent the night. We still went dancing and out to dinner once a week, but usually it was just us two.

I looked for work but didn't find another paying job. So I volunteered for the Camp Fire Day Camp, which was held five days a week, from nine to three, on the Reed College campus. It was a lengthy bus ride, but the best part was that I got to use the college pool for lap swims after three in the afternoon. Sometimes Fred picked me up downtown and we went to dinner, a movie, or a ride around Washington Park or Mt. Tabor, where we parked.

The war (which was called a "police action") in Korea heated up, and the draft board sent Fred a notice. He could avoid going into the army if he joined the National Guard. He was supposed to go to a meeting once a week, but he found them boring. (They just took roll call, played pool, drank beer, and went home.) When he missed three meetings, he received another draft notice. Mr. Ott was able to get Fred several deferments as an essential employee. Soon his deferments were used up.

We talked about our plans. I said I had hopes of going to college. He said if I did that, he would find another girl. This gave me something to think about. Each time I faced the reality of a life without Fred, I completely rejected the idea. Being with him was imperative for my happiness. I had no choice. Yet I was puzzled by his attitude about my further education.

Late one Friday night after Shabbat dinner at the Lindemanns, Fred and I were sitting on the couch looking out at the star-filled August night. "When I go into the army, we can't just go on like this," he said. I held my breath as I waited for him to tell me we needed to break up. Instead, I was thrilled to hear him say, "How about we get married?" When I didn't say anything because of the lump in my throat, he said, "After you finish high school, of course." I told him that was exactly what I wanted, and we were formally engaged.

One night, as we were parked at Mt. Tabor before going to dinner at the Top Hat, our favorite Chinese restaurant, he gave me a beautiful set of rings with stones set in platinum. I could hardly believe it, and I wasn't sure they were real. Fred was fond of playing tricks on people, so I said the first dumb thing that came to mind, a playful joke: "At which dime store did you get these?" It was something he might say to me.

He was terribly insulted, called me an ungrateful brat who didn't deserve such valuable rings, and asked how I could say such things. I abjectly apologized and praised the rings in every fashion, told him I was thrilled, and so forth. The evening was miserable but memorable. The restaurant menu was usually single-digit prices, but that night they had pheasant under glass, a double-digit dish that I had always wanted to try. Wearing that diamond engagement ring gave me the courage to order it. Of course I asked Fred first if it was okay to do so, and he growled a morose, "Go Ahead.'

That was the last word I heard from him all evening. (By the way, the pheasant was delicious.) He took me home and sat stiffly behind the steering wheel until I got out of the car. I thought about giving him back the rings, but I didn't want to antagonize him further. I probably cried that night, but the next day he came over and was his usual self. We went downtown to the Jolly Joan restaurant, and some of the Shanghai people saw us on their way out. I kept my hands in my lap while they talked to us. After they left, Fred asked if I was ashamed to show my ring. He was disappointed that I didn't show it to his friends. After that I made a habit of keeping it in sight as much as possible.

I couldn't get enough of looking at the engagement ring. When I combed my hair or dried my face and I saw it in the mirror, I could hardly believe it was on my own finger.

Chapter 56

The call came early in the morning before my parents and I had left the house. Lucy and Hugo had a new daughter—the first baby to be born in America from our family. After all the loss and devastation, a new life, a miracle. The next day at the hospital, Lucy asked me for a favor. Hugo had bought a baby basket, and would I make it comfortable for the baby so we could bring little Evelyn Irma (after Hugo's sister) Kohn home from the hospital in style.

Fred and I drove over to N.E. Russell Street and picked up the basket. I used a pillow and the remnant of an old sheet to make a mattress, bought several yards of wide, pink satin ribbon and wove it through the rim, and then wound it around the handle to make a giant pink bow at the top.

On the next Saturday morning, after I had stayed at Fred's for Shabbat, he carried the basket down the steps of the apartment house. Mrs. Wolf, our nosy neighbor from across the street, just happened to be talking with someone at the bottom of the steps as we walked down with Fred carrying the baby basket.

Mrs. Wolf looked us over with wide eyes and remarked to the friend in Yiddish, "They should get married before she has the baby." Maybe she didn't know that I understood her or maybe she didn't care. I was mortified and Fred looked angry.

Fred yelled at me all the way to the hospital about how I had embarrassed him by making him carry that basket. I could have reminded him that he offered to carry the baby basket, but by now I had learned to ignore those unreasonable outbreaks of hostility. I excused them as the result of seeing his father abuse his mother in this way.

After we delivered the basket to the hospital and admired little Evelyn Irma, we helped Lucy and Hugo carry the suitcase, flowers, and the baby to Fred's car. We drove them to N. E. Russell Street where they had found an apartment they could afford. This area was mostly populated by black people, and had a bad reputation. People stopped to stare at the new Studebaker, and some men even offered to buy the car. After depositing the basket, baby and suitcase, we made hurried good-byes and left the area as fast as possible.

One day after another session of insults because of something I had said or done, which I didn't even remember doing, I talked back. I said that I was not the same kind of woman as his mother and he was not to talk to me in that way again. I asked him how he could stand by and let his mother be harangued and insulted. Didn't he think his mother was stupid for quietly enduring such treatment?

His response was vicious. "Never call my mother stupid again," he blurted. "You will be sorry if you ever insult a member of my family again." We didn't talk again for several days, but as usual, after a fit of anger, he showed up at our house as if nothing had happened.

That fall I started my senior year in high school as an engaged woman. Almost half the girls in the senior class were engaged that year. Some of the girls got married and had to drop out of school; married women were not allowed in high school. (They might get pregnant and contaminate the virgins.) A few girls disappeared from our midst, ostensibly to visit relatives in another state. Sometimes they came back after a few months. We all knew they were pregnant, but no one spoke of it.

My grades were finally better as I dropped Home Economics and took a journalism class and another year of Latin, which was very helpful in expanding my English vocabulary. The most practical class was my second semester of Personal Finance. (Once again, I was the only girl in the class.) This curriculum went beyond learning how to write checks and balance a check book. We learned about loans, credit, and the high cost of borrowing money, as well as how and where to invest it. One of the most useful lessons was a graphic video showing the workings of the stock market.

English Literature was my favorite class, mostly because of Miss Winifred Casterline. She made the language come alive and urged us to write creative papers about subjects we knew. One assignment was to write about the most unforgettable person you knew. I chose to write about her.

She agreed, as did everyone who read it, that it was an excellent essay, but she gave me an A- (the only one that year). The first sentence in my paper was, "The most unique person I have ever known . . ."

Miss Casterline's note on the paper was emphatic, "Unique can't be modified! 'Unique' means one of a kind. You can modify "unusual," or "rare," but you would never say "this is the most one of a kind."

I completely got it. Never again would I modify "unique." It has been a lifelong aggravation for me, as almost daily I hear an announcer on the radio, a lecturer on television, or a friend say "The most unique . . ." while describing an event, object, or another person, and I want to scream, "No!"

My work on the school newspaper, procuring and creating ads for the Gresham Outlook, resulted in a scholarship in journalism to Whitman College in Walla Walla, Washington. Since Fred and I had no plans for a wedding anytime soon, the prospect of attending college suddenly seemed possible. When I told my parents about the scholarship, I saw no reaction.

One Saturday night while we were parked at the top of Mt. Tabor, talking about our plans, Fred said he didn't want to stay in Portland. He missed the excitement of a big city, a place more like Shanghai where he grew up. Portland was rather provincial during those days. Liquor by the drink was outlawed. Alcohol had to be bought by the bottle at a state-licensed liquor store (which had short hours), and you drank a cocktail at home. Many movies, books and plays were banned. Gambling was strictly forbidden, and even card games at home were in danger of being raided. More than once, I waited in someone's kitchen while Fred played a few hands of poker in the dining room to win money to take me out to dinner or a movie.

We also discussed having children and agreed that was definitely included in the plan. (I didn't consider who would take care of them.) Fred told me that men who had been in Shanghai had a bad reputation, and he was surprised that my parents raised no objection to my dating him. He told me that he had never gone to a brothel, as most of his friends had. "I wanted healthy children, so I kept myself very clean," he assured me.

We had a silver thaw in February of 1951, and although we knew it was dangerous, Fred and I decided to go to dinner at an Italian restaurant on Sandy Boulevard. It was a stupid decision, but we were young. Just as we arrived at the intersection of N.E. 39th Avenue and Sandy, the car started to skid on the glassy surface and spun around like a top several times, while we sat frozen in terror. When the car straightened out, Fred inched the car along until we reached our destination. We were the only patrons that night.

It took us two hours to get back to my house on 102nd Avenue, and Fred got home around two o'clock in the morning. He had promised to call me when he got home, so I had put the telephone under my pillow to muffle the ring. There was no chance that I would fall asleep before that call.

On one of those nights parked on Mt. Tabor, I told him about my scholarship to Whitman College. He didn't seem to hear me. After a minute he said that college was a waste of time. An engaged woman could not be seriously considering an education beyond high school. I didn't peruse the matter anymore that night. When I was in his arms, I could not think of anything except how good it felt to be there.

Now that we were engaged, Fred became more sexually demanding; he assured me that engaged couples had the right to be more intimate. That night while parked on top of Mt. Tabor, with the city lights like a glowing carpet below us, he put his hands up my skirt and eventually removed my panties. I was reluctant, but he was irresistible. Fred assured me that I would not get pregnant (which was my primary worry), and we spent a few passionate minutes before we heard a knock on the car window. Hurriedly we sat up. Fred opened the back door while I cringed into one corner of the back seat. One of the policemen shone the flashlight into the car.

The police checked this parking area intermittently, looking for minors who were out after the ten o'clock curfew. They may have forestalled an occasional rape, but mostly they just harassed the lovers looking for privacy.

Fred got out his driver's license, which showed him to be an adult. Fortunately, I had turned eighteen that winter and was no longer what the boys called "jailbait." However, I didn't have any identification papers with me. When the policeman asked my age, I told him I was eighteen. He played the flashlight around the car and found my panties on the floor.

"Are these yours?" he asked, then turned to his partner to show him the lacy undergarment. Both men laughed, then he made a point of handing me the panties. Instead of crying in embarrassment, I looked at his stupid face with a neutral expression. His disappointment was palpable. I had encountered much more dangerous bullies in uniform before. That incident became an inside joke between us.

Chapter 57

A few weeks later Fred took me out to dinner at "The Top Hat." It was quite a distance, out on Barbur Boulevard, but it had live music. (Fred always tried to find restaurants with live music. He wanted music to surround him all the time.) That night I ordered the pheasant under glass for $10.50 again. Fred commented that some girls were gold diggers and always ordered the most expensive meals on the menu. I offered to pay for my meal if he felt it cost too much. I knew it was the wrong thing to say, but it just slipped out. I should have just smiled as if he had meant it as a joke, which he probably did.

Driving back to my house on the other side of the river and, as Fred put it, "halfway to Mt. Hood," we hardly spoke, just listened to the music on the radio. Then I started more trouble. "If I decide to go to college, will you wait for me?" I asked.

"Girls just go to college to find a man." He growled. Then his voice rose. "I thought you were different, but you are just like the other gold-digging sluts, chasing after men."

I started to answer this slur with an even tone, trying to be reasonable, although I was highly insulted. I had not looked at another man since I met him, and now Fred was accusing me of being a slut. Was it because I let him touch me and kiss me?

It didn't matter what I said about my motives for going to college, he was not listening. He just kept yelling insults. Finally, about a mile from my house, I told him to stop the car and I got out and started walking along the dark, deserted road. I could hardly see where I was going, but I just kept walking, even while he pulled up beside me and "ordered' me to get back in the car. When it began to rain, I did get back into the car. At my house I didn't even turn around as I went in the door. I was done with this man. Tomorrow I would give back the beautiful ring. I might die an old maid, but I would be a famous, foreign correspondent, too busy for marriage.

By the time I got to my room I had decided that I couldn't live without Fred after all. I started to cry and curse myself for being so foolish as to possibly lose this wonderful man. I would do whatever he wanted so we could be together. I planned to wait until morning to call him, but just before midnight the telephone rang.

When the telephone was installed, it was hooked up to a thirty-foot cord so that I could take it into my bedroom for my nightly talks with Fred. I was almost afraid to answer because he might be asking me to return the ring. I knew better than to expect that he was calling to apologize.

During our fifty-eight years together I never heard him say "I'm sorry," "I apologize," or "Forgive me" for the insults, accusations and slights. I learned not to put him in a position of having to show gratitude because he found it difficult to say "Thank you." Eventually I adjusted to living without hearing the word "please" when he wanted something.

I picked up the telephone and said, "Hello."

"I got home okay," Fred said, as he usually did when he called me. He paused as I waited for him to, hopefully, apologize. "See you tomorrow" were his next words, and then he hung up.

When it was obvious that I would not be going to college since there was no support from my parents and strong opposition from my fiancé, I told Fred we needed to set a date for our wedding. Social pressure and Fred convinced me that marriage was the only legitimate profession for a respectable woman. I truly did not see any other option.

We decided to be married on July 22, 1951, at Ahavai Shalom Synagogue on SW Park Street. When Fred's father found out that we had set a date, he hardly reacted. Later I learned that he ardently tried to talk Fred out of getting married. When that didn't work, he took me to lunch one Saturday after services and talked to me quite earnestly of how he was only thinking of my welfare; that we should wait until Fred finished his army service before getting married.

"Fred might get killed in the war, and you would be a very young widow," he warned me. He continued, "You could spend the rest of your life alone." Leo Lindemann could be very charming. He had been a successful traveling salesman in Germany. Now every word he uttered was full of concern for my welfare.

When this argument didn't sway me, he started to paint a dire picture of what life would be like if Fred came home badly-wounded and I had to spend my life with a cripple. I tried to explain to Leo that our minds were made up and he was wasting his time. Then he begged me not to tell Fred about our meeting. When I told him that I didn't keep secrets from Fred, he sighed deeply, gave me one of his most ingratiating smiles, and even a hug.

One evening, a few weeks before the wedding, Leo Lindemann called my father. After my father hung up, he said, "Herr Lindemann wants to meet with me to discuss Ruth's dowry."

My father had put the phone down gently, but when he turned to look at my mother and me, his face was a mask of fury. The diatribe that followed was lengthy. My father ranted about the nerve of that arrogant *Pifke*[46] expecting him to pay his son for taking away his most precious possession.

---

[46] *Pifke*: an Austrian slur defining a rude, arrogant, German.

My mother tried to calm him down to no avail. "We are no longer in Europe!" my father yelled. "This is America! This is a new world, a new age. We don't need to bribe anyone to marry our daughter; she is worth her weight in gold."

It was the first time I had heard my father say I was worth anything. What a surprise. But the biggest surprise was yet to come.

One Sunday evening, right after dinner, Fred brought his father to our house to talk with my father, ostensibly, about my dowry. I was nervous about the situation. Although we didn't need our parents' signature to get married since I was now eighteen, and Fred was over twenty-one, we did want their blessing.

Our parents had met on one or two occasions, but they had never spoken. My mother had congratulated Rosa and Leo when we were at their twenty-fifth wedding anniversary party, but neither of the women made an effort to be sociable. Rosa only socialized with her German friends and had no interests beyond her circle, while my mother read the newspaper and we discussed world affairs. It was obvious that the Lindemanns considered Austrians a lower class, mentioning often that Fred was of "guten Hause."

As Leo came into our small living room it seemed to get smaller. He was a handsome, six-foot-tall man with military bearing, while my father was five feet and six inches with a slight frame and an easy smile.

The two men greeted each other cordially and sat down on chairs facing each other. My mother found an excuse to go into the bedroom while Fred and I went into the kitchen, closing the pocket door to the living room.

At first, we sat at the table holding hands, which soon moved to more intimate procedures. We kissed, our ears tuned to the goings-on in the living room. We heard low murmurings, chuckles that turned to hearty laughter. Not long after that, Leo Lindemann called to Fred that he was ready to leave. The two men shook hands, patted each other on the back, Fred gave me a hasty kiss and followed his father out to the car. I never knew what the two fathers discussed that night, but the dowry was never mentioned again.

Chapter 58

When I told Fred that it would be best if we got married in the rabbi's office with our parents as witnesses, he was appalled.

"We are going to have a regular, synagogue wedding," he proclaimed. "You will walk down the aisle in a white dress, and there will be a newspaper write-up about how beautiful you are."

I told him I was uncomfortable dressing like a virginal bride. He argued that, of course, I was technically a virgin. After all, he was a Kohan and required to marry a virgin. I said my parents didn't have the funds for a lavish wedding. He said he would help pay for the flowers and the rental of the hall. I countered that my parents didn't socialize and had no friends to invite. Fred said he had at least a hundred people who would need to be invited. Finally, I agreed to the synagogue wedding.

After talking to the Rabbi and reserving the hospitality room in the synagogue basement, we began to make up a guest list. Sure enough, the Lindemanns had at least a hundred people on their list, mostly from the Friendship Club. My side of the family invited Hugo and Lucy, the Klingers, the Kays, and the Foxes.

Once we all agreed on the date and time of the wedding, we decided to have fifty invitations printed, along with thank-you cards in case we got presents. We didn't know about bridal showers or a gift register. Even if we had known about such things, we would not have participated because, for us, asking for gifts was unseemly.

A few days later the rabbi called Fred and told him he couldn't marry us on July 22nd because it was Shavuot (a Jewish holiday to celebrate the receiving of the Torah). Could we move the wedding to July 15th? We had no choice. Fred had to ask to change his vacation schedule, and I needed to get the printer to change the date on the invitations.

Gresham High School Graduation, Thursday, May 24th 1951. (L - R) Zelma Mitchell, Shirley Ellis, Ruth Kohn, Lois Hawk.

At that time in May, my mind was on final exams, the senior prom, and the graduation ceremony. I studied every night, and Fred was outraged that I preferred my books to him. Most nights it was well after midnight before I got to really concentrate on my studies. I was also involved in decorating the gym for the prom, and that took about a week of after-school committee meetings and putting up the decorations. Lots of clouds and rainbows since the theme was "Dream" (a popular song that year).

With a few alterations, the white gown I had worn to the junior prom looked like an all-new dress. The prom was a success. Good music, great dancing, and Fred was in a good mood. He joked with my friends without getting crude and generally made a good impression.

The final exams went well, mostly because I was losing interest in being at the top of the class. Since I wasn't going to college, why should I care about my grades? The next big event was graduation on Thursday, May 24th. We had a brief rehearsal, and then it was graduation day.

I must admit I had a lump in my throat and mixed feelings about saying goodbye to my favorite teachers, like Miss Casterline who had taught us to love Shakespeare (not an easy feat); the typing teacher who had done her best to encourage me to type faster; and my friends who were all going their separate ways. Zelma and I were getting married; Shirley, Lois, Ruth, and Donna were off to various colleges.

A few days after graduation I got a job at Meier and Frank Department Store (now a Macy's) in the shipping room, wrapping packages for delivery. I was a terrible wrapper. Finally, one of the women (we were all women in that basement area) showed me how to make a tight knot, and that helped. But working with my hands was never my forte.

I was told that every month I could reapply for a transfer to another department, and if a vacancy came up, I might get the job—if I qualified. A month later, I filled out the application for an office job in the accounting department. For the second time, in the space marked "race," I wrote "Human." Did it occur to me that I might not get the job? Yes. But I refused to say anything else, knowing full well that "Negro" (the word for African Americans at that time) would get me a job cleaning toilets, and "Asian" would get me a job in the restaurant kitchen. I got a job as cashier for the women's apparel department. The floor manager was a stickler for accuracy. If I was off by a penny by the end of the day, I had to keep counting until I found that penny. (I sometimes put in the penny myself.)

Now it was time to concentrate on my wedding. I decided to remodel my prom dress. I bought several yards of white satin, lace border and decorative pearl strands. With the new sewing machine that Fred had bought me for my birthday, I made a long-sleeved, high-necked bolero to go over the strapless dress. Then I sewed on a scalloped train. I trimmed all the edges with lace I ruffled by hand. Then I attached beads to the pointed edges of the sleeves. It was a lengthy and tedious job, but I kept picturing how I would look walking down the aisle. For a veil, I bought a piece of sheer curtain material and fashioned it to fit my head. With my employee discount the whole outfit was less than ten dollars.

My mother gave Greta Kay and Blanka Klinger about a hundred dollars for refreshments. Lucy and Hugo were matron of honor and best man, respectively. Fred's sister, Inge, and Ruthie Klinger were bridesmaids, and Shirley Kay was the flower girl. (I told them to buy long dresses of their own choosing.) The groomsmen were Ludvig (Loui) Fox and Stephan Katzan. The wedding was set for one o'clock, after lunch, so we could serve only punch, wine, coffee, tea, home-baked cookies and a wedding cake at the reception.

One day before the invitations were to be mailed, the rabbi called and said he was not able to be at the wedding; he was sending Rabbi Kleinman from Nevah Zedick Synagogue to conduct the ceremony, and Rabbi Kleinman would not be available until three o'clock in the afternoon on July 15th. We steamed open the envelopes, and with a black pen changed the "1" to a "3."

Fred grumbled about the tackiness of doing this, but it was too late and too expensive to reprint the invitations. Everyone accepted—a gratifying surprise.

Near the end of June, Rabbi Kleinmann asked Fred and me to come to his office at Nevah Zedik. Since we all agreed on who was to take part and how, we had little discussion about procedures. We had a choice of *Katubbah* designs, and we chose a simple one. (The *Katubbah* is a Jewish marriage contract written in Hebrew.) Rabbi Kleinmann began to translate it for us. "I know all that," Fred interrupted him.

"I learned it in Yeshiva while studying for my Bar Mitzvah."

"That's commendable," the Rabbi smiled at us. "I need to make the bride aware of her husband's duties and also what is expected of her." He continued.

I learned that a husband's duties were to provide shelter, food, clothing, and protection, and to devote himself to the happiness of his wife. It was a big order, and I could tell by Fred's face that he took it seriously. A Jewish wife, the rabbi explained, was to fulfill her duties as a wife (with no explanation of what that might entail). We both had to agree to raise our children in the Jewish religion. I liked Rabbi Kleinmann, who had the same blue eyes as Fred and a soft voice, and kept assuring us that all was going to go well. He told us that he had married thousands of couples and they had all stayed married.

I was curious about the duties required of a wife. The Rabbi chuckled, then explained that girls learned what they needed to know from their mothers. Also, women had natural instincts about being wives and mothers, so they didn't need to go to Yeshiva to learn their duties. Meanwhile, boys had to be taught so that by the time they reached manhood (age thirteen) they would know what was involved in being a Jewish husband.

Chapter 59

Driving back to my house, that Sunday at the end of June, I began to think about what the rabbi had said. I wanted to be Fred's wife, mostly so we could spend our nights together. Apart from that, I had given no thought of what might be required of me as a wife. My mother had always done everything in the house, besides spending long hours at the grocery store. She had never taught me anything about housekeeping.

I had no interest in cooking. I was a master at warming up meals Mom had left for me. I could never wash or iron a garment to suit my mother's meticulous standards. My feeble attempts at dusting or vacuuming resulted in my disgusted mother taking over in the middle of the process.

We had no role models of domesticity in our family. My mother had been a secretary/bookkeeper, her mother was a successful seamstress, my paternal grandmother ran a grocery store. All these women had professional maids to run the household. Although my mother had been doing the cooking, cleaning and laundry since we arrived in the United States eleven years ago, she didn't think that I would be subjected to these duties. Her plan was that I should work in an office until I married a man who could afford a maid to do the housekeeping chores, and so forth. She thought Fred would eventually have those means.

About ten days before the wedding, I was beginning to have second thoughts. Also, I was not feeling well. My job as cashier required being indoors all day without a glimpse of daylight or the sky. I would come home and just lie out on a blanket in the back yard, staring at the sky for about an hour, then go indoors to work on my wedding dress. If Fred came over, we ate the dinner my mother had left me, and I tried to go back to my sewing.

This was not what Fred had in mind, and we began to argue about trivial matters. We had an altercation every night until the morning of our wedding day. One discussion I dreaded was what Fred would say about my working after we were married. I waited for him to bring up the subject. One evening, when I couldn't wait any longer, I told him that I expected to keep working at Meier & Frank after we were married. I was surprised and relieved when he said, "But of course. We need the money."

Driving over the Hawthorne Bridge that afternoon, I began to think about the next fifty years. I just saw a blank space. In those days we got married to *stay* married. The idea of "If it doesn't work out, we'll get divorced" never entered my mind. What did enter my mind was that I had forgotten my mother's orchid corsage in the refrigerator.

We arrived in front of the Synagogue. I got out of the car, clutching my plastic wrapped dress and veil. My mind was on what to do about my mother's corsage. Then I saw Fred going into the front door. I called out to him and he came down the steps. I told him about my forgetting the corsage and asked him if he would go out to our house to get it. "I'm not driving halfway to Mt. Hood to get a corsage," was his answer. Then he suggested I use the orchid from the middle of the bridal bouquet which was in the dressing room. I did just that, and if my mother noticed she never said anything.

As I started to get into my bridal gear, I had a sudden urge to use the restroom. To my horror, but not exactly a surprise, my period had started. That explained the hostile, edgy feelings and the cramps that I attributed to nervousness. The pads were in my suitcase, which was in the trunk of Fred's Studebaker. I searched in every room of the Synagogue but couldn't find Fred. Finally, I went outside, and found him leaning on the south side of the building, lighting a cigarette. I asked him for the car keys, and he gave me that annoyed look that meant, "Now what?"

I had no way out; I had to retrieve the Kotex in the car, but I was too embarrassed to tell him what I wanted. He seemed very reluctant to relinquish the car keys; I had to plead with him before I finally convinced him what I needed was vitally important. Perhaps he guessed what I needed because he opened the trunk and started to walk away. "Be sure to close the lid," he ordered over his shoulder.

We met again in the rabbi's office. Our parents, dressed in their festive garments, were to be witnesses to the signing of the Katubbah. I was wearing my wedding dress and veil, so not seeing the bride before the ceremony was no longer part of Jewish superstition. My Omama would have been shocked. She told me that she had only seen her future husband once before the wedding, at the engagement ceremony.

We all left the rabbi's office and went to our stations. The rabbi and Fred stood at the altar; our parents were in the back of the sanctuary where we gathered with the rest of the wedding party. A talented friend of Fred's sang a beautiful rendition of "Be My Love." It was not Mario Lanza, our favorite tenor, but came close. I had been told that crying on my wedding day was bad luck, so I fought to keep my eyes dry, but the lump in my throat made it hard to breathe. I was happy, proud, triumphant—so why those tears?

Fred's boss, Irving Ott, was filming the ceremony. The wedding participants all slowed down and hesitated as they approached the camera before they continued to the Bima.

When the two musicians started playing Mendelssohn's "Wedding March in C major," it was my turn to walk up the aisle with my father. He gripped my arm as if I were going to escape and pulled my veil sideways, almost off my head. I jerked away and this awkward moment, showing my displeased frown, is on that video forever.

As I stepped up next to Fred and my father took his place

beside my mother next to the *Chuppah*, I put my hand inside Fred's elbow. His arm was trembling so hard I had to clutch his sleeve. I tried to get him to look at me, so I could calm him down, but he stared straight ahead at the rabbi.

Rabbi Kleinmann was my height and, for a moment, he looked directly into my eyes. Then he looked at Fred and started to describe the duties of a Jewish husband, much as he had the day in his office. It was a lengthy list, and I could understand why a man might be nervous taking on such responsibilities.

The rabbi then turned to me. His blue eyes were sparkling, and he had a way of looking directly into my eyes that made me feel comfortable. Then he winked and asked if I would fulfill the duties of a Jewish wife. I said "yes" without having been given any details.

Fred slipped the diamond-studded wedding ring on my finger next to the engagement ring, and we kissed (for what seemed a long time).

At the ripe old age of eighteen, I had achieved the highest goal that all women were meant to strive for in that era. For all intents and purposes, my life must now be devoted to my husband's and society's expectations. The roller coaster ride would endure for the next fifty-six years.

Shirley Kay, Inge Lindemann, Ruth Klinger, Alice Kohn (Kern), Ruth & Fred, Hugo Kohn (Kern), Louis Fox, Steve Katzan, July 15, 1951.

If You Enjoyed

We Chose Survival, be sure to pick up *To Survive Is Not Enough* and *They Will Not Be Forgotten* available online, in stores, in gift shops and from the author.

To Survive is *Not* Enough

Snatched from a near certain death in a concentration camp, Hedy is taken to a totally strange environment in an opulent villa in Berlin. This is the residence of the Grand Mufti of Jerusalem, and she is forced to live in his harem for nearly 3 years. Here the rules were unknown but the punishment swift.

In a twist of events she is helped to escape by the Mufti's trusted secretary, the mysterious Omar. As a very young man Oskar Menkes becomes Omar Amadhi, a private secretary to the Grand Mufti of Jerusalem, one of the most evil men of the 20th Century. In that capacity, he risks his life on a daily basis to save the lives of countless Jewish children and help to further the Zionist cause.

Ruth Lindemann was born in 1933 in Vienna, Austria. After arriving in the United States in 1940, she grew up in the Pacific Northwest. After raising a family and graduating from Portland State University, she became Hadassah President in Portland, Oregon. Later in life, Ruth had a career as a tax consultant. Writing fiction and non-fiction has been a life-long hobby.

Since 1982, Ruth has been a lecturer on the Speaker's Bureau for the Holocaust Museum in Portland, Oregon, and recently at the Tolerance Education Center in Rancho Mirage, California.

To Survive is Not Enough is historical fiction based on the culmination of hundreds of stories told to Ruth over the last fifty years.

AquaZebra Book Publishing — Book Cover and Interior Design by AquaZebra.com

ISBN 978-0-9905827-5-5

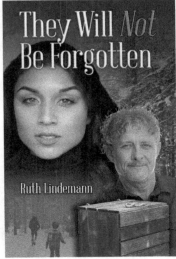

They Will *Not* Be Forgotten

In 1910 Estanza an adventurous Greek girl of 18, with a deep interest in German, classic literature is lured to Berlin by a highly placed German diplomat who loves her. Konrad joins her in Berlin and they consummate their forbidden love. Their daughter, Konstanza, whom Konrad refuses to acknowledge, is born in Switzerland. At eight years old, Konstanza is sent to a prestigious German boarding school where she learns about the brutality that lurks beneath the veneer of German culture. After her parents are murdered by the type of thugs who soon will rule Germany, Konstanza travels to Poland, to work for a loving Jewish family.

When Poland is occupied by Germany, the family is ripped apart and Konstanza is forced to become a housekeeper for a unit of German officers. Risking her life on a daily basis, Konstanza becomes instrumental in a plan to save Jewish children from certain death. *They Will Not Be Forgotten* reveals inconceivable cruelty by a population gone criminally insane and memorializes the brave people who have the courage to resist evil.

Ruth Lindemann was born in Vienna, Austria in 1933. Arrived in the U.S.A in 1940 and grew up in the Northwest. After raising a family she graduated from Portland State University, was president of her Hadassah Chapter, and a tax consultant. Writing is her passion.

They Will Not Be Forgotten joins her earlier book, *To Survive Is Not Enough.* Although historical fiction the books are based on the stories Ruth has heard from Holocaust survivors over 35 years.

Proceeds from the sale go to projects dedicated to teaching tolerance.

Book Cover and Interior Design by AquaZebra.com

ISBN 978-1-7324567-0-9

CPSIA information can be obtained
at www.ICGtesting.com
Printed in the USA
FSHW021609180621
82474FS

9 781954 604025